Power Performance
for Singers

Power Performance
for Singers

Transcending
the Barriers

SHIRLEE EMMONS
ALMA THOMAS

New York   Oxford

Oxford University Press

1998

Oxford University Press

Oxford   New York
Athens   Auckland   Bangkok   Bogota   Bombay
Buenos Aires   Calcutta   Cape Town   Dar es Salaam
Delhi   Florence   Hong Kong   Istanbul   Karachi
Kuala Lumpur   Madras   Madrid   Melbourne
Mexico City   Nairobi   Paris   Singapore
Taipei   Tokyo   Toronto   Warsaw

and associated companies in
Berlin   Ibadan

Library of Congress Cataloging-in-Publication Data
Emmons, Shirlee.
Power performance for singers : transcending the barriers
Shirlee Emmons, Alma Thomas.
p.   cm.
Includes bibliographical references and index.
ISBN 0-19-511224-5
1. Singing—Psychological aspects.   I. Thomas, Alma, 1939– .
II. Title.
MT892.E55   1998
783'.043—DC21   97-31732

9 8 7 6

Printed in the United States of America
on acid-free paper

[A performer is] one who joins body, mind, and spirit in the dance of existence; one who explores both inner and outer being, one who surpasses limitations and crosses boundaries in the process of a personal and social transformation; one who plays the larger game, the Game of Games, with full awareness, aware of life and death, and willing to accept the pain and joy that awareness brings.

G. Leonard,
The Ultimate Athlete (1975)

Preface

Within the first year that Alma Thomas, a performance psychologist, started working with singers in New York, her fame grew so rapidly that she was invited to adjudicate a New York State competition, which was an early stage of a prestigious national competition. There were to be five judges, four of them musicians and the fifth a nonmusician, Alma Thomas. Thomas demurred, declaring that she didn't have the necessary musical background with which to judge singers properly. Nevertheless, the competition chairperson insisted that Alma take part, advising her to define her own criteria, which she did.

Listening to the seventeen contestants, the four musician-judges busily juggled numbers (out of a perfect score of 100) for diction, tone quality, musicianship, and so on—the usual adjudication categories. Alma had no such categories or numbers, but she made notes. Hearing about the results later, I myself was astonished. Alma had ranked the first five contestants in exactly the same order as the composite score of the other four judges; had scrambled the order of the next three to 7, 6, 8 instead of the 6, 7, 8; and had ranked the remaining nine contestants just as the other judges had!

Although I knew what the official adjudication categories were, I couldn't wait to find out what Alma's criteria had been. "Apart from the mental skills demonstrated," she answered, "I had only one criterion: Whoever has best shown me *what he or she thinks the song is all about* is number one, and so on."

The Education of Shirlee

As many times as I have told this story since that day, it never fails to amaze me. For the adjudicated results to have come out as they did—virtually unanimous and this without any communication among the judges—the musicians must have been powerfully swayed (despite all the numerical calibrating of vocal and musical skills) by the same criterion that had influenced Alma—that is, the *quality of the performance.*

In 1990 my husband returned from an educational convention telling me that he had the answer to my longtime wish: the same kind of psychological help for singers as was routinely afforded athletes. He had met a certain Alma Thomas, a British performance psychologist, after a workshop she had conducted at the convention and had invited her to come to meet me in New York. As luck would have it, the day of our appointment found me signing autographs on copies of my Melchior biography, *Tristanissimo,* at the Metropolitan Opera Bookstore, something I had never expected to do in my lifetime and something I was enjoying immensely. Reluctantly I walked across the plaza to meet this British psychologist.

As a kind of test, I asked Alma to tell me what she would do to help two particular students of mine, whose problems I described in detail. Within five minutes I was enthralled; she had totally won me over. After she described what methods she would use with my two students, she asked gently, "Tell me, Shirlee, who *usually* does this sort of thing for your singers?"

Hesitantly I replied, "Why, I do, I guess, or the coach."

Ever so politely she said, "With all due respect, isn't that a bit amateurish?"

That was the first revelatory moment in our relationship, but not the last. Eventually my thorough understanding of the import of mental skills became directly proportional to the amount of time I spent watching and listening to Alma's workshops. As I watched her first "distraction" workshop in New York, for instance, I learned to my amazement that the big effort we singers make not to *show* that we are distracted in performance is more or less useless, because our concentration is then focused on pretending, and the performance suffers. What we must learn is not to *be* distracted. The competition that she adjudicated taught me what Alma already knew, that *everyone* is swayed by the performance, not just audience members. The biggest change came, however, when I made three discoveries: What singers routinely do before a performance is devote only one or two run-throughs to *performing* in practice sessions; most singers do not know how to take their minds off technical skills in performance; furthermore, conductors, judges, and auditioners of all kinds judge them on those very performance skills!

The Education of Alma

When I was asked to be on the judging panel for this competition, I was both honored and flattered, because (let's face it) I had only been working with singers a relatively short time. What did I know about it? Not a lot! I did give it some thought, because I really had to consider what I had to offer the panel and the singers who were competing. I felt very strongly that I had to give them some kind of feedback. What *did* I know about?

Well, I know a great deal about performance and the preparation of the individual for high-level performance, no matter the field: sports, education, the arts, or business. As far as I am concerned, the skills that performers require are the same, especially if the performer is aiming for excellence. I know what to look for when people are performing. I know when they are nervous and when they are trying to cover it up. I know when their focus and concentration are sharp, and I realize when that focus leaves the performer in the lurch! Above all, I know when they are thoroughly prepared, know what they are doing, and—in the arts—when they are communicating a message to me and allowing me to share their performance. I can also recognize talent, ability, and skill, no matter the field of performance. So I agreed to be on the panel.

At the suggestion of the chairperson, I prepared an observation sheet of mental attributes that I would observe in the competition, from which I would give feedback to the performer. The other members of the panel had their own agenda on a different attribute sheet. This meant that we would be observing the performance from very different angles and expertise: one vocal and musical, the other in terms of mental attributes and a completely synthesized performance.

On the day of the competition, as I was introduced to the other panel members there was little discussion about a joint understanding of the criteria of observation. (But then, I probably wouldn't have understood it anyway.) But how, I wondered, did my colleagues know that they all shared the same understanding of the criteria for observation? This wasn't at all like the major gymnastics competitions I'd judged! Once the competition began, I found it quite easy to observe the singers in relation to the observable "mental" aspects of their performance, but I knew I had to have some kind of a list of winners.

Because I did not at that time understand what the pieces sung were about, I decided that, apart from the mental aspects, my principle would be this: The singer who sang in such a way as to make me understand what he/she was singing about, who communicated the meaning clearly to me, and who made me listen—that singer would be higher up on the list than the ones whose renditions I did not understand. If the piece was about love or anger or depression or hopefulness and I understood that from the performance and the singer made me listen to him/her, that performer would rate highly.

Following the competition, when the panel members met to decide the winner and runners-up, I found that I had all but the middle three singers in the exact same order as the other judges!

The rest is history. At the time, I didn't know why Shirlee got so excited about the results. I do now! And I know much more about how singers prepare for and achieve excellence.

How to Use This Book

If you have a vocal technical problem, whom do you visit? A voice teacher. If you have a problem with expressive interpretation, where do you go? To a drama coach. If you have a problem with pitches or keeping a certain tempo, whom do you call? A musical coach. You don't think of these remedial visits as negative; you just go. If, on the other hand, you have a problem with concentrating in performance or are consumed by anxiety when performing, you simply conclude, fatalistically, that there is something basically wrong with *you*. Yet these issues are an integral part of your performance and must be faced, because if these problems are not solved, your vocal skills and interpretive abilities won't function optimally.

Some singers are good performers because they were gifted with great performing flair from birth. They usually have success, even when their technical skills are not exemplary. Some singers learned to be good performers by trial and error and lots of experience. If you are neither of these, you can still become a better performer by learning better performance skills.

This is not a book about performance anxiety, because anxiety is but *one* aspect of your total performance. This is not a book about how to sing, but rather a book about your performance, part of which is your singing. It does set out to explain exactly what constitutes performance. It is designed to help singers learn how to *perform* vocally, how to use what they have, how to enjoy their voices during performance, and how to perform consistently to the best of their ability. Although the performance skills within this book apply to all performers—experienced and developing—they will use these skills differently depending upon their present level. All performers can do better. World champions go on improving. Singers are late bloomers by the very nature of their instruments; they must go on improving. And even if you are a singer who has performing flair or who has learned to cope in performance through experience, you can still improve your performance.

This book has been written so that it follows the cycle of the performance through all its stages: preperformance, performance, and postperformance. Therefore, we recommend that you read the table of contents all the way through, initially, from beginning to end. This will give you an overall view of the nature and concept of mental preparation for performance, because that, too, follows the performance cycle. Specifically, we have made a studied effort to present the material in its most logical arrangement.

This book presents many choices for assessing the quality of your performance and for improving it in whatever way you find necessary. To that end, feel free to dip into its pages wherever you are interested "as if" you were requiring one part of the mental preparation process for your own immediate needs. A reading of the overview to each part will help you decide which chapters would best serve your personal needs. At the end of each chapter, you will find a list of other chapters to whose contents you can refer for more help with your immediate needs. Care has been taken to make each part, at the expense of some repetition, into something that can be read independently. However, you should know that most mental programs need thorough planning and much thought relative to your own individual preparation and performance requirements.

Teachers will find references throughout the text to "Teaching Points," which can be found in appendix 2 at the end of the book.

The term *collaborative pianist* has recently come to be the preferred designation for a pianist who accompanies another musician. We mean no disrespect by our use of the word *accompanist*, which was the preferred term as we wrote this book.

There is a detailed description in the afterword to help you with planning your mental journey to performance excellence.

Do it well. Do it thoughtfully. Practice it. It does work.

We hope that you enjoy your journey. Good luck!

New York City   S. E.
London   A. T.
November 1997

Acknowledgments

First, our thanks to Rollin Baldwin and David Weinstein, who, weary of hearing both of us exclaim endlessly about how much each had learned of the other's discipline, insisted that we write it all down and who, when we began to do that, helped with every kind of support, not least their enthusiasm.

Second, our gratitude to the clients of Alma Thomas and the students of Shirlee Emmons, who worked with one or both of us and, in the course of our relationship, clarified even more for us the needs of the singer regarding mental preparation. We especially thank those who shared their personal stories by writing them down for the book: Peri Chondeau, Brooke Elbein, Judith Engel, Christine Gengaro, Bernadette Jankauskas, Carolyn Kantor, Susan May, Debra Powell, Roberta Prada, and Mark Rehnstrom. Above all, we are grateful to Betsy Parrish, who gave so generously of her time while sharing her personal convictions—which are splendidly informed by her considerable talents as a singer—about searching out the deepest meaning behind songs and arias. We particularly appreciate her willingness to engage in the long and wide-ranging debate that eventually gave birth to the chapter on meaning.

Many thanks to those courageous athletes whose cogent words and unrelenting pursuit of excellence sustained us in this endeavor, and our appreciation to the many fine authors of the superb texts from which we have drawn both scholarly information and uplifting words.

To our husbands, David Thomas and Rollin Baldwin, deep appreciation for their unstinting generosity and loving support in all phases of the preparation. To our children—Justine Thomas, Hilary Baldwin, Gethin Thomas, and Joseph Guagliardo—who not only endured our endless progress reports and enthusiastic readings aloud but also rendered selfless and concrete help in producing the book, our gratitude.

We have been most fortunate in this work to have the expert assistance of our editor, Maribeth Anderson Payne, who immediately recognized the value of the book's concept, did everything in her power to aid us in its completion, and accompanied all advice with unfailing good humor and charm.

The authors would like to thank the following writers and researchers, who through their work in related fields have made valuable contributions to this book. We are especially indebted to these authors, some of whose work we have adapted for the use of singers:

S. J. Bull, J. G. Albinson, and O. J. Shambrook, authors of *The Mental Game Plan*, adapted in our chapter 4 and the afterword (see bibliography)

Richard J. Butler and Lew Hardy, authors of "The Performance Profile: Theory and Application," in *Sports Psychologist*, adapted in our chapter 4 (see bibliography)

Lew Hardy, author of "A Catastrophe Model of Performance in Sport," in *Stress and Performance in Sport*, adapted in our chapter 4 (see bibliography)

Lew Hardy and Dave Nelson, authors of the "Sports Related Psychological Skills Questionnaire" (SPSQ), developed in 1990, as yet unstandardized, adapted for singers with many thanks in our chapter 4 (see bibliography)

Tom Kubistant, author of *Performing Your Best*, adapted in our chapters 1, 8, 9, and 19 (see bibliography)

James E. Loehr, author of *Mental Toughness Training for Sports*, adapted in our chapter 3 (see bibliography)

Rainer Martens, author of *Coaches Guide to Sport Psychology*, adapted in our chapters 1 and 11 (see bibliography)

Saul Miller, author of *Performance under Pressure*, adapted in our chapters 6 and 11 (see bibliography)

Terry Orlick, author of *Psyching for Sport: Mental Training for Athletes* and *In Pursuit of Excellence*, adapted in our chapters 4 and 12 (see bibliography)

John Syer and Christopher Connolly, authors of *Sporting Body, Sporting Mind*, adapted in our chapters 6, 10, and 12 (see bibliography)

Contents

Power Performance
for Singers

I   THE POWER OF PERFORMANCE

Everyone would like to excel in something—personal life, relationships, sports, business, or the arts. Many people not only want to experience such excellence but actually live solely for the pursuit of excellence. Such is the power of performance. This desire to excel personally, to attain the highest standards, is seen to be a worthy "drive," especially in today's highly competitive world.

However, such excellence is not easy to achieve. It is only gained by grit, determination, talent, and sheer, unadulterated hard work. Referring to his conviction that high-level performance of any kind is only *partly* about skill, talent, and ability, Simon Barnes, a sportswriter from the London *Times*, said: "To think otherwise is to be taken in by sport's great illusion." These words were written in Barnes's report of a kick in the 1995 Rugby World Cup quarterfinal between England and Australia. The kick was famous, for it happened in the last moments of the game, when the score was tied. Taken from the Australian defensive players under tremendous pressure, this kick won a great victory for England.

Substitute vocal performance for sport and the sentiments remain the same. It is not only the superior talent and skills that separate the very high achiever from the also-ran but also the ability to respond in pressure situations, still sing your best, and do it with nerve, verve, and even risk, if need be. This is known as mental toughness, an inner strength that goes beyond talent and skill. Without this toughness, excellence is unobtainable.

These are the characteristics of peak performers, whatever their pursuit. The strength of their body–mind link is exhibited in the way they *think*, followed instantaneously by what they *do*. They are confident, positive, and optimistic. Not for them are concerns about failure or worry about others. Their sense of inner calm and their ability to remain in complete control separate them from other, lesser beings.

To be consistently good, elite performers plan assiduously and prepare in depth before, during, and after their performances. Then they do it all again and again. Their focus on pushing their own performance boundaries is relentless. They are "hooked" on excelling. Once they are in the performance cycle, they keep going around, looking for the place to add just a little more drive that will move the performance forward. This is their drug, and they take it daily, morning, noon, and night, throughout their performing lives. Their quest is unending.

Such is the power of performance.

1   This Thing Called Performance

> Performance is a basic level of communication in life as
> well as on the stage; performance is an activity in which
> we daily, routinely, and, all but inevitably, engage.
>
> Robert Cohen,
> *Acting Power*

Singers, professional or amateur, regard the spectacle of the Olympic Games as virtually identical to their own work. Even an inexperienced singer knows—as Gertrude Stein would say—that performance is performance is performance, whatever the field. It matters not that an athlete broke an Olympic record back home in Indiana on a Thursday afternoon at 2:00 P.M. It only counts when he or she does it at the appointed time and in the appointed place, under pressure, in Montreal or Atlanta, say, at 10:17 A.M. Similarly, it matters not how well the singer performed the aria at the Monday rehearsal; it only counts when he or she sings it well on Wednesday evening at 8:26 P.M. before an audience.

Professional and nonprofessional alike, everyone performs every day, be it in sports, singing, or acting, summing up before a jury, taking an examination, making a presentation at a conference, or presiding over a business meeting. You have "performed" if you have worked to achieve competence at some activity and then done it *before others.*

In order to become an outstanding performer you must learn how to perform your skills. The task is to learn how to perform. You cannot assume that once you have learned the music and become skilled at your singing you can just spurt those skills out coherently again and again in a performance situation. Ask one of those singers who panic when they see particular people on the audition panel. Ask those who suffer from severe muscle tension during performances that do not go as they should. Ask any singer who feels permanently frustrated because he/she is never able to sing as well in performance as in the studio with the voice teacher or coach.

Knowing how to learn and becoming more expert in the performance process are linked together, as performance psychologist
Tom Kubistant tells us: "If I know how to learn well, I can be in a
better position to perform what I have learned, and if I can perform
well, I can be in a better position to learn new things" (1986, p. 2).

You want to be the best you can be. Perhaps you have been told
that you have great potential. Nevertheless, in one normal lifetime
an average person actualizes only between 5 and 20 percent of his/
her potential (Otto, 1970). One might ask: Where does the other 80
to 95 percent go? Potential is a difficult concept. You never know
how much you actually have until you try to realize it. In their
book, *Maximum Performance*, researchers L. E. Morehouse and
L. Gross explain potential this way: "The better performer lies
dormant in us for three basic reasons. The first is that the various
cultural and social forces have conspired to keep it hidden. The
second is that it doesn't believe in itself. The third is that [the per-
son] literally doesn't know how to make use of potential" (1977,
p. 11).

It may not be possible to focus on your potential alone, but it is
certainly possible to focus on all your other qualities required for
good performance, such as discipline, creativity, persistence, and
sheer doggedness. These are the things you attend to, in addition
to knowing what you can achieve now. You don't have control over
whatever potential you do possess, but you do have control over
what you are capable of doing *now*. The answer, then, is to work at
all the other areas relating to performance, continuing to push the
boundaries of your performance abilities, perhaps using some of
that latent potential along the way. With this plan of action you
can become what you wish to become. You can experience the joy
of performing well, even though you might occasionally be frustrated or disappointed. Kubistant makes us realize: "No matter what
our roles and functions are in life, how we perform is as crucial to
our successes and development as individuals as are the outcomes
of our performances. These efforts define who we are as well as
give us indications of what we can become" (1986, p. 6).

Left- and Right-Brain Functions in Performance

The nature of your performance and the manner in which you work
to tap into that elusive potential can very often be traced to the
way you view your performance—purely analytically, purely creatively, or a combination of both. How you think will affect your
performance in many ways. Singing involves you in logical, analytical thought, simply because singing is a highly complex activity, during which *you really must think technically for some of the*

time, while constantly projecting creative, visual, nonverbal com-
munication and body language. When you perform, the two hemispheres of your brain organize different modes of thought and perception. The left hemisphere dominates your logical, analytical
thinking, strategies, evaluation and criticism, detailed specifics,
verbal effort, and thinking in the future and in the past. The right
hemisphere reigns over your insight, feelings, touch, tempo, intuition, positive feedback, imagery, living in the present, control by
goal, nonverbal understanding, and effortless flow.

Performance gives you plenty of opportunities to develop and
use (or misuse) both left-brain and right-brain functions. You require most, if not all, of these functions for your performance. Take
imagery as an example. This is a right-brain function. It can enhance your performance greatly. On the other hand, thinking clearly
about the next phrase or run or attack is correct use of both right-
and left-brain thinking. But perhaps your imagery takes you
repeatedly to a performance that was poor or you keep dwelling on
the vocal detail that didn't go well. These are examples of the misuse of the right and left hemispheres of the brain.

Clearly, one of your performance skills is learning to use the
correct brain function when you need it during performance. Staying only with the left-brain functions during performance is detrimental, because the performance may be very competent but will
lack meaning and expression. There will be perhaps little of the
correct type of thinking, using the right-brain functions (intuitive
responses, sensitivity of touch, imagery, positive feelings, and staying in the present), and perhaps too much negative thinking, too
much calibrating each note, each run, each phrase to get it right.

The left brain deals sequentially with input, while the right brain
deals simultaneously with input. When you look carefully at the
right-brain function (figure 1-1), you will see that it bears significant resemblances to performance.

Best performance results flow from the ability to use mainly the
right-brain (synthesizer) function, with occasional visits to the left-
brain (analyzer) function. A peak performance, where self-imposed
limitations are momentarily forgotten, goes by various nicknames
in sports. A basketball player talks about a "hot night." A tennis
player refers to "playing out of his/her head." An Australian football player reaches for the "purple patch," and Jimmy Connors tried
to "go into the tunnel" (Unestahl, 1983, p. 288).

Performance Levels

Your peak performance is a goal that you strive for, but before you
get to a peak performance level, there are other levels of perfor-

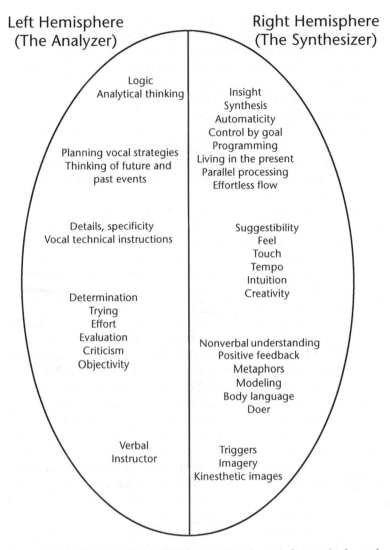

Left Hemisphere
(The Analyzer)

Right Hemisphere
(The Synthesizer)

Logic
Analytical thinking

Insight
Synthesis
Automaticity
Control by goal
Programming
Living in the present
Parallel processing
Effortless flow

Planning vocal strategies
Thinking of future and
past events

Details, specificity
Vocal technical instructions

Suggestibility
Feel
Touch
Tempo
Intuition
Creativity

Determination
Trying
Effort
Evaluation
Criticism
Objectivity

Nonverbal understanding
Positive feedback
Metaphors
Modeling
Body language
Doer

Verbal
Instructor

Triggers
Imagery
Kinesthetic images

Figure 1-1. The functions of the brain's two hemispheres. (Adapted from Unestahl, 1983, p. 284).

mance for which to strive. These have been termed *optimal* and *maximal* performance (Kubistant, 1986).

Optimal Performance

This is described as a performance that is as good as possible at that moment, bearing in mind that more experience might be wanted and that certain skills and techniques might still need to be learned or upgraded. An optimal performance builds up those specific skills and endurance levels that the specialty requires, achieving the most consistent and efficient results. Your new automobile is in the midst of an optimal performance when it is achieving its best gas consumption with minimal wear and tear at, say, fifty to sixty miles per hour.

Optimal performances can also be used as platforms for achieving greater things in performance later. You might think of optimal performance as learning to walk before you can run or learning the arias before the whole role or running many ten-kilometer races before you try to run a marathon. From your optimal performances you gain valuable experiences that will stand you in good stead for what is to come later. They have their own goals and can be complete within themselves. For example, singers are often encouraged to audition or to sing in workshops in order to appreciate how good their skills actually are. Particular goals are set at the singer's level, and the singer attempts to meet those goals. Many performing factors can be fine-tuned in this way. "Optimal performances are designed as consistent, progressive, integrative, efficient, and effective efforts that can be ends in themselves and/or be a means to an end," says Kubistant (1986, p. 13).

Maximal Performance

The next level of performance is one that makes great demands— both physical and mental—upon you as the performer. It is more consistent; it very often achieves the goals it sets out to attain; it extends your personal frontiers; it is an end in itself. Despite the requisite high mental and physical demands made upon you, a maximal performance gives the best quality, the best value, and the best results. This is like a new race car going flat out, the driver's foot depressing the accelerator pedal to the floor. A maximal performance is flat out, all or nothing.

While you can get to your goal more quickly this way, it does have its pitfalls. It uses up much more of your energy. All the wear and tear makes you become more anxious and, as a consequence, makes you break down more often. Your maximal performances, in which you push back your performance boundaries and really extend yourself, are very demanding. This is why it is important to plan and space your maximal performances judiciously. Important auditions, recitals, and stage performances may all require a maximal performance, regardless of the cost.

Track-and-field athletes plan carefully when during the season to give a maximal performance: It could be at the Olympic trials, at the major trials for the world championships, or even at the national championships, because they may lead to inclusion in the international squad. During 1996, the year of the Atlanta Olympics, the track-and-field athletes were very careful to plan their maximal performances. Too many, and they ended up giving poorer performances while becoming stale. Too few, and they didn't make the squad. Every performance doesn't have to be a maximal performance. You must plan carefully for those. At a very high level of ability, fewer is better.

Although optimal and maximal performances are subtly different from each other, they are equal in their intensity. Their outcomes are geared differently: A maximal performance seeks to achieve excellence across-the-board, whereas an optimal performance is more likely to be a means to an end. An optimal performance could be compared to your voice lesson, where you practice and refine certain parts, lines, phrases, or even one note within a piece of music. It's like taking an audition for a specific reason beyond getting the part, because you want to try something out or because you need the experience of auditioning, for example. You gain your experience in optimal performances, not in maximal performances.

High levels of individual performance combine optimal and maximal performances. As these two types of performance constantly improve, they open the gates for another higher level of performance, the peak performance.

Further information:

1. On the right-brain function of imagery, see chapter 12, "Imagery in Performance."
2. On solving the misuse of the right and left hemispheres of the brain, see chapter 15, "Exploring and Planning 'Meaning' for Performance."
3. On dealing in depth with peak performance, see chapter 2, "The Characteristics of Peak Performance."

2 The Characteristics of Peak Performance

> A successful performance is the pinnacle of achievement in your musical development. In one sense, performing entails a synthesis of thought, feeling, and physical movements; but in a broader sense, it signifies a supreme act of artistic giving.
>
> Seymour Bernstein,
> *With Your Own Two Hands*

A peak performance exhibits the strength of the mind–body link. For you as a peak performer *what you think* is echoed by *what you do.*

A peak performance is accompanied not by the fear of failure but rather by a confident and optimistic attitude, not by an unsettled state of mind but rather by a sense of inner calm and a high degree of concentration, not by an acceptance of powerlessness but rather by a feeling of being in control of an (apparently) effortless, unforced result, not by unmanageable tension but rather by a (learned technique of) physical relaxation and, at the same time, an extraordinary awareness of body and surroundings. As a singer, don't you long for such results? Wouldn't you be overjoyed to have this kind of experience?

The Effects of Peak Performance

These peak performances are exceptional and appear to surpass any ordinary level of performance. When such a performance happens to you, you will sing better than you have ever sung before. It will be a supreme high. It will be the moment toward which you, your voice teacher, and your coach have been working for many years. It will be the ultimate moment in your relentless search for excellence in performance.

Yet peak performances are rare occurrences and may be involuntary for some. When they do occur, they push you to a new level of experience that extends the boundaries of your performance into effortlessness. They enable you to tap further into your potential.

All your skills and abilities come together with your previous hard work. A peak performance integrates and synthesizes (a right-brain activity) all you know into one wonderful, complete whole. The experience is simply wonderful, say those who know. It's a floating sensation, blissful yet calm, as if you were standing outside yourself. You wonder: *What actually happened? Did I really do that? Was that my voice? Was that really me?*

When you give a peak performance your state of mind is actually altered; your perceptions are inverted. Time appears to slow down, and everything seems to be in slow motion, yet the event goes by so swiftly that you can scarcely believe it when it is over. Everything around you is in sharp focus. Colors are more vivid; sizes change. In golfers' peak performances that hole in the ground seems, they say, as "big as a bucket." For a weight lifter, weights become lighter. For a singer, there is a soaring ease. Senses become very acute; the victory of the performance can be smelled; the joy can be tasted. In a peak performance the boundaries of your performance are redefined.

Can You Train for Peak Performance?

In high-level sport and the arts one question has taxed researchers, athletes, and artists alike: Is it possible to train someone in such a way that peak performances occur more frequently?

As a singer, you are no different from an elite athlete. The same questions apply to you. Is there an "ideal performance state" (a phrase used repeatedly in sport psychology literature) for the singer? If so, does this "ideal state" vary from one singer to another? Are there common characteristics that distinguish the peak performance of the singer? Or are there common characteristics that all elite performers describe as a peak performance? Most important, if these common characteristics exist, can you learn them?

Any peak performance is an outcome of physical, technical, and mental factors. This means that the body and the mind cannot be separated in such a performance. In fact, the physical and technical aspects are *conditions* of high-level performance. There is no substitute for a complete mastery of the technical skills and, even in the arts, a certain level of physical well-being. The higher your level of physical well-being and your mastery of the vocal, musical, linguistic, and dramatic skills, the more control you have over your performance.

TEACHING POINT: See #1, Appendix 2.

However, the higher your level of physical and technical skills, the more important the mental aspects become. Aiming for peak performance, you would be wise to lavish a focus on the mental side that is equal to your usual concern with the physical and technical side. In high-level sport, most coaches and athletes will readily admit that 50 to 95 percent of success is due to mental factors. Now that the physical and technical aspects of sport are so advanced, it is the mental aspects, athletes believe, that differentiate between those who make it and those who do not. Mark Spitz, winner of seven gold medals at the Montreal Olympics, said on this subject, "At this level of physical skill, the difference between winning and losing is 99 percent psychological." And when Tiger Woods, on his way to being the youngest golfer ever to win the Masters Golf Tournament in 1997, played less well in game two and the press asked why, the young man replied simply, "I wasn't *thinking* right."

It is no different for singers. If the physical and technical aspects of your performance and that of your fellow singer are of high caliber, then the mental aspects will determine which of you will be successful and which will not.

Eventually there comes a point in performance preparation when your technical and physical skills are as good as they can be at that moment and there is little more to be done to improve these skills in the time remaining. But this does not indicate that you have nothing else to do. You must go on working at the mental aspects of your performance both before and during your performance.

Mental preparation is the single most critical element in peak performance.

Jack Nicklaus,
Golf My Way

Your Own "Ideal Performing State"

If, as the research states, the mental side of performance is so important for success, then it is up to you to determine what constitutes your own "ideal performing state" (Mahoney and Avanel, 1977). In particular, you must know what your own ideal performing state is *before* you begin a mental training program. We know from the research (Ravizza, 1977) that certain characteristics are present when peak performances occur.

High-level performers identify their own ideal performance state and learn, either consciously or unconsciously, to produce and retain this ideal state, which in turn allows them to prosper from their skills and abilities when under pressure. The chief psychological characteristics of high-achievement performers are:

- No feelings of fear
- An ability to regulate anxiety and arousal during performance
- Maintenance of positive thoughts and imagery throughout performance
- High confidence that is unshakable
- An ability to remain focused and concentrated, without distractions
- Determination to succeed
- Thinking that is committed and disciplined
- Control over the performance.

Allowing for many individual variations, these characteristics are generally acknowledged by most elite performers.

Because of these common factors in the psychological makeup of elite performers, sport psychologists like James E. Loehr (1984) conclude that there can be no room for a negative climate during performance. Negativity will trigger reactions that produce, among other things, tension in the body (fatal for the voice) and poor concentration (equally fatal). Rather, there must be a psychological and emotional atmosphere that allows for desirable physical and technical reactions. To create such an atmosphere, you must become conscious of your thought patterns.

Not only is your level of performance a direct reflection of your thinking and feeling before, during, and after performance, but also the relationship between performance and thinking behavior may be circular in nature. That is, your ideal mental state allows you to perform better; then your success returns the favor and reinforces the ideal mental state.

How You Can Stimulate and Encourage an Ideal Performing State

The ideal mental state does not just happen. Mental skills have to be learned, even as you have to learn the physical techniques of your vocal art. Mental skills are learned through practice just as your vocal skills were. You yourself may be able to perfect your special talents on your own, but most singers must be taught them through systematic and specific programs.

Although a peak performance happens without your predicting it, you can give it a chance to occur more often by working at the most appropriate mental skills. Your *aim* is always toward a peak performance, and your *task* is to create the proper climate within which it can happen. Inevitably there will be individual differences in performers and their performing activities, but certain mental skills should always be present and combined in the right dimensions at the right time in order to produce a peak performance:

- Your previous experiences during practice should have been at a very high level.
- Your goal setting and planning should have been specific and clear.
- Your self-confidence should be unquestionable.
- You should deal with your level of mental energy very efficiently.
- You should take advantage of each situation and of the opportunities it offers.
- You should accentuate your ability, your skills, and capitalize on your luck.
- You should keep a balance between your life as a person and your life as a performer, staying in harmony with your total self.
- You should make sure that you still enjoy what you do.
- You should be persistent.
- You should remain completely in the present moment, with no dwelling on past actions or future possibilities.
- You must remain noncritical of the ongoing performance (something that singers find extremely difficult to do!).

In other words, you must submit your total self to the experience of the performance.

A peak performance sets the standards for future performances. The more information you possess about the areas in your performance that must be improved, the more chance you have to give a peak-level performance. Clearly, the bases for such high-level performance are a development of your self-awareness and your need to be in complete control. As a singer you should learn, for example, to recognize your emotional state before, during, and after performance. You should learn to adjust it if and as necessary. You should learn to fine-tune your concentration by focusing on the appropriate critical points, not on the final result. If it is your habit to be concerned about the final outcome, you will find it difficult to remain in the present. The result is a waste of mental energy that could have been vital to a peak performance. Your aim is to gain control of every aspect of your performance—the functional vocal and breathing muscles as well as the extravocal musculature, your emotions, and your thoughts—so as to integrate them into one fine, smooth, joyous performance. As your awareness grows, so will your ability to make fine adjustments to your performance. Performance depends on *refinement* and *control*. Control of your self and your environment will increase as the understanding and awareness of your singing experiences deepen.

> The peak experience is an intrinsic experience that is
> self- validating. It is vital for the athlete [and the singer]
> to have some internal feelings of value rather than to
> rely on the evaluation of significant others, teachers,
> or coaches. The peak experience teaches the athlete
> [and the singer] an awareness of their [*sic*] own sig-
> nificance independent of what others have to say.
> Kenneth Ravizza, "Increasing Awareness
> for Sport Performance"

Practical Ways to Begin Acquiring Control of Your Performances

If you are ready to learn techniques that will help raise your own
level of awareness, if you are anxious to acquire the information
needed to gain control of your performing, if you cannot wait to
add peak performance to your singing life, try some of the following exercises.

Exercise 1

Keep a journal with a record of your auditions and other performances. You can use various headings to help structure your
thoughts. For example, you might write down what it felt like when
you sang or practiced at your best, a detailed description of your
reactions to the enjoyable experiences during performance, a list
of stress-inducing things that happened before, during, or after the
performance, and a measurement of the confidence you felt, of your
relaxation level, and of your focus and concentration. If you were
focused and concentrated on the right things, write down how you
did it. If you were unfocused or concentrated on the wrong things,
what happened? Where *was* your focus? Were you able to use other
skills, such as anxiety control or imagery? How did they work?
When did you use them? Keep your journal up-to-date. Use it for
practice sessions also. You can glean much information from a very
good practice session. Here is a sample checklist of your physical
and mental reactions that will help you assess the differences between the mental, physical, and technical facets of your best and
worst performances:

my muscles were relaxed	*or*	tight
my mind was quiet, and calm	*or*	frantic
my anxiety was low	*or*	high
my attitude was positive	*or*	negative
I experienced enjoyment	*or*	no enjoyment
performance felt effortless	*or*	effortful
performance was automatic	*or*	deliberate

I felt confident	or	a lack of confidence
I was alert	or	sluggish
performance was controlled	or	out of control
I was focused	or	unfocused
I sang well	or	poorly
I felt positive energy	or	negative energy

Exercise 2

Use the performance feedback sheet (figure 2-1) or a similar sheet, to process the information that you accumulate from the perfor-

---

Performance: _____ Date: _____

1. How anxious were you before today's performance? 0_____ 5_____10
$$\text{low \quad not bad \quad high}$$

2. What were the things that caused you stress?

3. When did you feel most stress—before, during, after?

4. How did you experience the stress? In thoughts, feelings, actions?

5. How did you manage your anxiety? How effective were you in controlling it using these techniques?

6. Describe in detail your self-talk. Remember key words and phrases you used.

7. What, if anything, have you learned from this performance that will help you plan for the next one? If you can, remember the details.

Figure 2-1. Sample performance feedback sheet.

mance. This will help you to be systematic about learning from each experience. It will also help you to plan for and focus on the next performance.

Exercise 3

Make an effort to discuss the performance and/or practice session in detail with others. Speak to another singer, your teacher, your coach, or a performance enhancement person. Sharing experiences, expertise, and perspectives can be an immense help in developing your self-awareness. Discussions will also help you to discover that there are many singers in the same boat; it's not just you!

Case Study

M.R., a dramatic tenor who developed from a high baritone, is a very intelligent, highly musical, laid-back, perhaps too laid-back, kind of person. He has professional management and is at the beginning of his career. We asked him to write down his recollections of his first peak performance experience.

I was performing the role of Canio in Leoncavallo's *I Pagliacci* in Michigan. This performance was my first time singing the role. I was very well prepared. The orchestra was also very good, especially considering it was a summertime music festival. The festival provided an atmosphere which was ideal for singing the role for the first time, and the camaraderie between the artists was enjoyable.

During my preparation for the opening night I was very positive. I told myself, "There is no one else on earth capable of doing this role as well as I." I have a distinct memory of my first entrance on stage and saying to myself, "This is what I have been preparing for all my life; this is where I want to be." At that moment a sense of calm came over me and much of my performance anxiety melted away.

Canio's second entrance is the point in the drama where he discovers his wife Nedda with another man. The music and the staging reflect the rage that has come over him. He threatens his wife with a knife and is restrained by another member of the troupe. He realizes he must get ready for the evening's performance. He sings the most famous tenor aria, "Vesti la giubba." He is wracked with pain, anger, and despair. I remember during the performance of this aria I allowed myself to give in to the full expression of my emotions and the full expression of my voice. During the "Ah" before the phrase "Ridi, pagliaccio," I experienced what can be best described as an *out-of-body* phenomenon. I was sobbing and writhing with the anger, pain, and despair of Canio, and yet as I performed I remember standing outside of myself watching my performance. I was giving myself directions: "Sing this note gently, then crescendo," "Open the vowel only this far," "Drive this phrase home." The character of Canio was one hundred percent given over to the moment and his emotions, and there I was watching and being one hundred percent calm. I also felt a great connection with the audience. I knew something exceptional was happening. I walked offstage with confidence, exhilaration, and a sense of peace.

Summary

A peak performance is within your power. It is not a gift of fate. It is not a reward for living a good life. It is a result of your attitudes and efforts in the entire cycle of performance—preperformance preparation, performance skills, and postperformance evaluation.

Further information:

1. On exercise 1 (assessing differences between best and worst performances), see chapter 8, "Developing Self-Confidence through Positive Thinking."
2. On exercise 2 (processing information accumulated from the performance), see chapter 8, "Developing Self-Confidence through Positive Thinking."

3 What Is Mental Toughness?

I realize that I have all the talent and technique, but unfortunately I was not born with the necessary competitive instincts and personality.

U.K. international
long jumper, 1994

When singers perform well, they are in a psychological state very different from that which accompanies a poor performance. In performance there are times when everything goes well and other times when it is difficult to put a foot right.

When your performance hasn't worked, what do *you* do? Most singers go back to their voice teachers to work yet again at the many technical things that they suspect are in need of correction, because they blame any problem with the performance on a technical fault. They check and recheck vocal technical problems; they tape; they listen; they tinker some more. They return to their coach to check and recheck the interpretation, the linguistic values, the dramatic qualities, the musical accuracy, and so on and on.

Perhaps you are very good at seeking out that left-brain function, technical perfection (if there is such a thing), as well as the utmost clarity of interpretation. However, high-level, consistently good performance is only partly to do with such things as technical skill, talent, and innate artistic ability—all those things that you admire so much. This view of performance is, in actuality, an all-pervasive misconception. Technical skill, talent, and innate artistic ability are not enough in any performance.

A classic example is that of the tenor's nine high Cs in Donizetti's *The Daughter of the Regiment*. Certainly he can successfully manage them time and time again in his studio and that of his teacher and coach. But perhaps he worries about doing it in audition when vying with other tenors for the role, or in the finals of a competition offering a $40,000 first prize. In these high-pressure situations things are not so easy.

21

As the skills of top teachers and singers become more equal across-the-board, as high-level coaching becomes ever more refined and more available to all, you need more than expert technical and coaching programs; you must also prepare very thoroughly in the psychological area. A combination of hard work, skill, and talent will continue to form you into a singer of quality. However, if in the future you wish to stay *ahead* of the pack, it will not be enough to perform consistently at a very high level. To be a winner, to remain in the zone of performing excellence as a singer, you will also need to refine your mental preparation and training. You must, in short, become mentally tough.

Once you have a swing or a stroke that works reasonably well, your mental and emotional approach becomes 95% of the package that determines how well and how consistently you score. That's a well known, often published, often discussed fact, but too many amateurs, as well as a few professionals, don't pay attention.

Ray Floyd, champion golfer,
From 60 Yards In

How often, following a mediocre or poor performance, do you evaluate your approach to the performance, then refine it, alter it, keep what works, jettison what doesn't, and rehearse it time and time again? You lavish this attention on technical and artistic matters. Do you devote the same attention to mental matters? Much of the research tells us that the primary reason a performance doesn't work is a mental one—at least 90 percent of the time. To become consistently very good at high-level performance, do not work harder; work smarter. Become mentally tough. Learn to apply to your singing the mental skills set forth in the following pages.

Performing to Potential

There is nothing more frustrating than continually performing below what you judge to be your actual potential (if you know what it is). This is especially true on those occasions when it is important to do well, for example a major audition, an opening night, or an important performance such as a debut. Such high-pressure situations can produce all the wrong kinds of emotion—self-doubt, frustration, anger, and poor self-esteem—all of which, in turn, erect at least one of the performance barriers that you may find difficult to surmount. Under these circumstances, many performers, older and experienced singers as well as young and inexperienced ones, become casualties, going no further.

It is at times like this when, weighed down by doubt and frustration, a singer will say, "If I can't overcome this problem, I simply will not be able to go on any longer. It's too demanding and too stressful trying to do your best when you suspect it won't be good enough. The most devastating thing about all this is that most of the time I am better than my performance would show, and I know it." Imagine how many talented singers have been lost to the art of singing and performance because of this impediment! Mental toughness may be the one decisive factor that keeps you performing.

Control and Consistency

When you decided to become a singer, wasn't that decision based at least in part upon the enjoyment singing gave you? Believing that it will go well, anticipating the pleasure of surrendering yourself to the performance with the knowledge that the result will be good—these things enhance the very act of singing and certainly the enjoyment of the audience. Part of the joy of singing is the expectation of a satisfying consistency in your efforts. Think back to the last time you were completely satisfied with your performance. Wasn't that a wonderful feeling? It can be that way most of the time!

Remember: The consistently good performer consistently *thinks* well under pressure. Consequently that performer is always in complete control of the performance. Control, together with consistency, is a measure of mental toughness.

If you wish to perform to the upper limits of your talent and skill day after day, performance after performance, then two things are required:

1. *Very good technical and artistic form.* If the technique is poor, performance inconsistencies occur no matter how good the mental approach.
2. *Good mental skills.* Especially mental toughness.

Contrary to common belief, mental toughness is a *learned* ability. It is not inherited; neither is it allied with general personality. It doesn't matter if you happen to be an introvert or an extrovert, thoughtful or arrogant, quiet or boastful, modest or pretentious. Happily, all such characteristics have very little to do with being successful in performance. Closely associated with confidence, mental toughness prevents you from being on a performance seesaw. "Mentally tough performers become consistent in their performances simply because they are psychologically consistent" (Loehr, 1984, p. 10).

Characteristics of Mental Toughness

The salient characteristics of mental toughness are related to being self-motivated and self-directed while possessing a stunningly strong belief and trust in self. Mentally tough performers are relaxed; they welcome challenge, rather than viewing difficult events and situations as threats. Performers who are mentally tough minimize errors and distractions and maximize strengths while learning from poor performances. They have unmistakable inner strength. It takes persistence, dedication, and courage to become a mentally tough performer.

All the great artists of sport exemplified this special kind of inner strength, a strength that goes well beyond the limits of their natural talent and skill. It is the thin line which separates the few who make it from the thousands who don't. The deciding factor is always the same, your INNER STRENGTH makes the ultimate difference.

James E. Loehr,
Mental Toughness Training for Sports

Elite, mentally tough performers (from team or individual sports as well as the performing arts, such as acting, singing, and dancing) are all characterized by specific mental skills. According to James E. Loehr, originator of the following mental toughness model for top tennis players, the mentally tough performer must be:

1. *Highly motivated and self-directed toward success.* You must be motivated from within. When you become this kind of performer, you will not require cajoling or persuading; you will be self-directed to go after success.
2. *Completely positive yet realistic and optimistic about him/ herself.* This means that you will build on the positive things that happen. You will tend to be rational and objective about what is possible, but you will look for success.
3. *In control of his/her emotions, but not an emotional performer.* Although many things happen within training and performance that might cause you to become angry, frustrated, or even frightened, as a mentally tough performer

you can control these emotions so that they do not interfere with the performance.

4. *Calm and relaxed, viewing pressure as a challenge, not a
   threat.* As this kind of performer, you will be motivated by
   the challenge, pushed by it to the limits of your potential,
   enjoying the opportunity to thrust against the boundaries
   of performance and further prove yourself.

5. *Focused and concentrated.* If you are a mentally tough
   singer, you will be able to concentrate intensively while
   remaining aware. You will be able to zero in on the most
   important things, to disregard the unimportant things. The
   control of focus is a vital skill in high-level performance,
   whether it be under pressure or not.

I'm not *involved* [authors' italics] in tennis; I am committed. Do you know the difference between involvement and commitment?

Martina Navratilova,
international tennis champion

---

6. *Utterly self-confident and incapable of being compromised.*
   To be mentally tough you *must* have an unfailing belief in
   yourself and your ability to do well. Then you will be full
   of self-confidence, always working your strengths in every
   aspect of your performance.

7. *In control and fully responsible for his/her own actions.*
   When you are responsible for your own actions, you will
   make no excuses. Nor will you allow others to control your
   performance, about which you will make your own decisions. You will take a risk if you must but be content to
   accept responsibility if things do not work out, because it
   was your decision.

8. *Resolute and determined to succeed.* As a mentally tough
   performer, you will set your goals and relentlessly aspire
   to them. Tending not to live in the past or the future, you
   will be in control of what you can do *now*. All incidents,
   even negative ones, will be acknowledged and taken in
   stride. As this kind of performer, you will learn from such
   incidents and proceed again toward your goal.

9. *Able to control and maintain the right level of mental energy.* The ability to reach the right level of mental energy,
   to control and maintain it however you are feeling, is a
   vital skill on the way to becoming mentally tough. You
   must be able to switch into and maintain the performance

mode, no matter what else has happened, no matter how you feel. This can be done despite the difficulties.

What mental toughness teaches you is that, for most of the time, the real challenge is to be able to deal with yourself. Sports people call it the ultimate challenge, and *it is no different for singers*. Like athletes, you must learn to master who you are, how you think. You must learn to stop being your own worst critic. Having learned to deal with yourself, no matter at what level you perform, you will always feel that you have done your best, that you have maintained a positive attitude, that you have felt completely in control, and that the full responsibility is yours—no need to blame or surrender credit to others around you.

This mental strength, together with your skill, talent, and artistic form, will allow you to be ahead of your "competitors" most of the time. This way lies success for you; this way you will have pleasure in your singing.

How to Become Mentally Tough, through a Four-Stage Success Process

But *how*, you ask, do you learn the skills that are so vital to your success? These skills are acquired through exactly the same process by which you acquired the skills of singing—intellectual understanding, practice, and hard work. If you want to be mentally tough, you can be. You must practice the performance skills; you must have knowledge about what you are attempting and its application to lessons, practice, and performance. It just takes time.

Most of the skills that will make you mentally tough are outlined elsewhere in this book, but, in addition to mastering these skills, you have to be committed to the following four-stage process, also adapted from Loehr (1987, p. 10).

Self-Discipline

Most, if not all, singers work very hard at trying to learn all the techniques required by their chosen art form. They accept the need to sacrifice some of the things they enjoy, to do whatever is necessary for the sake of success. It begins with self-discipline. Without this, you are lost as a performer. Your approach cannot be a halfhearted one. Unfortunately, it's all or nothing. You must be dedicated to your art. Sometimes it can be a lonely business, but at least you do find out who your real friends are and which of them understand that you can't go to a party, bar, or nightclub every night.

Self-Control

Self-discipline leads to self-control. After a time this control will become total. You will have control of how you practice, what you are doing, and, most important, how you think. Action follows thought. If you are able to control your thinking, then you also control the action. As a performer, you are what you think. Can you really become an outstanding performer without self-control? The answer is a resounding no.

Self-Confidence

After you have control, then you find self-confidence. You will see this word written many times in this book. There is no high-level performance without self-confidence, but you do not become self-confident unless you have self-discipline and are self-controlled. Your self-confidence must be completely unshatterable. This in turn comes from knowing exactly what you can do and being totally in control of yourself and your performance.

Self-Realization

Self-realization is the culmination of all your talent, skills, and hard work. True self-confidence allows you to have self-realization. Self-realization allows you to be the best you can be whenever you are called on in performance. Once you have self-confidence, once you know that you are in control, once you feel really good about yourself, then some of the potential within you will be tapped and you will continue to push the boundaries of your performance.

How to Use the Four-Stage Process and the Nine Characteristics of Mental Toughness

This simple four-stage process forms the strong base from which your mental toughness develops. The concept is a little like a stairway. Stepping from one stage to the other, you will eventually succeed in achieving the self-realization during performance that you crave.

Give yourself time to ponder each of the stages described earlier. Decide how each relates to you. What is your present status? At what stage are you? Do you need to be more self-disciplined, or are you doing well at that? Do you feel in control in some areas of your work but not in others? If so, what areas need work? At what level is your self-confidence?

Think about these stages in relation to your performance and, equally important, in relation to your life in general. The four stages

are no different for life than they are for performance. Your analytical thinking about both will not be a waste of time. Write down
your feelings about where you are in each stage at the present moment. This will generate a self-awareness that is imperative for the
development of mental strength. The better you know yourself, the
easier it is to make those adjustments and changes needed in order
to become really mentally tough. Knowing yourself better helps
you to erect a mental framework on which to start your work and
perhaps to set those all-important goals. You must start somewhere,
and this is the best place.

The exercise shown in figure 3-1 will help you to consider and
evaluate your own capacities as they relate to the nine characteristics of mental toughness outlined earlier in this chapter. Remember that you must evaluate yourself as you believe you are *now*, not
where you believe you may be in two months' time. Be honest.
Trying to fool yourself is counterproductive. Think about yourself
as a singer and rate yourself objectively.

You should always have a clear understanding of which area of
mental skills you need to improve. After doing this self-evaluation
exercise, use your self-discipline to work at those areas that need
work. Because they enhance your physical and technical skills,

Rate each factor on a continuum as follows:		
	0_____5_____10	
	poor average very good	
Highly motivated	0_____10	
Realistic and optimistic about self	0_____10	
In control of emotions	0_____10	
Calm and relaxed	0_____10	
Focused and concentrated	0_____10	
Self-confident	0_____10	
In control of own actions	0_____10	
Determined	0_____10	
Able to control mental energy	0_____10	

Figure 3-1. Personal evaluation graph.

mental skills complete the package that constitutes your performance. The better your mental skills, the more chance you give the other skills—vocal, musical, linguistic, and dramatic—to work for you, most especially when you are under pressure. All that potential you know to be yours can be uncovered; all that potential you didn't know how to get at previously will finally be drawn upon.

Case Study

P.C. is a twenty-seven-year-old petite, spirited, and very vivacious musical theater artist. She must work part-time as a waitress while she continues her training in New York. Although she has enjoyed some classical voice training, she prefers to make her way as a talented and sincere musical theater singer. We invited her to write about her experiences in trying to acquire mental toughness.

I have studied for years to be able to work in musical theater. I can't remember ever wanting to do anything else. My family were all in the theater either as actors or singers. It was my father who sang. I remember listening all the time to such great songwriters as Jerome Kern, Cole Porter, Stephen Sondheim, Harold Arlen, Rodgers and Hart, Hammerstein, and George and Ira Gershwin. Who could fail to fall in love with such lyrics and the shows for which these writers wrote?

I have always worked hard at becoming an all-round performer, in that I sang, danced, acted, I felt, at a reasonably high level. All my teachers and coaches for as long as I can remember were telling me that I had what it took to make it! Of course I believed them and naturally I got a lot of support from my family to do well and succeed.

I made my way from Buffalo to Manhattan, New York. I continued to study and waitress. I also began to audition in earnest. I'd had some small song and dance parts but not what I thought was big-time.

After being invited to audition many times and not getting a part, then I began to doubt myself. I think I had one callback in twenty-five auditions. I was very disheartened. The feedback from the auditions, when I could get any (Why are they so reluctant to give us feedback? How else can we improve our performance?) was very negative and nebulous. For example, "This song requires more than a pretty voice, and a smiling face. You have to mean it, and make a statement, not only with the song but with yourself." Or, "Remember, what we see is what we hear. You tend to wander out onstage not knowing what you want to do."

I had listened and seen some of the other auditionees, and I know they certainly weren't that much better than me if they were at all! I know you've all heard that before, but after all my training, I do have some idea of what is quality and what isn't! Why couldn't I perform in the audition to the level I know I can do in the studio? It was then I became aware of those other elements in performance which tended to be a bit difficult to define. Things like confidence, self-belief, mental attitude, mental toughness, presentation of self. It appeared that there was a whole section to do with performing well that I didn't know anything about. That's not strictly true; all my teachers and coaches had always talked about confidence and being thoroughly prepared and being able to project oneself with ease, but somehow no one ever taught me HOW to do these things. Aren't they a part of the performer?

I had to find out why I wasn't getting any callbacks at all, and it was then I began to work on this nebulous area of performance, called mental toughness. I did discover that I was already OK in some areas—for example, I was still as motivated as ever to get it right, though I did feel that if this process went on for much longer I might not be. My determination and dedication had not faltered either, thank goodness. It was, however, in the areas of control, especially of emotions and my own actions, together with not really understanding how to work to my strengths, that I was lacking, or rather, they were the areas which we decided were the priorities. I learned to my dismay that some of the other areas needed work, but for the time being they had to be left. I had to learn to deal with the urgent mental things first.

I learned very quickly that my "confidence" wasn't really that, rather a smoke screen to mask those doubts and fears, lack of self-belief and some deficiencies in both myself and the performance.

I learned that to be mentally tough as a performer, I had to minimize any errors and remain as focused as possible in the moment and not "flick" from the past to the future in my performance. I had to learn to maximize my strengths both in the performance and in myself, as well as use the past experiences in a positive way. Believe it or not, when I learned how to do this, I began to realize that my past auditions had had some very positive outcomes. In my disappointment, I just "threw the baby out with the bathwater."

After working in this way, I have learned to do what I do well, and to execute it always in the best way possible for me. I now know what I am actually confident in and that's what I do. I also believe it, because I know they are my strengths NOW. I'm still working at it, but I am being much more successful. I've had many more callbacks, and I've been in two major shows. The work goes on. It may be a nebulous area of performance. Mental toughness, what's that? Don't ignore it; it is the difference between me and some of the others who are auditioning with me. I know it, and I now recognize it. The work continues; watch this space. It will get better!

Summary

It is the conversation constantly going on between mind and body that the mental skills help to improve. Good mental skills *allow* your technical skills to function. They give you an appreciation and awareness of what works for you in certain situations. Your mind must speak to your body during every moment of your performance, because the body *always* does what the mind thinks. Your thoughts, images, and mental patterns act as a control mechanism; that is, they direct and the body follows.

Further information:

1. On performing below what you judge to be your actual potential, see chapter 1, "This Thing Called Performance."
2. On being self-directed toward success, see chapter 2, "The Characteristics of Peak Performance."
3. On being completely positive yet realistic about self, see chapter 8, "Developing Self-Confidence through Positive Thinking."
4. On being in control of your emotions, see chapter 11, "Dealing with Anxiety."
5. On being fully responsible for your own actions, see chapter 2, "The Characteristics of Peak Performance."
6. On achieving the right level of mental energy, see chapter 11, "Dealing with Anxiety."
7. On being resolute and determined to succeed, see chapter 1, "This Thing Called Performance."

II   PREPERFORMANCE

Every great human endeavor begins with dreams and visions. Before they surface and become reality, such visions are only fleeting. Dreams are crucial for elite performance because it is these very dreams that are the forerunners of reality. They feed on it. They may even create it.

All performers, singers in particular, have hopes and aspirations for excelling. They set goals so that they can continue to improve their performances. They try to tap into all the elusive potential they know to be theirs but must learn to unlock. They believe that, however good their abilities, they can always be better. At every level of performance, they seek to make their preparation even more complete. They face challenges: The competition is tougher; standards are higher. For many, their very being is at stake.

In today's competitive world, singers cannot just arrive on the scene and hope that their performance will be good enough. Unless the performance is thought about in detail, planned in detail and then re-planned, just turning up to sing is foolhardy, to say the least. Long before the actual performance there is much detail to be considered, filtered, retained, planned, and acted upon. All performances are only as good as the preparation that precedes them. The more thorough the preparation, the more possibility for a successful performance.

"Who am I?" is one very important, often intangible area of preparation for singers. Because the "performer self" is only one part of each person, a realistic, positive awareness of self—both person and performer—is a cornerstone of successful performance. Keeping the balance between performance and everyday life becomes a lifelong issue for all performers.

Mental skills (and their place in the entire performing cycle) allow for freedom from myriad vocal technicalities. Mental skills allow performers to *trust* what they are actually extremely good at—singing. When singers can learn to create and maintain a particular inner state of mind, they will have accomplished the single most important thing to ensure the best performance. To then *recapture* the same inner state of mind during every performance will result in consistently good performances.

A particular cluster of mental attitudes and skills allows performers to control their special insight and link it to belief in their own abilities.

All singers practice to improve their technical vocal faculties as much as possible. It is an ingrained part of their life as singers. They should also be sensitive to those other feelings and responses that relate to the meaning of the musical piece. They must be free to achieve the *expression* of their responses to the piece. It is, after all, the expression of these attitudes and feelings about the piece toward which all the technical work is directed. But this expression must be prepared. Preparation is patently the synthesis of all the aspects— physical, technical, and mental. This expression must be practiced. It should not be left to chance. One of the several ways we perceive greatness or artistry in singers lies in our own recognition of their ability to capture concisely the feelings they wish to convey to us. The sensations experienced by these great artists have become part of their automatic pilot, and they are able to reproduce under pressure everything that contributes to this kind of expression.

Once they have learned to use and maintain their mental skills, singers can look forward to becoming consistent performers, to performing at their best whatever their state of mind. Performers are mobile, dynamic integrators of moods, feelings, perceptions, contingencies, skills, and craft. Singers have to learn to integrate, synthesize, and organize these areas into some sort of useful structure. Otherwise, they and their performances would be chaotic. No one feeds excellence to performers from a silver spoon. They will earn it by being totally determined and, above all else, thorough in their planning, preparing, and thinking. The planning of the performance in each one of its many facets must begin long before any performance takes place.

Accordingly, the watchwords are: Prepare. Practice. Prepare and practice the performance techniques and skills for thorough preparation and performance.

On June 7, 1783 Wolfgang Amadeus Mozart wrote a letter to his father in which he described the playing of Muzio Clementi, one of the great composer/pianists of the day: "What he really does well are his passages in thirds; but he sweated over them day and night in London. Apart from this he can do nothing, absolutely nothing, for he has not the slightest expression or taste, still less feeling."

Seymour Bernstein,
With Your Own Two Hands

---

4   The Performing Cycle

Plans and Routines

All your performances are psychological as well as physical, because a performance is *led* by your thinking patterns and your mental images. In that moment in time when you must perform, both your body and your technique are at a certain level of excellence. Perhaps they might be better if you had been working longer at vocal technique or at your physical well-being, but regardless of your technical or physical capacity, when it comes to the actual performance it is to your mental ability that you must look in order to get the most out of yourself.

All the requisite hard work forms a cycle of performance. The performing cycle is a continuous, in-depth planning process comprising three segments:

> preperformance
> performance
> postperformance

Each segment has its own procedures and strategies. This separation into parts enables you to plan in fine detail your own individual approach to the performance. Each aspect of the performance cycle should be positive. High-level performers are separated from those who are less successful by the consistency of their performances. The planning of your performance cycle will foster such consistency.

You require mental skills that can be used to enhance your performance. Once you know what to practice, you need to practice only those particular mental skills regularly, after which your mind will be well prepared for almost everything the performance may "throw" at you. As with the acquiring of any new skill, these mental skills will cause a permanent change in behavior. You cannot expect the same effect if you fail to practice the training of your mind. Also, if you practice intermittently, the effect will soon wear off.

Try to think of your mental performance plan in the same way that you view your vocal training plan. To maintain the condition of your vocal technique, to keep it at a high level, you must practice regularly. It is exactly the same for the training of your mind for performance, except that, unlike your vocal skills, *mental skills do not demand lengthy practice periods*. Practicing the specific mental skills that you need for your performance just fifteen to twenty minutes a day, you will do very well. Some of this mental work can also be done in lessons and auditions, on the way to and from work, while shopping, and so on. True, these new skills will not become part of you overnight (neither did your vocal technique), but with belief in what you are doing, good time management, and perhaps even the help of a mental training log or diary, you will succeed in making your thinking an integral part of your performance cycle planning.

> Years ago, high performance amateur athletes may have been able to distinguish themselves in competition without developing a highly refined mental plan, but to hope for that today is much like hoping that God will come down during a time-out to tell you how to turn a game around. . . . God might be at another game.
>
> Terry Orlick,
> *Psyching for Sport: Mental Training for Athletes*

The Importance of Mental Plans and Routines for Performance

Would you ever embark upon a long, difficult journey without a good deal of preplanning? If you want the journey to be enjoyable and successful, making plans—what route to take, where to stay—will make it as stress-free as possible. Your performance, a journey of another kind, is no different. When you commence your journey toward good performing, start by uncovering your reasons for doing preperformance activities in certain ways and then plan your routines accordingly.

Your plans and routines will help you establish a good, consistent approach to your performances and will provide you with detailed focus cues to follow. They will keep your confidence high and your anxiety manageable. They will give you a dependable framework based on successful past experiences and on the evaluations that resulted from those experiences.

Too many singers settle for a belief that everything will fall into place once they get up onstage. Wrong. Not without planning it won't. You might be lucky once or twice, an audience might "inspire" you once or twice, but consistently good, spontaneous-sounding performances do not occur without thorough planning. Yes, it is possible that on the big day your performance may be so brilliant that you don't need your plans. But can you take that chance? One American sportswriter says that winning can be defined as the science of being totally prepared.

TEACHING
POINT
See #2,
Appendix 2

Three Time Frames for Mental Plans

These mental plans and routines are best considered in three different time frames: before, during, and after your performances.

1. *Preperformance.* A plan for the preperformance time includes the most appropriate mental warm-up, combined with your usual vocal and physical warm-up. Its purposes are to
   - *Strengthen the feeling of being prepared* to perform confidently and well
   - *Focus on personal strengths and qualities* in yourself and the piece you are about to sing
   - *Direct your mental energy* in the most appropriate, positive way, without giving in to negatives
   - *Establish the correct arousal level,* which feeling of readiness will set the right focus for your performance and allow you to perform well.

   This preperformance plan, possibly the most important of all your plans, sets the stage for everything to follow.
2. *Performance.* A detailed, thorough preparation plan for the performance itself—audition, competition, recital, or stage production—creates the possibility of a successful performance by avoiding unexpected happenings. Knowing that your preparation has been thorough and correct, that you have done everything possible to help yourself perform to the best of your ability, will provide the necessary mental security. Performance plans have as their purposes to
   - *Help you focus on the right things during* the performance. These plans answer questions as to the what, where, and why of your focus during performance.
   - *Guide your focus back to the performance* if, for some reason, it goes off the rails. With this type of refocus

plan you will feel confident, you will believe, that if you become distracted for any reason, you can get back to your performance plan more easily and without panic. You know what to do!

- *Help you put the energy into the performance*, where it is required. There may be a time when you need to mobilize all your efforts for the next segment of the performance—the signature or final aria, the third piece in an audition, or those crucial notes in the aria. (Examples: The Queen of the Night in *The Magic Flute* must ace the high Fs in her two arias, or all the rest of her work is for naught. The Duke in *Rigoletto* rests his reputation on the last B♮, "pen-SIER!" Having sung two other pieces in approximately six minutes, an auditioner is justifiably tired but cannot do less well on the third one. Whatever else Rodolfo does in *La Bohème*, he can never make up for failing on "Che gelida manina.") Pushing yourself to the limits of your ability, with the help of your performance plan, may be the final decider between you and the next performer.

Together, the preperformance and the performance plans are designed to give you the best possible chance of being consistently good in your performances. Implementation of these plans, individually developed and refined according to the nature of the performance, will always encourage you to do well because they make you feel so confident, so thoroughly prepared, so in control.

3. *Postperformance*. Postperformance is either (a) the time following the actual performance or (b) the time between pieces in an audition, recital, or competition. Postperformance is in some ways a very neglected area of the full performance cycle. It is a crucial time for evaluation, resting, preparing mentally for what is to follow (a repeat performance or preparation and planning for another performance), and acquiring a working knowledge of your own postperformance needs. Postperformance plans help you

- *Evaluate your performance in all its aspects*. It makes good sense to improve your forthcoming performances by knowing where the problems arose in the present performance—the vocal, mental, or physical aspects or any combination of these. It makes little sense to go back and rework areas of the performance that are fine, such as a vocal skill, when, for example, the whole problem may actually lie in your inability to remain focused at key times during the performance.

- *Relax and regain some energy* in preparation for the next performance. Giving yourself some free time or doing something completely different and having fun for a short time may be just the tonic your next performance needs.
- *Learn to deal with postperformance tension and emotion*, thus avoiding a state of staleness in your future performances.
- *Devise short refocus plans for the next piece.* It is important to view each piece as a separate performance, especially in auditions and recitals, rather than thinking of, say, three pieces as one performance.

Where and How to Begin Performance Planning

Preperformance plans guide your focus for performing. Their objective is to put you into a perfect performance condition, which can be described as follows:

- You have learned your professional craft by hard work.
- You know what your strengths are and where they lie in the pieces you are going to sing.
- You feel very confident about your ability.
- You are excited by the forthcoming performance.
- You feel very well prepared.

When beginning to plan, your first step is to review your past good performances. Go over them in detail. Write down how you prepared for them, recalling in as much detail as possible your thoughts, your feelings, and your actions preceding those successful performances. Base your beginning plans on those things that *do* work for you.

As you write down everything you can remember, what you did will become clearer. And you will have a valuable record. (You might believe that you will remember everything without notes, but you won't.) With this written record you can begin to apply some of the things that worked and refine your new plan.

You may find it easier to write down your feelings, actions, and thoughts if you organize them under the three headings of performance: physical, technical, mental.

Under *physical*, for example, you might write answers to these questions: What did I do for my physical well-being before my performance? How much time did I give to this area of preparation? Did I do stretching exercises? Did I work out? Did I meditate? For how many days in the period immediately before the performance did I do these things? What did I eat? At what hour? How much did I sleep?

Under *technical*: How did I warm up? How long did I warm up? How long before the performance? What exercises did I do? In what order? Do I really need all that vocal warm-up? Did I do breathing exercises? How much time did I spend on getting into head voice? How many low-range exercises did I do? What did I do about hydration?

Extend this type of thinking into all the areas so that you begin to build up a picture of exactly what you did before the performance, perhaps as far back as one, two, or even three weeks. Now begin to look at the actual performance, trying to recall details. Write down how this performance felt in *all* aspects. You must be absolutely certain that any plan you develop and refine is going to suit your own personal needs for performance. You may have to take into account the nature of the piece as well. For example, do you need to feel more relaxed and calm in order to sing quiet, serene, and calming pieces like Strauss's "Muttertändelei" or "Ruhe, meine Seele," as compared with his vibrant and fast-moving "Frühlingsfeier," for which you may need to feel more activated and excited? If this is the case, then each does require you to prepare yourself in a different way.

Two Different Kinds of Preperformance Plan—General and Specific

1. *General.* Here you decide, usually approximately seven to ten days before the performance, the general areas you must include in your plan. This list will include such things as:
   - Information about the performance venue
   - Detailed plans about your travel to the venue
   - The clothing you will wear
   - Dietary and sleep requirements
   - Practicing in performance mode so that you can feel that your preparation is as good as possible
   - No stopping during your simulation of the performance, no matter what mistakes you make (performance does require that you *not* go back and try again)
   - The mental warm-up, including positive self-talk, mental rehearsal of areas of both individual pieces and the full performance, imagery used for self-confidence, dealing with anxiety, and enhancement of the pieces to be sung.
2. *Specific.* There are two time frames, and therefore two plans, to be dealt with: the plan for the day of the performance and the plan for the time at the performance venue.

The plan for the day of performance may have to be adjusted to cover varying amounts of time from few to many hours. It will cover some of the following areas:

- Positive thought routine on waking
- Personal preparation, for example, showering, dressing, makeup, and so forth
- What to eat and when to eat
- A check of all gear, for example, music, panty hose, antistatic spray, reading matter, personal stereo, tapes, apple, comb, performance clothing and accessories, hairbrush, and so forth
- Preperformance routines geared to physical well-being, remaining mentally focused, and positive self-talk
- Mental rehearsal of all pieces for performance
- Mental rehearsal for presentation of self
- Vocalizing and technical work geared to vocal readiness.

The performance venue plan would cover some of the following areas:

- Refreshing your memory of the venue
- A check for any unexpected distractions
- A check of the bathrooms and facilities for vocal warm-up
- A decision about where you want to locate and the staking of your claim (you may have an aversion to being crowded, or you may need to be among others; try to get as close to your ideal as possible)
- Any routine for physical well-being, for example, stretching
- A final mental rehearsal of individual pieces
- Positive self-talk and use of imagery for confidence
- Positive key words and phrases
- Any arousal management that's called for.

A preperformance planning sheet (figure 4-1) will help to order your thoughts. Include the types of activities, feelings, thoughts, and images that are in your plan. Write down the most important positive factors that you recall in all areas of your best performances from the past.

Ideal, Normal, and Emergency Preperformance Plans

You are encouraged to have three preperformance plans available:

1. *An ideal plan.* Use this one if you have plenty of time and wish to do everything very thoroughly. This is the plan

General Physical	General Mental	General Vocal Technical

Specific Physical	Specific Mental	Specific Vocal Technical

Figure 4-1. Preperformance planning sheet.

you have formulated from all the detailed work described previously.

2. *A normal plan.* This one you would use most of the time, precisely because you do not often have all the time you need. Developed from your ideal plan, this plan frequently doesn't cover as many things because the available time is shorter. Just make sure it includes what you really need.

3. *An emergency plan.* This plan, based on your normal plan, is a very important plan that requires much thought and includes only the things you know you cannot do without. You may have to be quite ruthless in formulating it. Perhaps you must limit it, for example, to your imagery work, a very short vocal warm-up, and your positive self-talk. All of this may even have to be done in the taxi, on the subway, or in the street!

You never know exactly when you'll need each of these three plans, because you never know what is going to happen at the last minute. It is not enough to formulate your three plans; you must also practice them. Perhaps you will find it expedient to practice your emergency plan on the way to your final voice lesson and/or coaching just before your performance. Treat these last two sessions "as if" they were your performance and see how you get on. To repeat, the simulation of your preperformance plans is very necessary.

Once you have the general plan, you should begin to prepare in detail:

- A general plan and routine for the week or so before the performance
- A detailed plan and routine for the day of the performance
- A detailed plan and routine for the time at the performance venue.

At this time you can prepare your normal plan (based on the preceding ideal plan) and your emergency plan (based on your normal plan).

This process can be *very time-consuming*, but it is well worth your effort. The first time you try it, the plan may cover several sheets of paper. However, as you become more aware of your needs and know exactly what works for you, you will prepare your routines more swiftly. Eventually they will fit on very small cards. Always write them down and carry them with you so that you can practice parts of them at any time in any place.

In appendix 1 you will find two preperformance planning sheets: chart #1, which will help you to plan ten days before the event up to the day before the performance, and chart #2, which will record what you want to do on the day of the performance and at the performance venue.

Here is one singer's preperformance plan (audition time: 3:30 P.M.):

Night before *the night before the audition*: Go to bed late after working hard all day. No singing repertoire on this day. Very basic, short vocalization. Lots of hydration.

Night before: Check bag and contents thoroughly. Make sure I have an apple for tomorrow. Relax. Watch a video. Early to bed. Run through some mental rehearsal of two pianissimo high notes in second piece and very low passage in last piece to remind myself how good my dynamic control and range extremes are. Use imagery required for interpretive enhancement of aria. Set alarm for preplanned hour.

8:30 A.M.: Wake up. Hydration. Go over positive self-talk and positive affirmations about my own performance and how well I have prepared. Smile! I feel good!

9:00 A.M.: Five minutes easy vocalizing. Hydration. Go for early-morning walk, listening to my pieces sung by favorite singer on my personal stereo. At same time, image myself at audition singing very well. I feel very confident.

9:45 A.M.: Five minutes vocalizing. Shower. Eat light breakfast, mostly protein.

11:00 A.M.: Five minutes vocalizing. Relaxation, stretching exercises. Watch TV.

12:00 P.M.: Full warm-up. Check vocal strengths in each piece. With no last-minute changes, sing each piece through in performance mode. Light lunch, protein, clear soup, no sweets. Check gear bag again. Dress. Makeup.

2:00 P.M.: Final easy vocalizing. Bite of the apple.

2:30 P.M.: Leave for audition. Read novel on subway. Check anxiety level. Use breathing exercises if necessary. Bite of the apple.

3:05 P.M.: Arrive. Check venue. Settle into own space. Bite of the apple.

3:15 P.M.: Confidence check, using positive words and phrases. Bite of the apple. Stretching exercises while sitting. I feel great!

3:25 P.M.: Imagery of past very good performance. Final checks for self-confidence and arousal/anxiety levels. Use key words and breathing exercises if necessary. Apple bites.

3:29 P.M.: On way to the stage, confident image of myself. This is me. It is my performance. I'm ready.

3:30 P.M.: *Let's do it!*

The foregoing example is an *ideal* plan. Clearly, it must be flexible, since things do not always work out as a timetable has predicted. For example, it is a very common occurrence for auditions to run very late. When this is the situation in which you find yourself, simply recycle important parts of your preperformance routine. This is easy because you will have it with you!

Developing Performance Plans/Routines

Performance plans guide your focus, give you mental security throughout your performance, and allow you to be in complete control. Develop your plans in the following way:

1. Go over each piece that you are going to sing and make a list of your strengths and qualities for each piece. This must be done, whatever the type of performance. Make your lists in the order in which you will perform the pieces. (In a staged performance, this decision is, of course, made for you.) In order to simulate your performance, practicing in the performance mode, you may have to make an early decision about the order in which you will sing the pieces. Initially, use the Song/Aria/Piece Strengths and Qualities Exercise Sheet (chart #3, which can be found in appendix 1) to help with this process. Eventually, make your lists on separate three-by-five index cards, each card representing one piece of music. These cards will provide you with a record and can be adjusted to reflect your improvements as you use them in the future.

2. Remember that each piece of music is a small performance in its own right. Dealing with your performance this way helps you to stay in the present and prevents your focus from slipping backward or forward. Thus a small refocus plan followed by a performance plan for the next piece is called for. Make a note of what you need to refocus on after each piece you sing. As an example of such a routine:

- Focus on vocal and physical/mental strengths in the first piece.

  Sing the piece, ending the performance.
- Refocus on vocal and physical/mental strengths of the next piece.

  Sing the piece, ending the performance.
- Refocus on vocal and physical/mental strengths of the third piece.

  Sing the piece, ending the performance.

When you begin each piece by focusing only on your specific strengths and qualities in that particular piece, you divide your performance into manageable blocks.

During auditions, recitals, and competitions, it is your choice how much time to take between each piece. Don't be tempted to hurry because the pause seems lengthy to you. Actually, it probably isn't. Depending on the type of performance, an acceptable gap between pieces can be anything from one minute to twenty minutes. Switch from the previous piece, refocus on the next piece, and stay in the present. The principle is always the same: one piece at a time.

3. Go over each piece in detail, making a note of where you may need some help with your focus. You should be able to divide up the piece in relation to the nature of the focus—vocal, mental, or physical. Try to keep your vocal focuses to a minimum, while allowing most of your focus cues to relate to your confidence, imagery, feeling relaxed, and experiencing pleasure. Some pieces may not need such detailed focus plans for performance (energy thoughts and images, key words cuing you into your proper focus, thoughts based on your strengths and qualities, vocal cues for difficult areas, and images you need to enhance your performance), but you should get into the good habit of making plans for all your pieces. Plan as follows:

- Plan the presentation of yourself as confident, calm, and in control. Base the presentation of self on your strengths and good qualities.
- Deal with the accompanist, if necessary; then begin to focus on the strengths of your first piece. Go over your confidence check-list in your head, and image yourself singing the piece very well.
- During the pause between pieces one and two, refocus on piece number two.
- Remind yourself what your strengths are in this piece.
- Go over the positive self-talk about this piece while imaging yourself singing it very well.
- Indicate that you are ready to begin. Your start is very important. It will dictate whether or not the audition panel, judges, or even audience listens to you. Consequently, always try to have a very good cue for the start. You must establish yourself right from the beginning. The cue can be key words (such as *smooth, delicate, sing this red*), the choice of words dependent upon the piece and your individual plan. Although this sounds long and involved, the whole process only takes seconds when you are performing.
- Then simply sing the piece, and allow yourself to sing well. Use your planned cues for your focus if and when you need them. The vocal resting places in the pieces—especially the prelude, introduction, or any long piano or orchestral

interludes—are a dangerous time because it is easy to allow the performance to drop. To keep your performance alive, you must know where your focus is going to be during those nonsinging moments. On some occasions you may not need to remind yourself of cues because you are singing so well. On other occasions you will need help from your planned focuses.

Sample Performance Plan

Here is an example of a performance plan for one piece, including some of the cues and focuses that this singer feels he needs:

> *Performance*: Song competition
> *Date*: Six months from tomorrow
> *Song*: "Morgen," Opus 21, No. 4, Richard Strauss

During the very long thirteen-bar introduction the dramatic cues, establishing the mood, and the invocation of my positive self by using positive words and imagery are most important.

As I enter in bar 14, I will be completely in the mood and, although I breathe exactly on the first beat of the bar, the taking of the breath will not interfere with the established mood.

In bars 17 and 18, I will make sure that the [e] vowels in *Wege* and *gehen* are properly executed and all the glottals are done correctly.

In bar 19, my high note on *Glücklichen* will be piano, with a vowel shape that is anticipated on the word *die*.

In bar 25, *wogen* will be a supported pianissimo because of my imaging of the breath and the sound.

In bars 27 and 28, the lengthening of the expressive "sh" sound that begins the words *stille* and *steigen* will be exquisite, supporting linguistically the musical and dramatic mood I have established through imagery.

During bars 29, 30, and part of 31, the dramatic focus will clearly change to a much more intimate focus, helped by my imaging of the very blue eyes of the person I love.

The last phrase will be dramatically evocative, because I will use my color image to enhance it. The inhalation in bar 34 will be more than adequate and will bring me to the end. My "what if?" answer for the unlikely happening that I do not make it to the end is to take an emergency breath between *Glückes* and *stummes*, using the special image I have concocted to make it a great dramatic moment. (See the next section in this chapter for "what ifs?")

Once you have finished the plan for one piece, you then continue to plan all of your program in the same way, paying special attention to preludes, your starts, interludes, postludes, and the pause between the end of one piece and the beginning of the next. At a certain level of excellence there will be very little to separate you from all the other singers. Therefore, you must be very well prepared mentally, which in turn will permit you to push yourself to the limits of your potential when performing. By identifying your critical points in your total performance and planning *where* you will focus and on *what* you will focus during those times, you will make your performance a vital one.

"What Ifs?"

Because performance is uncertain and often very risky, you should prepare for anything that may happen. You should be able to give yourself the confidence that, whatever happens, you will cope and produce your best performance. Thorough preparation is the key, and this includes "what if?" situations. The better performer will be the one who can deal with any change or disruption with calmness and the confident knowledge that he/she can cope with anything. Spend some time thinking about the things that could happen to you and how you might handle them. Here are some examples of "what ifs?" given us by singers:

> What if . . .
> > . . . I missed my train and the next one would make me an hour late?
> > . . . the accompanist provided is so poor that he cannot play my Poulenc?
> > . . . I don't manage the first of my six high notes?
> > . . . the importance of this audition makes me feel very nervous?
> > . . . the soprano upstages me in the second act yet again?
> > . . . I can't manage to rid myself of worry about my mother's illness?
> > . . . my old problem (having no voice when I start to warm up) is still there?
> > . . . the tenor blows his odorous breath in my face *again* during our duet?
> > . . . my allergy medicine dries out my cords disastrously?

The "what if?" sheet will help you plan how you would cope with any disruptions occurring before or during your performance. Give them some very deep thought before making a decision. Always make sure that your actions—answers to the "what ifs?"—are written and spoken in a positive manner, whether physical, technical, or mental. Perhaps you can ask your voice teacher or coach to go over them with you. Employ *every method you possess* to use your energy wisely. This means not wasting your energy on things that are not important or on things you haven't planned for. A "What If?" Plans Sheet (chart #4) can be found in appendix 1.

Postperformance Plans

Are you aware that the time following your performance is a very important time for you as a singer? All that emotion accompanying your performance does not cease just because the performance does. (For this reason, you will find it advantageous to have some kind of understanding of the relationship between postperformance syndrome and staleness and burnout.)

It is unfortunate but true that you habitually spend a great deal of time preparing thoroughly for your performances, especially in the vocal and technical aspects of your music, but very rarely do you spend the same amount of time planning and preparing for the time *following* the performance. This type of planning, however, will allow you to conserve the reserves of your energy for future preparation and performances to come.

Here are some suggestions that can help you to alleviate postperformance tension and emotion and to preserve your energy:

1. *Make a decision, a very personal decision, about how much time you need to yourself after the performance.* You may need one day, half a day, or just one hour. Work out why you need this time, this relaxation, why you must get away from the performance mode. To come down emotionally after a thrilling performance, treat yourself to something quite different, something that you enjoy but, until that moment, have not had the time for.

2. *Take the opportunity to become part of a group activity, if that appeals to you.* Meet new friends for lunch, go to visit a favorite place, et cetera. This is one way to keep family and close friends *away*. Why would you want to do that? Because such people are usually either very critical or overly vociferous in their praise. This can aggravate latent emotions and produce detrimental effects in the future.

3. *Provide yourself with an unemotional, objective, and realistic evaluation of your performance.* Using a postperformance evaluation form is a simple but very effective way of being *objective* about your performance. You need not complete this form immediately after the performance; it is much better to do it when you are feeling quieter emo-

tionally and will have a better chance of getting sound information. This list of things about your performance—some positive, others negative—gives some kind of structure to your thoughts. Three ways of doing this evaluation are given here:

- Complete a postperformance evaluation form. Figure 4-2 is an example of a thorough evaluation couched in the form of questions.
- Or write your own evaluation in another way, for example, as a part of a diary or mental log. Write down your feelings, thoughts, and actions elicited by the key areas of your performance and the mental skills you used. Be objective and honest with yourself, taking care to write all the positive as well as the negative things. Singers are often very good at remembering each and every negative aspect of their performance but do not give themselves the same treatment for the good things they do. Try not to let your feelings of perfectionism get in the way of performing your best. Seeking perfection is not an efficient way of dealing with performance. Just do the things you do well.
- Or use another type of performance evaluation (like chart #5, Postperformance Evaluation Form 2, in appendix 1), which is merely a list of positive points and negative points.

Each of the three methods of evaluation will tend to vary in length, but you must write down all the things that you found positive in your performance. If you find it easier, use the three headings of physical, mental, and technical. After completing your evaluation, adopt this process:

1. Read both lists carefully, positive and negative.
2. Read the bad points list once again and think how you can use this information for your next performance and its preparation. Write your conclusions down.
3. Cross out the negative list once you have done this. Forget it.
4. Read the positive list once again. Try to remember what those feelings were like and how you managed to achieve them.
5. Develop some mental images from items on the positive list. Keep this list and use it for planning your next performance.
6. Read this list as many times as you like. It will act as a confidence checklist. Try always to focus on the positive aspects. Use them to improve.

Performance: _____

Date: _____ Venue: _____

List the positive things in your performance:

List the things that caused you stress in this performance:

How did this stress feel? (in terms of thoughts, actions, body responses)

What was your level of anxiety like? Describe.

How effective were you in dealing with this anxiety? How did you do it?

How did you feel before, during, after the performance?

Figure 4-2. Postperformance evaluation form.

7. Include items from this list when preparing your focus for the next preparation. It will clarify your strengths and personal qualities.

8. Get on with the next item on your performing agenda, with the help of your teacher and/or coach. It could be preparation for the next audition, concert, or competition or learning a new piece or a new role. Or it might be more appropriate for you to update your materials and photographs to be sent to other companies, conductors, competitions, and so forth. Most important is that you do *plan* your next step with regard to upcoming performances. Once you have evaluated your performance objectively, it is much more efficient to move on into the present. This is within your control. Deal with it as it is.

How the Voice Teacher and Coach Can Help with the Postperformance Evaluation

Time permitting, there should be communication among the three members of the triumvirate—voice teacher, coach, and you—about what happened at the performance. The singer, whose artistic development hinges upon feedback from the teachers, should act as liaison in order to collate the information before decisions are made as to how future work should proceed. The very best and most productive method would be a meeting *à trois*, if at all possible, because the combined strength of all three members of the team is the most helpful.

In order for your postperformance evaluation to function efficiently, all parties should be enthusiastic participants. You have a right to expect an ongoing amicable and cooperative relationship between your coach(es) and your voice teacher. A mere lack of tension between these members of your team is not sufficient. Actual feelings of enmity (not unheard of) would be totally disruptive to your progress. You should take the responsibility for building a team that works together in harmony, the common goal being your progress. Should you be philosophically dismayed at all this attention and effort being focused on you, remember that, as a performer, you deserve to have what you need to perform well. You can be a modest, generous, and self-effacing person if you wish, but for you the performer, selective selfishness is rather necessary.

After everyone has communicated, be sure to report back to your voice teacher and coach about your conclusions. Let them help you to devise a plan for your next period of development. Once you and your teachers have drawn up new goals for you and a plan for their implementation, the whole process will start all over again.

New repertoire will be learned and prepared in an ever more efficient manner so that you are free to think more about the dramatic and interpretive facets of your performance. You and your voice teacher will make an effort to improve even further your command of the singing craft. With the help of your coach(es) you will aspire to a greater linguistic, musical, and stylistic authority.

TEACHING POINT: See #3, appendix 2.

Recycling

Having these performance plans ready and practiced means that you know what works and what doesn't. When there are delays during your performance, you have an unexpected break between pieces, or the audition panel decides that they want you to stay a little longer in order to hear more from you, go over your performance preparation again. Extract from the plan those parts that you *need* to do and *can* do under the circumstances, recycling part of your prepared plan. This should not inspire worry. Just give yourself a little time to think it through. You do actually have all the relevant knowledge. You don't have to plan new material. Recycling part of your preparation plans is a good habit to get into. Those plans allow you to be confident about what you know you do well.

Case Study

B.J. is a young dramatic soprano, well trained, with a large, beautiful voice, who is poised to make an audition tour in Germany. She is such an apt student of these new methods and planning techniques that we asked her to write down for us what kind of planning *she* now habitually does.

In thinking about what I do to prepare for auditions or performances, it seems to me the process breaks down into five basic components:

1. Deciding what it is I need to focus on.
2. Allowing for things to go wrong.
3. Setting the necessary goals to get me where I want to be.
4. Efficient management of time and resources.
5. Regrouping.

Deciding What It Is I Need to Focus On

This seems like a fairly obvious thing to do, but I can't tell you how many times I've walked into an audition with a piece, thinking all the preparation I needed was to sing straight through it twenty times or so (we all know that won't fly!). I now force myself to choose a plan of action for an audition two weeks in advance (time permitting) and stick to it. For me it takes a lot of self-discipline not to be making last-minute changes, especially where technique is concerned. However, having a concrete plan of action that's really clear in my mind has carried me through some rather harrowing performance situations, so I've become a Believer. Therefore, if I'm preparing a new aria for an audition, I know a certain percentage of my concentration will necessarily have to be spent on remembering entrances and words and such. If it's a piece I've done a number of times, I can afford to focus on something like color imagery or incorporating a new acting technique. It's really important for me to decide right away what I'm going to do about the most technically difficult parts of the piece so that: (1) I take a lot of psychological pressure off myself, and (2) the whole piece will then make a quantum leap.

Allowing for Things to Go Wrong

This covers everything from carrying an extra pair of panty hose with you to an audition to memorizing the other person's part in a duet so if he/she forgets a line, you won't be thrown off. I find if you can say with a clear conscience that you prepared yourself for every eventuality and something beyond your control still went wrong, you won't feel bad because, after all, you gave it your best shot.

Setting the Necessary Goals to Get Me Where I Want to Be

This is where my daily planner comes in. I buy the kind where you get two sheets for each day of the month, so there's plenty of space to make notes about things. Say, for example, I want to learn a new role. I choose the date where I want to have the whole thing memorized cold and write that down. Then I backtrack and make reminders to myself along the way: "Need to have Act I memorized by the end of this week." This can be a real pain in the neck, but it does force me to get things accomplished that would otherwise slide and also lets me learn how much time I need to gauge for preparing things.

Efficient Management of Time and Resources

This is perhaps the most important skill for a singer to develop, because we have such a tremendous amount of material to learn and most of us have such little time in which to do it. Wherever possible I kill two birds with one stone. There's a great crossover between singing and language study. A lot of operatic composers used the literature of their time for subject material, so by reading the text in the original language I not only glean important nuances of character or plot that may have had to be sacrificed in the libretto but also develop language skills. I make flash cards for the words I don't know in an aria and incorporate them with the flash cards from my other language study. I always carry the following in my bag in case I find a few minutes of extra time on my hands: (1) a notebook with copies of music I am currently working on, (2) flash cards from languages I am currently working on, (3) my Walkman with either a foreign language tape or a tape of myself playing the cues of a piece I'm trying to learn, and (4) a book that is background literature for an opera or a historically related subject. It's important to have a number of different things on you because, say, you may be just too tired to read something like *Le roi s'amuse* on your way home from work on the subway, but you may have the energy to listen to a tape.

One method I have found very valuable is to type out the words of an aria or role triple-spaced on plain paper—just the words. I then go through and make notes on where I need to modify a vowel, where I'm going to do a relaxation technique, where I'm going to move or do a gesture, how many beats is it between the end of one phrase and the beginning of another, what image I'm thinking of on a certain phrase, or what have you. This seems to give my mind a very clear, composite picture to go by, so when the time for performance comes I find it much easier to split my concentration when necessary.

Regrouping

This is where I move onto the next project and start the process all over again. The only note I would make here is that I find when I focus on what I did *right*, I make a lot more progress.

Summary

The performance cycle is continuous. It comprises

- preperformance (before)
- performance (during)
- postperformance (after).

Each has its own procedures and strategies. Planning your performance cycle fosters consistency in performance and gives you mental security. Work at it as you do at your vocal technique.

Mental plans and routines are your journey to good consistent performances. There are three preperformance plans: ideal, normal, and emergency. Learn to organize your thinking and planning for each segment of performance under these headings: physical, technical, and mental. View each piece as a "new" performance; six pieces means six performances. Prepare some "what ifs?" for the uncertainties.

Learn to evaluate your performance in detail and with objectivity. Be sure to be aware of and plan for the time following your performance, a crucial part of the whole performance cycle.

Further information:

1. On your travel to the venue, see chapter 16, "The Audition and the Competition."
2. On the clothing you will wear, see chapter 16, "The Audition and the Competition."
3. On dietary and sleep requirements, see chapter 16, "The Audition and the Competition."
4. On practicing in the performance mode, see chapter 14, "The Coach's Place in Singers' Preperformance Work."
5. On what to eat and when to eat, see chapter 16, "The Audition and the Competition."
6. On mental rehearsal for presentation of self, see chapter 16, "The Audition and the Competition."
7. On vocalizing and technical work, see chapter 16, "The Audition and the Competition."
8. On arousal management, see chapter 11, "Dealing with Anxiety."
9. On focusing only on your specific strengths, see chapter 8, "Developing Self-Confidence through Positive Thinking."
10. On presentation of yourself as confident, calm, and in control, see chapter 5, "The Self and Performance: You, the Person; You, the Performer."
11. On the relationship between postperformance syndrome and staleness and burnout, see chapter 21, "Staleness and Burnout in Performers."

5   The Self and Performance

You, the Person; You, the Performer

Life itself mandates that human beings have an awareness of self, that is, the ability to form an identity and then attach worth to it. So performers must define themselves as persons and then decide whether they like those identities or not. Yet the human propensity to be judgmental creates a problem. In the same way that they would protect themselves from a physical wound, human beings protect themselves from self-rejection by avoidance of anything that might cause pain for the self. Judging and rejecting oneself can be a very painful experience. Under such circumstances, one may avoid taking risks, such as meeting with other people; one may find it difficult to be the center of attention or to even hear criticism. Present in the performer, these factors soon interfere with the performance itself. The performer has to learn to take from the person all positive strengths and qualities so as to use them in performance when necessary. "To avoid judgments and self-rejection, [performers] erect barriers of defense, perhaps [invent] blame and get angry, or bury themselves in perfectionistic work" (McKay and Fanning, 1992, p. 2).

How the Concept of Self Influences Your Behavior as a Performer

There are many ways of looking at the concept of self, but for performers it is helpful to take a humanistic approach, delineating how the concept of self influences your behavior as a performer. This approach is not based solely on behavior seen by the external observer but, rather, on the subjective view of the individual doing the "behaving."

How do you interpret your own self, the person you are? This is an important issue, because the self constitutes a central and ever-present focal point, which is built into a uniquely meaningful construction. It is evident that discovering the identity of self is not only a real human need but also an imperative issue for you as a performer. You must understand how you perceive yourself and what consequent effects this perception has on your behavior in life as well as in your performance. This self is uniquely yours, and yours alone. It is also "the focal object within your experience, because of its primacy, centrality, continuity" (Burns, 1988, p. 51), and predominant in all aspects of your behavior. Through this basic human capacity for self-awareness each of you acknowledges his or her self-identity. It is the premise behind the philosopher Descartes's most important sentence: "Cogito, ergo sum" (I think, therefore I am), which, according to R. B. Burns, compels all of us to turn "towards an intellectual and emotional commitment to the existence of Self" (1988, p. 51).

Theories relating to the self are fascinating if you are interested in this area of your work. Without going into all the psychological doctrines, suffice to say that common elements constantly emerge:

- You are a person, an entity separate from other people and existing in time.
- You have a knowledge about yourself (your self-concept), and you are able to evaluate yourself (your self-esteem). Both are basic circumstances of any self-awareness.
- Both self-knowledge and self-evaluation are learned through experience, mainly socially interactive experience, especially with significant others.

We propose that you view your self-concept as a set of attitudes, using what is known as the Burns Model, that states that your self-concept can be viewed as the attitudes you have toward the following three important areas of self:

1. The *cognized self,* or that self within you, known only to you.
2. The *other self,* or that self you believe other people perceive.
3. The *ideal self,* or that self you would like to be.

Now, to be possessed of attitudes about things, you must have a belief or knowledge, an affective or emotional response, an evaluative process, and an inclination to respond. According to researchers D. Kretch, R. S. Crutchfield, and E. L. Ballachey (1962, p. 117), an attitude is "an enduring system of positive and negative evaluations, emotional feelings and pro and con action tendencies with respect to a social object." That is, you have an attitude about these different selves. You have a belief and knowledge that you feel emotional about, one that you can certainly evaluate. You can respond to your cognized, other, or ideal self. What's more, *both* you the person and you the performer have a cognized self, an other self, and an ideal self.

Exercise

To further clarify the three selves for yourself try the following exercises.

- Focus on yourself as a person. Write down a list of descriptions and attributes that describe your
  1. cognized self (known only to you),
  2. other self (as you believe others see you),
  3. ideal self (as you would like to be).
- Now do the same for yourself as a performer.
- Take a look at the lists you have made. Which of the attributes elicited a strong positive emotion, which a negative emotion?

For the sake of better understanding, let's take an example. You may have written down "five feet tall." Because you don't enjoy being that short, this description may arouse negative emotions in you. Further, this attitude may restrict your personal views of people in society as well as about yourself. That is, this emotion is aroused by your attitude to your stature. This type of reaction happens all the time. If you have many things you do not like about yourself, it may lead to a low self-concept and possibly low self-esteem. You will automatically think that other people also view you in a negative fashion.

Let's transfer this reasoning to your performance. From the list you have written down, which things elicited a negative emotion in you? Perhaps you have perceived that others see you as a singer who has failed because you haven't sung in a major house or taken part in a major opera performance. Thus you have evaluated yourself with some disapproval. This is an indication of the extent to which you believe yourself capable, successful, or worthy of being termed a singer. Imagine this scene at a party. Someone says to you, "What do you do?" You answer, "I am a singer." Now comes the inevitable and ever-present question: "Where have you performed?" "Well . . . ," you mumble. (This is a scenario that every burgeoning singer has experienced and one that singers who are still struggling know well.)

Your self-esteem implies several things: whether you feel you are worthy or not, whether you have respect for yourself or not, and whether you will condemn yourself for what you are not. Low self-esteem suggests that you are rejecting yourself, that you are derogatory about yourself, and that you have a negative self-evaluation. How's that as a platform for a performer? Don't laugh. This is mild in comparison with some issues you must deal with.

What is important in all of this is that you must become more aware of yourself both as a person and as a performer. Without doubt, this is one of the most difficult exercises for you do to. This is mainly because you are not accustomed to focusing on yourself and asking, "What am I really like?" As you can now begin to see, it becomes crucial for you to feel capable, worthy of yourself, and positive about yourself. Self-worth can be defined as a feeling that the self is important and effective in all areas of your life. You should be aware of yourself; you should be a master of your own actions, with a sense of your own competence. This does not depend upon extrinsic support; it is intrinsic. Remember Descartes? "I think, therefore I am."

Evaluating your relative success or failure at doing what your identity entails does not necessitate a judgment that what you do is good in itself, but rather that you are good at what you do—which is sing. You the performer are only one manifestation of your total person. How you feel about yourself reflects your essential thoughts and feelings about you in your world. It also reflects your choice of how to approach your performance.

We all have a tendency, a motivation, to evaluate ourselves—especially in relation to others around us. The belief that you build your self-evaluation based on feedback received from others has validity. That is, if you constantly receive negative feedback without any seeming justification or without any reminder about what was good about your performance, then your self-esteem lowers. If you are told negative things often enough, you actually begin to believe them. You do need to be aware of favorable attitudes toward you and your work. The more favorable attitudes are denied you, the more passionately you will wish to hear them. If your self-esteem is low, you will be more likely to hunger for positive feedback. Moreover, you will become even more frustrated and angry if you don't get it. You will respond very positively to good feedback, but you will also respond more despondently to failure than do your colleagues who have high self-esteem.

All of this, in turn, explains how you behave in auditions, why you want approval, and why you need to please other people. You want positive feedback! This is why auditions can be very frustrating. You work very hard to get your repertoire ready. You are delighted to be given the opportunity to sing, and you want to do well. Yet on most occasions you will get no feedback at all unless there is someone present who will report to you. This can be very disheartening. If you are unable to enter into a positive self-evaluation about what you did well and if you view yourself as a failure because you did something wrong, then you add to your negative view of self.

There is another important issue here. That has to do with the way in which you perceive those who give you feedback. You will tend to be attracted to the people who evaluate you positively and to dislike those who provide negative feedback. If you are not aware of self in all its aspects, then you may be missing out on some very valuable information from those who occasionally give negative feedback. If you feel that you have failed and that this failure was observed by an "expert," your self-evaluation lowers. If you are the kind of singer who becomes sensitive to the opinions of others, especially when you think you have failed, then your feelings are affected by the validity you attribute to the judgments of others (e.g., an audition panel or your voice teacher).

TEACHING POINT: See #4, appendix 2.

Practical Conclusions

The general rule is this: Surround yourself with positive people and learn from them. View yourself always from a positive standpoint. Everything will not always be perfect, but you will see mistakes as just that—mistakes. Learn from them, and then move on. If you have high self-esteem, you will defend yourself more vigorously against the negative feedback. You will be less vulnerable to the impact of outside events. You will be more responsive to experiences of success. Positive feedback is more rapidly learned and more quickly forgotten than negative appraisals. But if your self-concept is negative, then you are more likely to linger over the negatives and eventually begin to believe them.

If you tend to have a negative self-concept, there are other performance-related issues for you. There appears to be some association between this negative self-concept and your anxiety level. If you are anxious, you may feel less free to examine your own performance behavior. As a consequence, you will be prevented from acquiring a *realistic* self-concept. So the argument is: Anxiety tends to generate low self-esteem. During performance, when you are under pressure, you are more likely to experience some of the physiological symptoms of anxiety, such as sweaty palms, trembling, fast heart rate, et cetera. Where did all this come from? An unstable self-concept creates it. Having to present a false front to the world—and if you have low self-esteem you often do—places a tremendous strain on you. This strain creates tension, with anxiety as a by-product. Worthlessness and inadequacy create isolation—both physical and emotional—in you. You feel unable to share yourself with others. This is particularly unfortunate in a performing context, because one of your main reasons for singing is to communicate your talent and love for that art to an audience.

You know yourself better than anyone else in the world, despite what your mother, father, granny, partner, husband, or wife says to you. Be open. Researcher H. Otto in his *Guide to Developing Your Potential* says: "Change and growth take place when a person has risked himself and dares to become involved with experimenting with his own life" (1970, p. 8). Allow yourself to tune in to who you really are and how you really think. You may get some answers about why you think as you do, why you tend to react as you do in certain circumstances, or even how you react to other people. Get to know yourself in your normal everyday life and your performing life as well. How are you inclined to behave in a performing situation or when you are under pressure? Have you any idea why you behave that way? What can you change? Ask yourself what you *want* to change. Focus on an area that you would like to improve. Perhaps you would like to have more personal control. Whatever it is, choose the target, set your sights, and go for the positive change you want. Many exercises in this book will help you with this pursuit.

You must remember that by making a positive change in your person, you also give the performer within you a better chance of success (and vice versa). The final choice for positive change in self is in your own hands. Only you can make the decision to do it. You may need help from others, but that's the easy part. Making the decision to change to the positive is the difficult part.

TEACHING POINT: See #5, appendix 2.

Your pathway to excellence in singing must begin by getting to know yourself in all aspects—the self that is known only to you, the self that others perceive, and the ideal self that you want.

Case Study

B.P. is an actress who sings and a singer who acts, both very well. She is no longer an ingenue, but she has the verve and pizzazz, as well as the beauty, of a youngster. She has had such spectacular success bringing her performance up to a splendid standard by means of mental skills that we asked her to write the story of her study.

In a moment of collapse and seeming disaster in my life, I decided to create and give a cabaret performance! Madness, some of my friends said. But I had to, and I did. And it went so well that I was surprised! Pleased . . . but surprised. Shocked, even.

Who did that? Not the helpless, desperate to please, fighting for survival me! The performer in me did that.

How is that possible? Can it be true that I can give a very good performance and, at the same time, block out, lock out, bury, keep back and in the dark . . . the person that I really am?

Is this the Glass Ceiling . . . the invisible Performance Barrier that we bump up against, that knocks us back, and down, and possibly out?

And how can we release that forbidden self into the Performance, and transcend that Performance Barrier?

What can I *do* to make that happen?

So, without much understanding, but in a state of trust and need, I began to work at the techniques in relation to Self, through which a series of insights seem to create waves in the psyche, and to culminate in small actions . . . beginning to release the mystery of Self.

I made lists of my strengths and weaknesses: who I think I am, who I want to be; my goals, long and short, how I worked with the Problem Frame and the Outcome Frame, how I worked with "trigger" words and ideas. Stay in the present. Positive thinking is a skill. "Own" yourself. And above all, I began to build into daily life, every morning, time for "Self-Talk."

If the reservoir of potential in the Person is unconscious, then all this work must be an effort to get that reservoir to bubble up and manifest itself! So much so that in a well-crafted performance the Person that I am won't be locked away, denied, ignored . . . silenced!

"You the Person, You the Performer!" What a seemingly schizophrenic conundrum! Are there two of us for me to deal with? And who is this "me"? That's the "Self" I'm trying to discover . . . and release into the Performance.

Further information:

1. On going for a positive change, see chapter 8, "Developing Self-Confidence through Positive Thinking."

6 Physical Well-Being and Relaxation

Of the many things you can do to enhance your performance, some have a greater impact than others, especially when you perform under pressure. Your whole lifestyle is an important factor in nurturing your ability to deal with pressure. Of the many factors that could limit your success in performance, one—rarely dealt with during your training for performance—is your physical well-being and your health. You want to be able to perform well under all circumstances, but if you are ill in any way, you will not perform well. At worst, you may not be able to perform at all.

How you live your life outside performance directly affects your ability to focus, handle pressure, and think consistently well. Feeling good—physically and mentally—is very important for you, in your life and in your performing. Feeling too tight, too tense, or too stressed interferes with your focus; therefore, your performance suffers. Because the best performances occur when mind and muscles are combined and free-flowing, you require a state of calm. Physical well-being helps you to enter into and remain in the comfort zone. Developing the ability to relax the body and calm the mind is very important for your performing life.

Areas That Allow for a Feeling of Well-Being

Each of you is an individual, uniquely different from the next individual. You each respond to pressure in different ways from other singers. Perhaps you feel tension in the neck and shoulders; perhaps you feel sick to your stomach or physically shake. (Singers often report that their knees and legs shake when they wait to perform.)

65

Take note of the key areas that allow for a feeling of well-being: diet, exercise, fun and recreation, relaxation, relationships, and a positive, healthy perspective on life in general. All have an intense effect on how you deal with your life; therefore, they affect your performance. Think carefully about each of these areas. Deal with each of them in turn. Watch your diet carefully, everything within reason. Exercise prudently, intelligently, and regularly. It is an excellent way to increase your resistance to stress and stay in good physical shape. Learn to relax in all parts of your life. Enjoy your friends and relations; you need to have a balance in your life, and relationships can be truly empowering. Try to remain positive. The ability to keep a healthy perspective will enable you to succeed in life and rise to the challenge of performance. It may even have a positive effect on the voice.

In the 1970s Elmer and Alyce Green (1977) conducted experiments that measured the influence of mental control on body functions. In 1977 they published *Beyond Biofeedback*, in which they reported that Indian yogis were able to alter their brain waves, heart rate, breathing, blood pressure, and body temperature voluntarily. They had discovered that voluntary control of these body processes can be taught quite easily and the skill acquired in a very short time. Sport psychologist Dorothy V. Harris (1986) reported in "Relaxation and Energizing Techniques for Regulation of Arousal" that all individuals possess a "highly complex, sophisticated and effectively integrated network between the mind and the body." It is also well-known that changes in the mental and emotional state are consciously or unconsciously accompanied by an appropriate change within the body. In other words, there is strong evidence to support the notion that *we think with our entire body*.

Therefore, as a singer, you should learn how to exercise greater mastery and control over all your functions and responses. Your body must do what you want it to do. Consequently, you should be more efficient at communicating with your body if you wish it to help you perform well. If you become worried or anxious, then your muscles contract involuntarily, and, as a consequence, are less effective when you want to use them. In addition, the contraction involves nerves as well, as Harris tells us: "Approximately one half of the nerves alert the muscles to respond to the messages from the brain, and the other half carry the messages back to the brain. Human nerve circuits have no automatic regulators: there are no signals to alert one to too much tension."

Body Awareness

The quality of this important body–mind relationship is crucial to your preparation and performance, as you have read previously.

Actually, in the end, it is the quality of this relationship that determines how much you will be able to draw from your full potential as a performer. Try to be aware of the demands of the mind and what it is saying to you. It will intrude somewhere along the way. You cannot shut it down; it will not go away. You should try to learn how to deal with it.

However, it is also important to understand the demands of your body, to learn what the body also is trying to tell you. Becoming aware of your body is the first step toward feeling relaxed and good; it also sets the stage for all the important mental preparation. A large part of your training as a singer involves learning to recognize and isolate bad habits in order to interrupt or prevent them. Cultivating good habits in the body and eliminating bad ones is just as important for a singer as it is for an elite athlete.

For you as a singer, the physical side of your performance preparation has two benefits:

1. Achievement of more physical fitness, strengthening and toning all muscle groups
2. Increase of your ability to utilize your vocal skills in performance.

When you practice your vocal skills, you are training more than your muscles. The repetition of your vocal skills sends a constant stream of signals via the nervous system to your brain, familiarizing it with the movements: "What repetition really does is to train the nervous system and the brain. . . . When you move, your body sends thousands of signals every second to the brain, which, in turn, collects, organizes and distills them into some cohesive whole" (Syer and Connolly, 1984, p. 24).

This kind of conversation between the brain, the nervous system, and the body is continuous. The brain makes the decision, then sends the message via the nervous system, and the muscles react. (Action follows the thought!) All your training and repetition allows you to "parcel" the information appropriately so that the nervous system and body can take over. This way you do not have to think about how to be vocally correct *all* the time. Yes, this is possible! Once you have the ability to perform the skill, all you then have to do is maintain it.

It becomes necessary, then, to change *only the things that you do not need or those that do not work*. Here are three exercises (adapted from Syer and Connolly's *Sporting Body, Sporting Mind,* 1984) that will help you:

1. Become bodily aware when you sing your pieces
2. Gain some insight into the mind–body relationship
3. See what effect the body is having on your performance.

Exercise 1.   Kinesthetic Body Inventory

In this exercise you simply check all your body parts. How do they feel? Can you distinguish one from the other? Feel one toe or finger as separate from the others. Check the front of the neck and the muscles leading down into the sternum. Switch to the back of the neck. Begin with the feet, either lying down or sitting down. You can extend this exercise by doing it while you are practicing. While singing or vocalizing, begin to pay attention to the different parts of the body. See how they are working. This can be a very useful experience, focusing on the muscle groups you use for singing. It can substantially enhance your efficiency.

Exercise 2.   Eyes Closed

Select two or three movements that you have done or some that you are using in a stage performance. They can be anything: walking and turning to look, kneeling and lifting arms, reaching up and lifting something down. Do each movement with your eyes open and re-peat it a number of times. Now close your eyes and repeat the move-ment in exactly the same way. Be aware of how it feels. How are you using the nonvisual senses to organize your movement? Repeat with eyes open. Focus on the body, muscles, and so forth, and become very aware. Repeat with eyes closed and become even more aware.

Exercise 3.   Color-Coding the Body

This exercise will help body awareness but will also enhance your mental rehearsal imagery. Sit comfortably and watch yourself sing-ing the most recent piece you have learned. Make sure that you are watching yourself from the outside (as if you are on a video). Keep it positive. Now imagine that you see each area of your body sur-rounded by a color. Sing the piece and focus on head, neck, arms, and shoulders enveloped in blue. Then focus on torso, waist, pel-vis, and hips surrounded by green. Move on to focus on thighs, knees, calves, ankles, and feet surrounded by red. Does the color change, become paler or more intense? Is the change in color asso-ciated with tension, either growing or decreasing? What effect is this having on your performance?

These are but a few—you may have more of your own—examples of how you can train yourself to become more aware of your body–mind relationship. The more aware you become, the greater your ability to deal quickly with any tension in the body during perfor-mance and to feel in physical control of what you are performing or practicing.

Relaxation through Breathing

Acquiring the ability to deal with tension in your life and in your performance can be done quite simply through breathing. Have you ever noticed what happens to your breathing when you are under pressure, trying too hard, or simply driven to push and push again? You hold it; it becomes shallow; it becomes more rapid. This is a version of the "fight or flight" syndrome. Result: You are impatient, worried, nervous, and less effective in all you do.

When this happens, the most effective thing to do is be aware of your own breathing. A very talented world-class tennis player has said that tapping into his own breathing, getting it to revert to its normal rhythm, is the key skill he uses all the time, because it always allows him to return to being in control. During performance and at other high-pressure times in life, the mind may often run ahead of the body. Returning to your normal breathing rhythm will allow you to relax.

When under pressure, remember to *breathe*. Breathe through your nose. Keep it as simple as you can. Don't think of anything but breathing. What your chest and abdomen are doing is quite beside the point and unimportant in this instance. Take some time to tune in to your own breathing pattern. Always allow the breath to execute a complete cycle. Take time for a complete inhalation. Allow your breath to come all the way in and go all the way out. Doing this about five or six times will keep you focused and in control of the situation. Really concentrate on your breathing cycle—all the way in, all the way out. As Saul Miller (1992) says, breathing is like the waves and "the waves never rush." Build a nice, easy rhythm, *your* rhythm, always giving yourself time to allow the full breath in and out. The waves never rush and neither should your breathing. It deserves your attention and time. Miller's three axioms for breathing are:

> There's power in rhythm.
> The waves never rush.
> I deserve my time.

If, at the same moment as you take your time to breathe, you can also think positive thoughts, then you will begin to feel even more relaxed. You will be able to enjoy that wonderful feeling of physical well-being that tells you, "I can conquer anything." Give yourself permission to take your time. Don't hurry! Tell yourself, "I am in control; I feel good; I feel relaxed; I am allowed to take my time" (Miller, 1992, p. 38).

Relaxation through Release of Tension

Another way to keep a feeling of well-being and relaxation is to acquire the ability to scan your body for tension and then release it. (This skill is linked to your body awareness, outlined earlier.) First, recognize how certain areas of the body feel when they are tense. Do this by deliberately creating tension in your hands. Form a clenched fist; know what that tension feels like; then allow the tension to melt away. Release it; then breathe carefully and deeply, fully in and out. This is the feeling you want to recognize and re-create, this wonderful sensation of freedom when the muscles are relaxed.

Scan the body for the area of tension. Then focus on it. Then release the tension and allow yourself to refocus on the freedom within the muscles. You can repeat this exercise for all different parts of your body (e.g., focus on an area of the body used in sing-ing, tense those muscles, relax, and focus on how good they feel when relaxed). When you excel at this, you will be able to release tension from all parts of the body at will, even during your perfor-mance. As can be seen, scanning for and then releasing tension is geared to your ability to use the breath efficiently. It is the key to relaxation and to most of your feelings of well-being.

In his book *Progressive Muscular Relaxation* (1974) Edmund Jacobson describes his deep muscle relaxation technique. It works on the premise that if you have a feeling of warmth and well-being in your body or parts of your body, you cannot also feel anxious and stressed. This method of relaxation is used widely in elite sports and by all who advocate and teach stress-reducing techniques. It provides you with a way of identifying the difference between tense and relaxed muscles. One muscle group at a time is tensed for about six to eight seconds, then relaxed for twenty to thirty seconds; then the whole process is repeated at least once. If tension remains, an-other repeat is in order. To allow the relaxation to deepen, posi-tive self-talk or imagery can be used at the same time. The fol-lowing method is adapted from Jacobson's *Progressive Muscular Relaxation*:

1. Get into a comfortable, supported position, sitting or lying.
2. Close your eyes, relax, and focus on your breathing. Al-low the breathing to become a steady rhythm. As you con-tinue to breathe out, let the tension drain from the body until you are fully relaxed.
3. Clench your right fist tighter and tighter, focusing on the tension in your fist, hand, and forearm. Now relax by slowly opening your fingers. Feel the looseness in your right hand and arm; feel its heaviness. Repeat this proce-

dure with the right fist and arm, always paying special attention to the differences between relaxation and tension. Repeat the process with your left fist and arm.

4. Now tighten your buttocks and thighs. Relax; feel the difference. Focus on your right leg. Curl your toes downward, tensing the calves; focus on the tension. Slowly relax. Tighten the muscles in the whole leg; hold the tension; then allow the muscles to relax completely. Allow the leg to go heavy and relax deeply. Repeat this procedure. Once again, pay special attention to the contrast between the relaxation and the tension. Repeat with your left leg. Feel the heaviness throughout your lower body. Relax feet, ankles, calves, knees, thighs, and buttocks.

5. Now focus on your face, neck, and shoulders. Wrinkle your forehead as tight as you can. Relax and smooth it out. Clench your jaw; bite hard; focus on the tension. Relax and feel the contrast between tension and relaxation. Shrug your shoulders; hold the tension. Now relax them; drop them back until you can feel the heaviness and the relaxation spreading throughout your neck, face, and shoulders. This should be deep relaxation.

6. Focus on allowing your entire body to relax. Enjoy the feeling of heaviness from head to toe. Breathe in; hold your breath; feel and notice the tension. Exhale and feel the relaxation. Repeat several times, allowing the body to become more relaxed each time you exhale. Drain the tension away.

7. Enjoy the feeling of complete relaxation for some minutes. Become aware of the feeling of calmness in your whole body. You are now completely at ease and free from tension.

8. Now allow yourself to stretch parts of the body slowly, gradually becoming fully aware again, and open your eyes. As you do this, also tell yourself how wonderful you feel, how relaxed and at ease with yourself.

Relaxation by "Breathing in Power"

You can also relax yourself by "breathing in power." Based on an exercise devised by Saul Miller (1992), it works like this: Focus on your breathing as a rhythm, making sure that you take time, allowing the breath to go in and out in a full cycle. Keep doing this until your body feels calm and loose. Now, as you breathe in through your nose, try to be aware that you can breathe in your own power; you can allow it into the body. It is a form of energy forever available to you. Then you can use this inhaled power and energy to give yourself permission to do almost anything you wish. Use it to inspire yourself, to enrich your performance, or to enhance something in your everyday life. On the exhalation, talk positively to yourself. Or watch an image that makes you feel great, one that turns loose all your power and energy.

As you are aware, one of the main reasons you become tense and tight is because your breathing is wrong in some way. Working at your breathing in the way described previously, you will be able to breathe in your own power and energy, then use it to enhance whatever you are doing. The amount of power and energy available to you is infinite. You must simply learn how to use it to your advantage.

Learn to relax in all high-pressure situations by:

- Not focusing on the importance of the outcome
- Slowing down what you are doing, breathing fully in a full cycle
- Breathing easily and slowly, remembering that "the waves don't hurry"
- Taking your time so that you are in control
- Letting your body be free and loose
- Staying in the moment, focusing only on what you are doing in that moment.

(Should you be interested in following up on the excellent breath techniques taught by Saul Miller, they can be found in his book *Performance under Pressure*.)

Performing consistently well and enjoying a feeling of well-being should go together and work to your advantage. Try to remember to:

- Save energy and use it efficiently, especially in preparation for a performance
- Enjoy deep, restful sleep, especially the night before a performance
- Keep your body and mind clear, open to all positive thoughts
- Facilitate the use of imagery for good, consistent performance.

Summary

Put together a plan for your total well-being by learning to become aware of your body.

Relax nonessential muscles; contract only the muscles you need to save energy and use more effectively the energy you have.

Scan your body. Breathe to release all the tension.

Use your breath well; take your time; give yourself permission to get into a rhythm.

Breathe in your own power and energy; breathe to empower yourself; use it to enhance your lifestyle.

Sing relaxed.

Further information:

1. On color-coding the body to enhance your mental rehearsal imagery, see chapter 12, "Imagery in Performance."
2. On learning to relax, see chapter 11, "Dealing with Anxiety."

7 Setting Goals

"Would you tell me, please, which way I ought to go
from here?"
"That depends a good deal on where you want to
get to."

Lewis Carroll,
Alice's Adventures in Wonderland

Where do *you* want to get with your singing? What do *you* want to
achieve in the long term, in the short term?

A 1953 Yale University study revealed that of all the graduating
seniors, only 3 percent had set goals and planned how to achieve
them. These seniors were conspicuous in their class because they
alone focused on the very important questions linked with goal
setting, such as what it was that they really wanted to accomplish
and how they planned to achieve the goals they had set. Furthermore, it is clear that this top 3 percent of "goal setters" were by far
the most successful of their class. In terms of money, this 3 percent
earned more than all the other 97 percent of the whole class. While
success cannot always be viewed in terms of money, the process
used to achieve the success *is* important.

Noting the number of books and articles written about goal setting, we have to conclude that it is no secret just how important
the process is. Neither is there any doubt that individuals who are
achievers have a capacity for successful goal setting. Goal setting's
positive influence on behavior stems from the fact that the establishing of goals will:

1. *Direct your attention to the important elements of the skill
   itself.* For example, as you set specific goals, you must isolate particular vocal aspects that need upgrading, such as
   your legato.
2. *Mobilize your efforts.* For example, you might not wish to
   practice on a particular day, finding it difficult to gather
   your energy to do so even though you know it is really
   necessary. By dividing up the piece you wish to work at,

setting goals for one section at a time, you provide incentives that seem sensible to you and will therefore motivate you to satisfying work.

3. *Strengthen your persistence.* For example, having to learn four new pieces in a very short time may seem an insurmountable obstacle, but by setting subgoals of learning smaller chunks of the pieces and charting your progress, you will be much more likely to remain motivated. You will persist and you will achieve the goals you set.

4. *Encourage the development of new learning strategies (a hidden bonus of goal setting).* For example, while responding to your effort to achieve a goal you might learn new ways of dealing with a problem. You will then set a new goal: to continue to think about and deal with that problem in the same way in the future. This indirect thought process resulting from goal setting influences performance indirectly by affecting the psychological state, including such factors as confidence level, anxiety, and satisfaction.

How to Be Successful at Goal Setting

Perhaps you are already accustomed to setting goals for both long-term and short-term achievements. Some of these goals will have been easily identified and set, but others may have taken some time to plan in order to ensure achievement. Such programs have had very good results. Why, then, are some individuals very successful in setting and achieving their goals while others are not?

According to Gary Blair, author of *What Are Your Goals?* (1993), the answer lies in the nature of the questions you ask yourself when starting the process of a goal-setting program. In order to clarify what your dreams are and how you want to achieve them, you need to know what questions to ask yourself. Blair calls goal setting a journey—the journey of clarification, analysis, and, finally, achievement. Most important, it is the major means of remaining motivated in relation to your performance.

Goal setting is a major feature in all programs of mental preparation for performance excellence, imperative for the performance whether before, during, or after it. If you set the appropriate goals and plan how to achieve them, you will be successful. Although you have set goals in relation to your singing, it is the process of planning to achieve them that is all-important, because your planning will dictate how you think in relation to goals. This in turn keeps you motivated, allows you to maintain your drive to be successful, and guides your planning for the next stage of achievement.

Goals as a Focus of Attention

Goals give you a focus of attention. They allow you to expand your own horizons. Performing excellence can be achieved and earned through planning and persistence. This journey toward excellence begins with your dreams, your visions of what you want to achieve, and your goals. The more penetrating your vision, the greater the goal you will be able to achieve.

The following kinds of goals are immediately recognizable to you. You may even have set some like them for yourself.

> My goal is to sing for a major opera company.
> I intend to improve my agility so that I can offer "Let the Bright Seraphim" for my audition next month.
> My objective is to become an outstandingly good voice teacher.
> I want to sing with the San Francisco Opera.
> I want to be able to audition well and consistently.
> I want to earn my living as a singer.

Your primary task is to set the right kind of goal, the kind that provides direction and enhances motivation. Once you have done this, your next step is to plan an appropriate program to help you achieve your goal.

Subjective and Objective Goals

What is a goal? An objective, a target, a standard, or a level of performance or proficiency to be aimed for or reached.

Of the many different types of goals, you might set a very subjective one, such as having fun, enjoying yourself, or simply doing the best you can. This subjective type of goal does not give you the direction that can help you to achieve (although the subjective goal of having fun is important and should always be on a goal list). An objective goal, on the other hand, gives a very clear target to aim for, such as reaching a particular standard ("I will learn to cover or not cover my high notes at will"), learning a new piece in a certain time ("knowing that memorization depends upon repetition, I will not allow myself to be tempted into proceeding before repeating each section twenty times"), or spending daily a certain amount of time at a specific skill ("I will practice my Garcia velocity exercises every day for fifteen minutes").

In order to enhance your performance and to push it to the limits that you want to achieve, you should learn how to set and fulfill objective goals. They in turn will help you to achieve a specific standard of proficiency within a specified time. Here are some examples of objective goals:

> I will learn three new arias for audition purposes within
> the coming four months.
> Within the next two weeks I will discuss with my
> management new arrangements for my auditions.
> For a whole week I'll make two phone calls a day with
> the purpose of finding a venue for my showcase recital.

Outcome Goals and Performance Goals

Outcome and performance goals are the two different kinds of objective goals that you can set. Outcome goals are exactly that—your focus is on the outcome: being called back, being offered a particular role, getting the job, winning the competition. While such goals could be important for you, you must accept the fact that such goals are often not met because of other people. For example, you may have sung *your* best ever in the competition, but it happened that another singer sang better. He won; you didn't. Therefore, you failed to achieve your outcome goal, winning the competition. This outcome goal was beyond your control because it depended on other people. (Remember that good performances are always within your own control, not the control of others. Other singers, judges, and singing conditions all affect your performance but cannot be under your control.)

While setting an outcome goal—win or lose—is certainly not pointless, setting *only* this type of goal can lead to a slump in performance, frustration, unwanted anxiety, and even de-motivation. A lack of success can make you think that you are not very talented or that you are much less talented than you actually are. This is a very negative cycle for you to be in and a very difficult one to break. Winning is a habit, based on positive thinking and confidence. Losing is also a habit, but it is based on negative thinking and feelings of inferiority. Outcome goals only have two levels, win and lose.

On the other hand, performance goals (what to do) and process goals (how to attain your objectives) focus your attention on attaining certain standards or performance objectives, which can be compared with your own previous performances. Unlike outcome goals, performance goals remain firmly within your own control and lend themselves to being much more flexible. For example, if you set a goal of improving the percentage of times you sing your high notes in a certain piece with beauty and clarity to a level between 70 and 80 percent, then you will be able to adjust this kind of goal more precisely—

perhaps raising it to 84 percent—than you would have with an out-come goal such as "I want to have great high notes." (For some guidance on how to increase percentages through goal setting, see "Performance Profiling" in this chapter.) Research also tells us that performance goals, especially during competition, are generally associated with less anxiety and higher performance than outcome goals.

Goal setting and planning are important not only because they define your performance objectives but also because they develop and reaffirm your sense of mission, vision, purpose, and direction. If you can learn to set goals that relate to your own priorities in performance, then you can actually increase your commitment to achieving them.

As you can see, it is always best to focus your attention on and put your energy into those specific aspects of performance that are potentially within your control, such as your singing skills, your preparation (physical, technical and mental), your execution, and your performance routines, the best you can do in that moment of time or on that particular day.

Often, performance issues such as motivation, drive, ambition, persistence, dedication, and willpower become critical only when the singer has neither set the goals appropriately nor fully integrated them into a program of priorities.

TEACHING POINT: see #6, appendix 2.

Designing and Planning for a Goal-Setting Program

Designing and planning for a goal-setting program are really not very difficult if you follow a few rules. Initially such a program will demand time and honesty from you. Before you can decide where you want to go, you must first know where you are now. Consequently, the starting point and essence of successful goal setting is an accurate assessment of your skill level now, gained by asking yourself the right questions. Some of the questions may be painful, even challenging, for you to answer. If the questions actually appear to be difficult, they are more likely to "clear the path" that you follow to achieve your most important goals.

Self-Assessment Questions

Exercise

Ask yourself the following questions about you and your singing:

1. Why do I sing?
2. What personal needs are met by my singing?

3. How does singing fit in with the rest of my life?
4. What sacrifices have I made to pursue my singing?
5. Has it been worth it?
6. Do I honestly enjoy singing for its own sake?
7. When I sing, how does it make me feel?

These questions are designed to make you think deeply about the meaning of your singing. The issue is important because in your pursuit of excellence as a singer you will often come up against obstacles and periods of wondering if all your hard work is worth it. Only when you understand the deeper meaning your singing has for you will you remain motivated to succeed and gear yourself to surmount any obstacle. "Why do I sing?" sounds like a very obvious thing to ask. However, it's amazing how many singers when faced with such a question do not know the answer or haven't given it any thought for a long time. Your reasons for singing may change over time, and that, of course, will alter your horizons and the goals you set.

Visions and Dreams

Once you know why you sing, then you can begin to put this fact into perspective with your own visions and dreams. Of prime importance in your goal-setting program are your visions and dreams of where you want to go and of what, ideally, you want to achieve (as well as the aspect of where you are now). Such visions and dreams give to you your drive, desire, aspirations, and direction.

Exercise

What, then, are your visions and dreams for your singing? Think carefully about the following questions. Allow your thoughts to wander. Dream a little.

1. What is it that I ultimately want to achieve in my singing?
2. Precisely how would I feel if I excelled at singing?
3. Which singer do I endeavor to be most like?
4. When I become the singer of my dreams, what kinds of opportunities will present themselves to me?
5. What will I do when I have achieved my visions and dreams?

Your honest assessment of your own ability and of the reasons you sing is the rock upon which your goal-setting program is based. It sculpts the explicitness of what will be your performance goals and will in turn determine how you plan your program. Thinking about your dreams and aspirations allows you to accept such things as real possibilities. If you never dream, you will never strive for the best you can be.

Goals can be set in many diverse areas other than outcome and performance goals, which you know about. For example, there are:

- *Individual skills* (all the technical skills linked with fine vocal production)
- *Group skills* (skills you use as part of a singing group, choir, or cast)
- *Physical fitness* (very important, even in singing, because of the very close link between mind and body and the feeling of well-being)
- *Enjoyment*
- *Mental skills* (all of which you will find outlined in this book)
- *Singing time* (the number of auditions or competitions you want to do in any given time, the amount of practicing time you want to put in, the number of voice lessons, coachings, etc.).

The next stage asks you to identify the most appropriate mental skills that need help. There are various methods to help you do this, two of which are outlined for you here: performance profiling and the mental skills questionnaire.

Performance Profiling

Performance profiling is another approach to becoming aware of how you currently feel about your preparation and your performances. The following method for performance profiling was originally developed in 1989 by Richard J. Butler of High Royds Hospital in England (Butler and Hardy, 1992) and has been widely used and developed in all areas of performance.

Improvement in some areas of your performance is easily recognized: feeling physically stronger, observing measurable improvement in your technical vocal skills, and receiving positive endorsement from voice teachers and coaches about your progress. On the other hand, it is not so easy to recognize improvement in your mental skills or psychological development, which is far more intangible. Perhaps all you know is that you have some kind of feeling that things are better: you had the impression that you were better focused, your confidence seemed higher, and you felt more at ease in the performing arena.

With performance profiling you can particularize your true strengths and the specific areas that need more work and then set goals accordingly. A graphic method, it enables you to see quite clearly how you perceive yourself in all areas of your singing performance—physically, technically, emotionally, socially, and psychologically.

To get the most out of this method, you must be open and honest during your evaluation, so that you view the information positively and see its value clearly. No matter what your level as a singer—still developing or experienced—you can gather valuable information about all aspects of your performance. Most important, this information can also act as a shared understanding among you, your voice teacher, and your coach (or your mental skills consultant, if you are in touch with one) as to where your priorities about improvement should be placed.

Using Performance Profiles

Be as specific as you wish. Include aspects of your performance other than mental or, if you wish, use a performance profile for each area of performance—physical, technical, social, and personal.

Exercise 1

Identify all key performance qualities in the area that you have decided to deal with. Identify those qualities and factors of the desired area that, in your estimation, contribute to your peak performance. (Remember that top-level performance is not limited to experienced singers.) This identification can be carried out in one of two ways: (a) Think of the most outstanding singer whom you would wish to emulate and list all the qualities that make that performer the ultimate singer for you, or, (b) Imagine yourself when you are singing at the peak of your own potential, and list all the qualities needed to be that accomplished a performer—consistently.

Exercise 2

Write down all the performance qualities you are considering. Using the form of a circle as shown in figures 7-1, 7-2, and 7-3, note all the performance qualities that you consider important for you in the area named at the top of the page. Indicate how you currently see yourself on a scale of 1 to 10 for each quality. Draw a line at that level. Any score below 7 indicates that further development is required in that quality. For your guidance, each of figures 7-1, 7-2, and 7-3 is an example of a particular singer's profile, physical, technical, and mental.

If you can persuade your teacher, coach, and mental skills expert to fill out profiles of you from their point of view, it would be very productive. You could then review the profiles together and agree

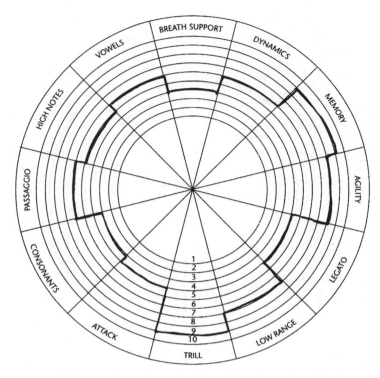

Figure 7-1. Performance profile: Technical vocal skills. At the present moment, this singer feels that her consonants are the weakest of her skills. Her breath support, her high notes, her attacks, and her legato are next on the list of skills needing attention. A conclusion could be drawn that the lack of command over consonants plays a part in her problems with breath control, attack, and legato. Agility, memory, trills, and low range are above average, and control of dynamics, vowels, and *passaggio* are on the borderline.

about which areas of your performance are the real priorities. Their time is very valuable, but at this point performance profiling might well be more valuable to you than the voice lesson or coaching itself.

In the three performance profiles here, each is an example of what one particular singer believes his or her skills to be like at the present moment. If you wish to profile your own performance, you will find a blank graph (chart #6) in appendix 1.

Performance profiles do not necessarily have to be displayed as circular graphs. As in figure 7-4, you can also show your performance profile as a series of lines, on the scale of 1 to 10, in two ways:

1. You can draw a line to indicate your ideal performance in each category listed and then draw a line beneath these to point out where you believe your performance is *now*. The difference between the two lines is the amount of improvement you have still to make.

TEACHING POINT: see #7, appendix 2.

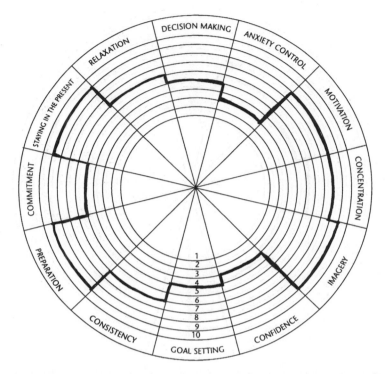

Figure 7-2. Performance profile: Mental skills. At the present moment, this singer feels that the mental skills of staying in the present, imagery, and preparation are his mental strengths, with motivation and concentration also being quite good. However, because it is difficult to work on everything at once, he would be advised to spend time working at anxiety control and confidence. These two skills will have a marked effect on his performance.

2. You can draw your own line to indicate where your performance is at the present time in the categories listed. Then ask your voice teacher or coach to draw a line indicating where he or she thinks your performance standard is. You can then use the results as a discussion to identify which areas have to be worked at and set your goals accordingly.

Figures 7-4 and 7-5 are two samples of linear performance profiles, representing two particular singers' assessments of the performance qualities, vocal and mental, that are meaningful for them as well as the teacher's assessment of the same performance.

In figure 7-4 the singer believed his musical memory to be exemplary, but the teacher disagreed by a small degree. The same small difference existed in the categories of language pronunciation; linguistic authority, flavor; musical accuracy; control of all dynamics; body and facial tranquility; and ensemble with pianist. In all cases the teacher felt that the singer had overestimated his

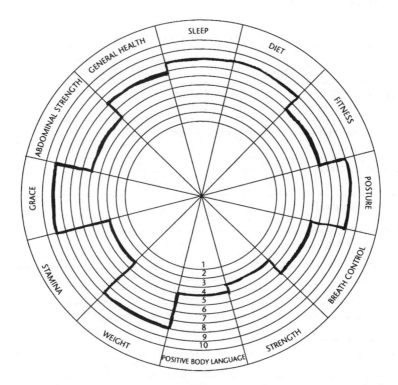

Figure 7-3. Performance profile: Physical factors. At the present moment, this singer feels that her posture and grace are her best physical elements. She is keeping her weight down reasonably well. She got enough sleep and ate properly before the performance. Because her general health is only adequate, although her fitness is slightly better, her stamina, strength, and abdominal strength are not what they should be and will need work, as will her positive body language.

skills by a small amount. In those cases where the differences were small or nonexistent, the singer's skills are validated and he can be reassured. The teacher and the student agreed in their assessment of these subjects: text memory; language enunciation; high, low, medium ranges; and agility, melisma; but they were very far apart in their assessments of the student's legato; cantabile; musical style; and physical elements of drama. Is there a debate here, or should he just accede to the teacher's view and try to improve those skills in the future? There were, in addition, three categories in which the teacher found the singer to be actually better than his own assessment: breath support; *appoggio*; dramatic commitment; and presentation of self. He needs to have a discussion with his teacher about the skills he underestimated.

In figure 7-5, as can be seen quite clearly, the voice teacher's and the singer's impressions of the mental strengths at the moment coincide in many instances. They agree on the singer's motivation,

Name: _____	Aria: _____	Date: _____

QUALITY	Assessment: 0 2 4 6 8 10
musical memory	========================== ////////////////////////////////
text memory	============== ///////////////////
language pronunciation	================= ///////////////////
language enunciation	================= //////////////////////////
linguistic authority, flavor	============== ////////////////
high, low, medium ranges	================= ////////////////////////
legato, cantabile	======================== ///////////////////////
agility, melisma	===================== ///////////////////////////
musical accuracy	=========================== ////////////////////////////////////
musical style	========================== //////////////////////
breath support, appoggio	=============== ///////////////////////////
control of all dynamics	=============== ////////////////
body and facial tranquility	================= //////////////////////
dramatic commitment	======================== ///
physical elements of drama	============================ //////////////////
presentation of self	======= /////////////
ensemble with pianist	================= ///////////////////

QUALITIES TO WORK ON:

1. _____   2. _____
3. _____   4. _____

========== Performer's Assessment   /////////////////// Teacher's Assessment

Figure 7-4. Vocal performance profile.

SKILL	0 1 2 3 4 5 6 7 8 9 10
Motivation	================= ///////////////////////////
Anxiety	===================== /////////////////////
Relaxation skills	============================== ////////////////////////
Concentration/focus	================= ///////////////////////
Use of imagery	===================== //////////////////
Determination	========= ////////////////
Confidence	=================== ///
Physical well-being	======= ////////////
Distractions	========= ////////////
Enjoyment	================== ////////////////////

Key:

Singer's perception of performance ======
Teacher's perception of performance //////////

Figure 7-5. Mental performance profile.

her ability to cope with distractions, her determination, her concentration/focus, and her physical well-being. However, there are some serious discrepancies that dictate a discussion between singer and teacher before action can be taken: anxiety, relaxation skills, use of imagery, confidence, and enjoyment. Not all these skills can be dealt with at the same time. Therefore, the ones causing the biggest problems should be attended to first.

After reviewing figures 7-4. and 7-5, if you find that you prefer the linear form to the circular graph, you will find in appendix 1 blank copies (chart #7 and chart #8) of the linear performance profiles. If there are some differences of opinion revealed in figure 7-4.

or 7-5, they can be debated by you and your teacher. The outcome can be used as a basis for your goal-setting strategy.

One of the unique features of performance profiling is that its final analysis is actually yours, is designed by you, and contains your selection of what is important in your performance. It is a wonderfully clear analysis of what areas you consider to be important and whether those areas require more work or not.

The Mental Skills Questionnaire

Another method regularly used to identify those mental strengths that require more work from you and to monitor your progress is the mental skills questionnaire.

Many different types of questionnaire are used, especially in sports. The following one (figure 7-6) has been adapted for use by singers from a questionnaire designed by two British sport psychology researchers, Lew Hardy and Dave Nelson (1990). The questionnaire measures eight important aspects of the mental side of singing performance. Each aspect has a series of statements about your own experiences linked with singing. A particular singer completed the questionnaire by circling the appropriate number. He then followed the scoring instructions and completed figure 7-7. As can be seen, he needs to work on anxiety and fear, relaxation, and motivation.

If you would like to use these two forms yourself, you will find blank copies of them (chart #9a and chart #9b) in appendix 1.

Scoring Instructions

Work out your score by adding up the numbers you have circled in each of the sections. Now calculate your percentage score for each category. Do this by dividing your score by 35, then moving the decimal point two digits to the right. For example, if you have scored 14 out of the possible 35, you will calculate your percentage score as 14 / 35 = .40. Move the decimal point two digits to the right: 40 percent. These percentage scores do not represent a right or wrong score as in an exam. They simply show you where you are now. You should use them in the future to assess whether you have progressed from this starting point.

What to Do Now?

With your eight percentage scores calculated, decide what skills you need to work on.

From these methods of performance profiling you will be able to see the areas in which you will need to do more work, and you

Feel free to fill in statements in each category that would better apply to *your* singing.

Questionnaire: Mental Skills for Singing	Strongly Disagree				Strongly Agree

Motivation

1. In performance I usually manage my mental energy well enough to sing my best.   1   2   ③   4   5
2. I really enjoy performing when the other singers are of high caliber.   ①   2   3   4   5
3. I am good at motivating myself.   1   2   3   ④   5
4. I find that I usually try my hardest.   1   2   ③   4   5
5. I normally have a clear idea of WHY I sing.   1   2   3   4   ⑤

Goal Setting

6. I always set myself goals in my lessons and coachings.   1   2   3   ④   5
7. My goals are always very specific.   1   2   ③   4   5
8. I always analyze and evaluate the outcome after a performance.   1   2   3   4   ⑤
9. I usually set goals that I can achieve   1   2   ③   4   5

Self-Confidence

10. I suffer from lack of confidence about my performance abilities.   5   4   3   ②   1
11. I approach all auditions, competitions, and performances with confident thoughts.   1   2   ③   4   5
12. My confidence wavers as auditions, competitions, and performances draw nearer.   5   ④   3   2   1
13. Throughout all performances I keep a positive attitude.   1   2   3   ④   5

Anxiety and Fear

14. I often experience fears about failing in performance.   5   ④   3   2   1
15. I worry that I will disgrace myself when singing in public.   ⑤   4   3   2   1
16. I let my mistakes and omissions distract me while I perform.   5   4   3   ②   1
17. My anxiety is harder to control in the presence of other singers.   5   4   3   2   ①

Relaxation

18. I am able to relax myself before a performance.   1   2   ③   4   5
19. I become too tense before performance.   5   4   ③   2   1
20. Being able to calm myself down is one of my strong points.   1   2   ③   4   5
21. I know how to relax in difficult circumstances.   1   2   ③   4   5

Concentration and Focusing

22. My thoughts are often elsewhere during performance.   ⑤   4   3   2   1
23. My concentration lets me down during performance.   5   4   3   ②   1
24. Unexpected noises and sights distract me during performance.   5   4   3   ②   1
25. I am good at pretending to be focused even though I'm distracted.   5   ④   3   2   1
26. Despite distractions, I can control my focus during performance.   1   2   ③   4   5

Imagery

27. I can rehearse my repertoire in my imagination.   1   2   ③   4   5
28. I rehearse my musical, vocal, and dramatic skills in my head before I use them.   ①   2   3   4   5
29. It is difficult for me to form mental pictures.   ⑤   4   3   2   1
30. I can easily imagine how technical vocal and dramatic maneuvers feel.   1   2   3   ④   5

Expression and Meaning

31. I am good at personalizing the text of my music.   1   2   3   ④   5
32. I have difficulty expressing my intended emotional state with my body.   5   4   3   ②   1
33. My face reflects my emotions accurately and expressively.   1   2   ③   4   5
34. Without props, costumes, and sets I find it difficult to summon up dramatic truth.   5   4   ③   2   1
35. I can usually understand the musical and textual clues that give dramatic meaning.   ①   2   3   4   5

Figure 7-6. Mental skills questionnaire.

MENTAL SKILLS QUESTIONNAIRE RESULTS		
Date: *Feb. 22, 1998*	SCORE	PERCENTAGE
Motivation	*12*	*34%*
Goal Setting	*15*	*42%*
Self-Confidence	*13*	*36%*
Anxiety and Fear	*12*	*33%*
Relaxation	*12*	*33%*
Concentration and Focusing	*16*	*45%*
Imagery	*13*	*36%*
Expression and Meaning	*13*	*36%*
MENTAL SKILLS TO FOCUS ON:		
1. *Anxiety and Fear*		
2. *Relaxation*		
3. *Motivation*		

Figure 7-7. Mental skills questionnaire results.

can set goals accordingly. For example, if you scored yourself low on concentration and focusing, you will have to do the following things:

1. Go back over the performance and check where your concentration was poor and what actually happened to your focus at that time.
2. Work out what you need to refocus on. Then learn and practice the new, relevant focusing skills so that when you perform again you will be less likely to make the same mistake.
3. Practice this concentration and focusing skill in the piece under performance conditions, if possible—in a voice lesson, workshop, or master class. Try to simulate the performance situation if you can, and then practice and practice!

When looking at your assessments in either your performance profile or the mental skills questionnaire (or perhaps both), if there are a number of areas that need extra work then you should either (a) enter into an overall general program of performing skills in order to enhance your singing, or (b) prioritize those areas that are really urgent and work at those without trying to worry about the rest. This can be done in partnership with your voice teacher or coach or, possibly, a mental skills consultant.

Now let's take some time to summarize what you have already done:

Stage 1. You have grasped the importance of goal setting for performance excellence.

Stage 2. You have become aware that you can set many different kinds of goals.

Stage 3. You have followed the steps to designing a goal setting program for yourself, which are:

    a. *Self-assessment.* You have asked the right questions, for example: "Why do I sing?"

    b. *Visions and dreams.* You have given yourself permission to dream.

    c. *Performance assessment.* You have been very thorough about your performance assessment, through either performance profiling or the mental skills questionnaire or both, and are aware of the areas that need to be improved.

Now you are ready to set your targets and design your goal-setting program.

Setting Targets and Designing a Goal-Setting Program

This is not as difficult as it first seems. However, in order to give your goal-setting program some direction and also to know whether or not you are making progress, you must follow some very simple basic principles. These goal-setting principles have been identified from research and practice. Their correct application provides a very strong foundation for designing your program.

Here is an acronym to aid your work: SMARTER. The acronym *SMARTER* will help you remember what the basic principles of goal setting are. It will also facilitate your evaluation of whether or not your goals are working successfully.

    S (specific)
    M (measurable)
    A (acceptable and adjustable)
    R (realistic)
    T (time-phased)
    E (exciting)
    R (recorded)

If you had set as a goal for yourself "I will improve the mental side of my auditioning," it would not prove to be very efficient, because it doesn't fulfill all of the *SMARTER* requirements. They are:

S[pecific]   *Be as* specific *as you can be when identifying your goals.* When the goal is too vague, assessment of its success is hindered. *The mental side of auditioning* is far too inexact a term. The "mental side" could be almost anything.

M[easurable]   *You should be able to* measure *all your goals in an objective way.* In this goal, mentioned earlier, objective measurement is not possible. The word *improvement* is not helpful. How *much* improvement is required? Objective measurement is easier in some areas than others. For example, you will find it quite simple to assess how many times you manage to sing those A♮s at the end of "Una furtiva lagrima" in your lessons or in performance, but mental skills are not so easy to assess in this way. The percentage scores from the mental skills questionnaire or the more subjective measurement used on the performance profiling sheet might make it possible, as long as you use the same evaluative criteria each time. Be sure that you always use the same 1–10 scale for your assessment. Then you will be able to assess your progress.

A[cceptable] and A[djustable]   *You will be more likely to* accept *your goals if you are instrumental in designing them.* You should believe that you can achieve your goals and that you *want* to achieve them. Goal setting should not be done only by the voice teacher, musical coach, or mental skills coach but should be a decision shared with you. You do need to feel that you have control over your destiny. This way you are more likely to accept the outcome.

Always adjust *your goals if you need to.* Goals are not written in stone. They can and should be changed when you feel that your progress is faster or slower than you had originally intended. For example, you may set yourself a technical goal such as learning a new piece for an audition four weeks away. But anything could happen before then. You might catch a cold or have a family problem, either of which would dictate that this goal could not be achieved. It will need some adjustment, and that's fine. On the other hand, you might make such good progress with the piece that you need to extend your goals!

R[ealistic]   *Your goals should be* realistic *yet challenging for you in the time available.* If the goal you set is very difficult, you may be inclined to give up or may even fail. Such a result might lead to losing confidence in yourself and not wanting to try again. On the other hand, if the goal is too easy, you will gain no satisfaction from achieving it. Ideally, you should aim to set your goals slightly higher than your present ability. This will make you work to achieve them and also help you to be persistent in trying to achieve your targets.

T[ime-phased]   *The progression of your goals should be planned in* timed phases. In order for you to achieve a long-term goal, you need to plan shorter term goals in a step-by-step progression. Each short-term goal should have a target date, by which you identify a goal achievable within a specific time. If a time frame is not set, you may consider putting things off or postponing those good intentions. In short, you will have less motivation to achieve.

E[xciting]   *When you achieve your goals, especially short-term progressive goals, you should feel* excited *by your achievement— and justifiably so.* If you don't feel excited by your achievements, then you may be setting goals that you find too difficult to achieve. Pat yourself on the back. Feel good about your progress. It's exciting to be in control of your own achievements.

R[ecorded]   *Always* record *the goals that you set for yourself.* Write down your goals. Be very precise about the wording itself and about the time frame you have set. When you are assessing and reviewing your progress, it will be much easier to refer to this written record. It will also help you, your voice teacher, and your coach to remember the details of your goal-setting program.

The following is an example of a goal-setting schedule that uses the *SMARTER* acronym:

Long-Term Goal, set on October 23:   I will improve my use of imagery during the audition on December 18, especially as Dorabella in the aria "Smanie implacabili."

Intermediate Goal, set on October 23:   By November 20 I will have reviewed my work on the use of imagery in performance with the help of my mental skills consultant; I will have listed all the sensory perceptions that this piece stimulates and practiced them; I will have developed my imagery strategy for this aria and begun to put it into my practice sessions and voice lessons.

Short-Term Goals for the week of October 27–November 3:

1. I will stimulate the sensory perceptions for the imagery required for this aria for ten minutes every day. To help the process, I will use recordings and videos of my "ultimate" performer singing this aria.
2. During my practice sessions I will spend twenty minutes working at using in the aria some of the images that have emerged and evaluating them for their vividness.

3. I will share my findings with my coach during my session and seek advice regarding his/her opinion about the outcomes.
4. I will practice singing the complete aria in performance mode, using the images that have the most potential, and then evaluate the result.

Based on the assessment of this entire program, I will plan the short-term goals for the next week to achieve my intermediate goal.

Summary

Setting goals of many different kinds holds great importance in your quest for enhancement of your performance. The steps to be followed in designing a goal-setting program of your own are:

> Self-assessment (asking the right questions)
> Visions and dreams (giving yourself permission to dream)
> Performance assessment (learning which areas need improvement)

The basic principles of goal setting are reinforced by using the acronym *SMARTER*: (S)pecific; (M)easurable; (A)cceptable and adjustable; (R)ealistic; (T)ime-phased; (E)xciting; (R)ecorded. The use of these principles will also contribute eventually to the evaluation of your goal-setting program.

Further information:

1. On physical fitness, see chapter 6, "Physical Well-Being and Relaxation."

8   Developing Self-Confidence through Positive Thinking

> We ask ourselves, who am I to be brilliant, gorgeous, talented, and fabulous? Actually, who are you *not* to be? . . . There's nothing enlightened about shrinking so that other people won't feel insecure around you. . . . As we are liberated from our own fears, our presence automatically liberates others.
>
> Nelson Mandela

Is your self-confidence already soaring? Then you needn't read this chapter. (The best maxim is: If it's working well, don't tinker with it!) Those of you who wish to continue, gather round with those singers who do, from time to time, suffer from self-doubt.

Explaining self-confidence is almost unnecessary. In some singers it is visible for all to see, so obvious that it is very nearly tangible—in the way they look, walk, and talk, what they say, and even the very thoughts they think. But did you ever think of confidence in the following way? Confidence is the assuredness that comes from feeling *equal* to the task you are about to complete, an assuredness usually characterized by unshakable belief in yourself and your ability. In practical singers' terms, it is the serenity of knowing that even your worst four bars are going to be pretty good.

You probably know some who fit this description. Their self-belief is truly unalterable, and their egos resist the severest misfortunes. They appear very resilient, bouncing back like a rubber ball—the harder it's hit, the quicker it bounces back. Remember Muhammad Ali? "I'm the greatest," he kept saying. He carried this aura around with him, and in the end, even his opponents believed that he was indeed the greatest. The same with Tiger Woods's golf performance in 1997: "I was in between a B and a C [in my playing]. Winning that meant a lot. It shows *if you think well* [authors' italics] and have a good short game, you can win."

When you study successful singers, you realize that they do not necessarily have better voices than you do, nor have they studied with better voice teachers, nor have they had better backgrounds in preparation for their lives as singers. Actually, they have simply developed a greater belief in themselves and their ability and have acted upon that belief. They have trained their thinking. It allows them to believe that they can achieve anything. Having constantly told themselves that they can and will achieve, inevitably they do!

On many occasions you hear singers saying that their audition or performance wasn't as good as their rehearsal in the studio. Part of the reason for this underperforming is lack of self-confidence and positive self-belief. In order to tap your own potential, you must believe that you control whatever happens to you and that you can change your singing life for the better.

Many elite performers firmly believe that being positive and feeling positive about yourself and your abilities is the cornerstone of outstanding performance, at whatever level you perform. That is, even developing performers can give good, consistent performances at their level *if they have confidence in their own abilities.* Recognizing what it is that you can do, believing in what you can do, and doing those things well—even under pressure—is a major part of good performance.

Self-Confidence and Positive Self-Enhancement as Skills

> The dancer with conviction has power; many a dance of poor quality has been "put across" just by the superb belief of the performer in the work. . . . If you believe in yourself, everybody else probably will, too.
>
> Doris Humphrey,
> *The Art of Making Dances*

Some individuals have a more resilient self-concept than others. Some are inclined to think the worst of themselves, while others are kinder in their self-perceptions. Some are more prone to anxiety, while others are either carefree or simply very laid-back. Such tendencies can change over time, but the changes will not be sudden. Confidence tends to be extremely specific. Very few people are full of confidence or totally lacking confidence in all situations or all the time in any particular situation. Imagine Placido Domingo on a skateboard or Renée Fleming diving from a highboard. Surely their resolute confidence might abandon them in such circumstances. Even those who are the epitome of confidence can lose it quickly in unfamiliar surroundings.

Sometimes successful singers suffer a run of poor performances (as do Olympic performers) and, perhaps as a result, experience some feelings of lack of confidence. In all forms of performance the pendulum of success swings one way and then the other, toward you and away from you. All too often it takes your confidence with it. It is this fluctuation in your self-confidence and self-belief that you should learn to manage.

The ability to think positively is one of the most powerful skills and tools that you have as a singer. Once you have learned this skill, you can use it to help yourself not only in your performance but also in your life, especially at those times when you come under pressure. *Confidence arouses positive emotions and positive thinking habits.* Successful singers often will things to happen the way they want. They're positive thinkers. According to Canadian performance consultant Saul Miller (1992), positive performers tend to say things like "I can" and "I will," and, of course, by and large they can and they do! Miller also believes that positive performers live by a basic rule: You get more of what you think. Abiding by his rule will give you confidence not only in your singing ability but also in yourself. It will allow you to value your own worth.

To Be Positive Takes Courage

It takes much more courage, dedication, and conscious awareness to be positive than to be negative. Singing performances do not exist in isolation. They reflect your inner attitudes, your daily behavior, and, above all, your basic views of yourself. If you are to remain positive about yourself and your singing, then your unremitting effort must be to reinforce and affirm yourself constantly and consciously.

Even if your vocal technique is very good, even if you feel physically able to stand the rigors of performance, when you do not *believe* that you can perform well, you will not make use of all your abilities or your full potential. Therefore, it is essential not only that you learn the technical and physical skills demanded of you as a singer but also that you learn to instill in yourself confidence about your ability to perform those skills.

How Do You Become Positive and Gain in Self-Confidence?

There are no secret formulas. Begin by looking at the good things you already do and want to do in the future. Start looking on the bright side of your singing life. Take a new perspective. You have to make a conscious decision always to view yourself and each singing situation in the best possible light. In this way you begin to create a *habit* of being positive.

Self-confidence is derived mainly from one or more of the following sources:

- Interaction with other people who always give you positive feedback when you deserve it
- Previous successful performances and singing experiences
- Involvement with other successful people who act as good role models and whose success rubs off on you
- Verbal persuasion, whether done by you or others, a fundamental means of attempting to change attitudes and behavior in the direction of self-confidence
- The ability to control negative thinking and emotions.

If you now perform consistently close to your potential, you have already learned to control such things as your mental focus. You can channel your emotions. You can recover from your mistakes in a constructive way, that is, without defeating yourself. What you have is the ability to shift quickly from negative thinking to a positive focus, particularly in response to increased anxiety, distractions, mistakes, and worries.

If, on the other hand, you have *not* mastered such matters, then you need to learn some mental skills that will help you with this shift of focus from negative to positive thinking. This begins with your self-confidence. The following series of principles and exercises will help you develop positive-thinking skills and become much more self-confident.

Positive Self-Talk and Positive Affirmations

Where your mind goes, negative or positive, your performance will follow.

As has been said, one of the most crucial determinants in developing a positive thinking pattern (and therefore maintaining confidence) is what you say to yourself, that is, *self-talk*. This self-talk either improves or worsens your thinking and therefore your confidence. If you have a strong mental attitude, emphasizing your positive characteristics, positive traits, and positive skills, then you will be confident. If you are confident, your performance will be enhanced. If, on the other hand, you have a negative attitude, then your confidence will drop. When your confidence drops, the performance suffers.

Self-affirmation is the process of directing your self-talk to affirm and confirm all your positive strengths, qualities, abilities, and skills. It can also be used to affirm the quality of the preparation that you have done, as well as the quality of your training as a singer. Self-affirmation allows you to plant in the conscious mind positive thoughts, which you then connect to giving an excellent performance.

When you repeat these positive self-affirmations and use them, they become part of the subconscious. Therefore, they affect *your own perception* of your strengths, qualities, skills, and ability. This expanded positive perception heightens your confidence during all the circumstances of performance—before, during, and after. Therefore, your performance has a better chance for improvement.

As you begin to compile your affirmations, don't be modest! Remember that they are yours and they need not be shown to or discussed with anyone else. Don't let yourself feel embarrassed by this new confidence. You are not being a show-off; you are not being arrogant. It is important for you to develop a strong, unshakable self-belief.

While there are a number of exercises and techniques that work well at helping you improve your self-confidence, not all techniques work for all singers. The following exercises have proven to be successful across a range of singers at all different levels of performance—from beginners through advanced.

How to Develop Personal Lists of Positive Affirmations

A list of positive affirmations will help you begin the process of becoming *aware* of all your positive qualities and strengths, both as a person and as a singer. Three different types of affirmation can be developed and used as part of your self-confidence program:

1. General affirmations
2. Performance achievement affirmations
3. Triggers, or process affirmations.

General Affirmations (type 1) are positive self-statements that you use to confirm your own good qualities. Try to draw up a list of five to ten general affirmations relating to yourself as a person and as a singer. If you feel that you need help with this, use the form (chart #10) that appears in appendix 1 to aid you with this. Some examples are:

> I am a strong person.
> I have trained well to become a good singer.
> I have a sense of humor.
> I can perform well in tough situations.
> I am very loyal to my friends.
> I feel good about my singing skills.
> I can say "no!" when I need to.
> I enjoy the challenge of an audition.

Using these affirmations on a daily basis makes it easier to repeat them with conviction and intensity. You will soon feel confident using your affirmations. You will be able to use them during your voice lessons, auditions, performances, or even your ordinary day job, if you have one. To summarize:

- Write down a list of positive affirmations for yourself as a person and a singer. (chart #10 in appendix 1 may be helpful in making this list.)
- Use your affirmations daily by repeating them on a regular basis.
- Use them in voice lessons, coachings, and performance when you feel comfortable saying them to yourself.
- Feel free to change your affirmations, if you wish to, as you grow more confident. They are not written in stone. It is most important that they continue to help you in your performance.
- Continue to use your affirmation training, even when you are feeling very confident. Although things may be going very well for you, you never know what further challenges are in store for you.

If it seems that it will be useful, make another kind of affirmations list, one with reference to your *performance achievement affirmations (type 2)* only. You will find a Performance Achievement Affirmations form (chart #11) in appendix 1. This kind of affirmation is specific to your singing, having to do with auditions and other kinds of performance. This list acts as a reminder of how well you did and what you should remember for future good performances. It also gives you a pat on the back for the improvements you have made. It really doesn't matter whether the performance was successful in terms of getting an engagement. What matters is this: Since you felt that things went well for you, you must keep this reminder of your own worthiness. Performance achievement affirmations also act as a further reinforcement of your confidence, which you can reuse for your performance. The Performance Achievement Affirmations form (chart #11 in appendix 1) will help with that list. Some examples of performance achievement affirmations are:

> I sang very well and with joy.
> My mental training is working.
> I performed really well, considering who was on the audition panel.
> I managed getting in and out of cover very well.
> I am a creative singer, and I sing with great expression.
> I am a good singer.
> My high notes were great, especially the last B♮.
> I felt very confident throughout.

Working to Your Strengths

Another way of listing your positive strengths and qualities in relation to your performance achievements is to organize them under three headings: physical, technical, and mental. Having listed your strengths, you can then use them for positive affirmations during performance or when you practice in the performance mode (which is to simulate a performance during the preparation period).

It is recommended that you draw up this kind of positive list for each piece you prepare for an audition, for each of your main arias or duets in an operatic performance, for each song in your recital, and for each piece you sing with an orchestra. It takes surprisingly little time to do.

Under the heading of *physical*, write down in as much detail as possible all the things that you believe to be positive in the physical aspects of the piece. Some examples might be:

> My body language is very confident during this piece.
> I know that I look good in this dress.
> My body language and facial expressions reflect really
>   well the character I'm playing.
> I walk with confidence and I look good.
> I've conquered that old nervous habit of flexing my thumb.
> This jacket makes me look really great.
> I'm proud of how I enter and present myself.

This area of your performance is extremely important and should not be underestimated. Always remember that you are seen before you are heard. Looking good, walking tall, and exuding confidence are all key parts of your performance. It does require practice if you are not accustomed to doing it.

Under the heading of *technical*, write down all the positive aspects of your technical skills on each particular piece. Some examples are:

> The musical requirements of this piece are totally under
>   my control.
> My French has improved so much that it is both accurate
>   *and* authoritative in this song.
> I managed the low notes well enough to make them
>   powerful but not vulgar.
> I don't have to take any extra breaths in the entire aria!
> I'm finally at home in the bel canto style.
> My rubatos were under control and well synchronized
>   with the accompanist.

"Knowing that you know" your technical skills is a great confidence builder, and accepting the positive truths about your technique will make you execute those skills even better. Let us use Susanna's aria "Deh, vieni, non tardar" as an example, knowing that this piece is sung by sopranos at all levels of technical proficiency. A very experienced singer, whose standards are extremely high, might make out a list like this after a good performance of the aria:

> I finally achieved a totally natural delivery of the first line of this recitative. At the same time I kept all the stresses in the right place and added Italian flavor with the single and double consonants.
>
> In the second page of the recitative, I managed a completely successful transition from a Susanna playacting for Figaro's sake to a Susanna who has melted, honestly captivated by the beauty of the night and the garden.
>
> My breath was ready to go and functioning splendidly from the very first note of the first line of the aria.
>
> I was able to keep the legato line very even throughout all the zigzags of the tune.
>
> Although the pianissimo F "vieni" was not the best I have done, the other three places—the high A, the long decrescendo on F, and the last soft F—were ravishingly soft and yet supported.
>
> During the entire aria, I did not allow my technical concerns to tense up my calm face and body.

A less experienced soprano might make out the following list:

> I got every double consonant in that hard stuff on page one of the recitative.
>
> My recitative style is really improving. It doesn't sound so studied.
>
> I remembered the double r in "susurro" and the closed e in "fioretti" and the open o in "rosa."
>
> I didn't get louder on the high A. I couldn't get softer, but I didn't get louder.

Under the heading of *mental*, write down in detail the positive mental skills of each piece. Some examples are:

> I am well prepared. I know this piece well.
>
> I am focused for this piece and will not easily be distracted.
>
> I enjoy singing this piece so much that I don't care who is on the panel.
>
> This is *my* performance. I own it, and I will sing well.
>
> The audience is going to love what I do.

Once you have all the details noted, then you can begin to structure them into a positive self-talk program for each piece. Keep reading the lists, and keep saying to yourself those positive phrases that are crucial for you.

Always complete the lists when you are feeling calm, logical, and thoughtful about your singing. They should be unemotional and unbiased, because it would not help you to remain positive if you did your lists when you were feeling angry or frustrated about your singing. Use the Working to Your Strengths Sheet (chart #12 in appendix 1) to help your thinking. Just jot down some reminders. Soon you will think this way automatically.

Triggers, or Process Affirmations (type 3), normally consist of one or two positive words or images that you can use during the performance or during your preparation for the performance. This type of affirmation helps the mind to focus on the important things within the performance. You can arrive at your own triggers—positive words or images—by going back over a very good performance or practice session and reminding yourself what it felt like. Write down the key words that come to mind. You may find that you use different words at different times during the performance. For example, during your warm-up your words may be softer, such as: *relax, easy, smooth, serene, and tranquil.* Later on in your preparation you may be using words that have a little more force or spark to them, such as: *do it, strong, concentrate,* and *go for it.* The image you choose as a trigger will be one that comes to mind when you attempt to describe the feelings or images invoked by your successful execution of a technical skill. Remember: One word or image can often ignite the performance if you learn to use these triggers efficiently.

Let's use the third item on the experienced soprano's list of affirmations as an example of how to choose and implement a trigger: "My breath was ready to go and functioning splendidly from the very first note of the first line of the aria." Given the zigzag contour of the "Deh, vieni" tune, the problem of the first phrase might be described as keeping the air flow at a steady rate so that the legato can be exemplary and making sure that the legato starts immediately on the first note. One might image this straight-ahead, never-faltering air flow to be like a bulldozer that you observe moving at a snail's pace—three miles an hour—across a terrain filled with boulders, bushes, trees, and hillocks. As you watch the bulldozer make its powerful and stately progress across the land, tossing the rocks and bushes it encounters to either side, it levels the plot of earth to a uniform flatness. Now you must choose the correct moment to employ the trigger. If you are accustomed to inhaling on the final three eighth notes after the last sixteenth note run, then you must *image* the bulldozer and its very slow movement before you take your breath (on the last group of ascending sixteenth notes). This way the sense of steady air flow will be with you before you sing the first note. Having a clear-cut, invariable musical moment in which to trigger this image will help to assure a fine legato and make each performance of this aria more telling.

A Triggers or Process Affirmations Sheet (chart #13 in appendix 1) will make it easy to record your choice of triggers, if you believe that it will be helpful to you.

Changing Self-Talk

It is very important to devise and phrase affirmations properly. They should always be positive, based on your own positive aspects and those of your performance. Changing self-talk from negative to positive is a valuable skill, but in order to change it you must be aware of it. Monitor yourself so that you are aware of how much negative talk you speak, and make sure that you restructure it. Don't ignore the fact that there is a problem. Try to think about the source of your negativity in a much more positive way, as if it were a *challenge* to replace it with a more positive statement or word. You may find this difficult and awkward at first, but when you have practiced it, it will get easier. You will have positive alternatives ready. Some examples appear in figure 8-1.

Now make a list of the typically negative things you say to yourself, especially during practice and performance. Then try to reword them in a positive form. When you do this, remember that the opening words of the statement are very important. For example:

I can't . . . should become	*I can* . . .
If only . . . should become	*When* . . .
I find it very difficult to . . . should become	*It is a challenge for me to* . . .
I worry about . . . should become	*I will be OK because* . . .

This bears repeating: Practice these affirmation skills so that you can replace that negative thought with a positive one before it can do any damage to your performance.

NEGATIVE	POSITIVE
I can't sing for that conductor again.	I'll be okay with him. My attitude is already better.
I hate auditioning in that room.	I can sing well there because I prepared thoroughly.
I never get the agility right in this piece.	This is a new audition; I will not make the same old mistakes.

Figure 8-1. Changing self-talk.

Becoming a Positive Listener

Very often, because of the nature of their training, singers may have an inclination to hear only the negative things that are spoken to them. The ability to hear the positive things that are being said is an important skill to learn.

Voice teachers and coaches are very busy people. It is their job to help you improve your vocal and performance skills. There seems never to be enough time for the work that must be done in the lesson, so there may be occasions when the positive things they have said become buried. It is not your teacher's job to keep reminding you just how wonderful you are. You must learn to do that for yourself. Your job is to become independent of the teacher and coach, so that you can survive alone under pressure. Help yourself to develop the skill of listening by doing the following:

- Listen for the positive things that are said to you. No matter how small they seem, they are important to you.
- Set yourself this goal before you go to your lesson or coaching: to listen for and hear the positive things that are said to you.
- Try to practice this skill in all areas of your life—at work and at home, as well as in your singing—so that you become accustomed to what it feels like.
- Always acknowledge any compliments that are paid to you, no matter how small or who has said them. Get used to saying, "Thank you," without feeling embarrassed. If you can acknowledge compliments calmly and graciously, it signifies that you have heard the positive things that are said to you. Do not fall into the trap of saying, "Thank you, but my ——— wasn't very good today." Take the positive compliment for what it is worth and feel good.

Thought Stopping

It is often difficult to prevent negative thoughts coming into your head, but the skill of thought stopping might help you to replace those negative thoughts immediately with positive ones. Here are a few techniques used by performers to help themselves with this problem. Perhaps one or more will prove useful for you.

- Just saying *STOP!* silently as a negative thought comes into the performer's head
- Using the image of a red traffic light to symbolize stopping those negative thoughts or seeing a large stop sign right in front of him or her.

Both of the preceding techniques work better if they are accompanied by a physical sign as well. For example, at the same time

that you say *Stop!* to yourself, you can also clench your fist, slap
your thigh, or stamp your foot. This acts as a physical reminder to
focus properly. This particular combination worked very well for a
soprano who was singing at a major international opera house in
1995. She was bedeviled by negative thoughts but trained herself
to stop the thoughts by combining the word *Stop!* with a clenched
fist. She became so good at it that in the end all she had to do was
clench her fist and the negative thought stopped. Of course, you
must be ready to follow your *Stop!* with the necessary positive
statements.

Accepting Mistakes

> To avoid more judgments and self-rejection, [perform-
> ers] erect barriers of defense, perhaps [invent] blame
> and get angry, or bury themselves in perfectionistic
> work.
>
> Matthew McKay and Patrick Fanning,
> *Self-Esteem*

As a result of their training, singers tend to crave perfection in
their practice and performances and are enormously depressed
when they cannot achieve it. While you are obsessed with achieving perfection and a fault-free performance you will often lose sight
of the *good* things that you do. And there will be many good things.
Major-league baseball player Doug Frobel once said, "Don't let perfection get in the way of performance excellence. . . . Just get on
first base."

Being satisfied with your performance as it is in that moment in
time is a skill. Taking note during performance of all the things
that need improvement will only make the situation worse. This
can cause tension and negative thoughts during the performance,
which will then lead to frustration for you, because you will never
appear to be doing as well as you can. The answer is this: Know
what you do well and do *only that*; do what is necessary from among
all the positive things that you know you can do. Without being
"perfect" you can still give a good performance and feel happy
about it.

Learning to accept mistakes is an integral part of performance.
Yes, you *will* make mistakes, and that's perfectly all right. Not learning from the mistakes is what is not all right. In the golfing world
there is an old saying: "Golf is a game about mistakes. You just
hope that your mistakes aren't as big as the next guy's." Singing is
a little like golf; both are very technical disciplines fraught with

possible mistakes. The best performer focuses on what he or she does well and doesn't worry about mistakes or perfection. This is the process:

- *Know what you do well in your vocal pieces.* Identify your strengths and the good things that happen. ("I know I trill very well. I'm just going to enjoy my trills.")
- *Recognize the critical moments in your pieces.* Think the positive words and phrases that you need at that time. ("If I just think my positive words: *Alive! Up!* every time I approach the ends of the phrases, I can prevent the usual sagging of my breath at those ending moments.")
- *Stay in the moment.* Don't allow your thoughts to wander forward to what is coming up or to linger back with any mistake you may have made. Instead, remain focused on what you do well. ("I know why I began the second repeat with the orchestra instead of one beat later than the orchestra. Just before that repeat I thought to myself, *This is going really well tonight. I'm going to make it with room to spare.* And then I lost my concentration.")
- *Learn about your mistakes.* Take some time to make a list of the mistakes you tend to make in your pieces. If you look hard enough, you may find that a pattern is emerging, that the mistakes happen in the same place every time. What are your patterns of mistakes? When you know that, you will be able to begin to minimize them. Use positive words and phrases to help you in those moments. ("My mistake has been that I always forget to breathe in the same place in my aria. My breath in the aria is now going to be right every time.")

Reviewing Your Performance

Reviewing your performance can be a simple but effective way of developing your self-confidence relative to both preparation and performance. Following the performance, whether you believed it to be good or bad, you should take some time to review what and how you did. This can be done alone or with your voice teacher, your pianist, or another person who attended the performance. Make two lists: Good Points and Bad Points. (In appendix 1 you will find chart #14, a Performance Review List form, which may be of help.)

- *Good Points* (positive). Put everything you did in the performance that you viewed as good and positive on this list. Be as detailed as possible. Take into account all aspects of the performance. Some examples, in addition to your actual singing, are: the clothes you were wearing, the way you walked onstage, the way you handled the audition panel, the pieces you sang, your relationship with singing colleagues, and your attitude toward the judges.

- *Bad points* (negative). Follow the same process as you did for good points, but this time put on your list all the things that you viewed as bad or negative about your performance. Once again, try to think in detail. Don't forget the small things that you might find insignificant on first viewing.

Start by reading the negative list aloud. Think carefully about how you can improve on some of the issues in future performances. Write your thoughts down so that you can see which parts you should discuss with your voice teacher and which with your coach and in which ways you can change your performance for the better. With this procedure you at least get something positive from your "bad" list. You learn from your mistakes. You do something about them.

Now forget your bad list. Throw it away; it has served its purpose. Dwelling on the bad results will not help. They are in the past and outside your control. You can do nothing about them anymore. You will not improve your performance by continuing to think about them. Just implement the insights that the "bad" list gave you.

Now is the time to read the good, positive list. Try to remember all the good feelings associated with the good parts of the performance. If you can, you should try to create an image of yourself doing this performance, using the things that you have written on your good list. Keep this list and continue to read it at regular intervals to remind yourself of the performance's good points. Work hard at focusing on the positive elements of that performance; then integrate them into your next vocal practice session and performance. Continue to work *to your strengths*.

Enjoying Your Performance

One of the easiest things for people to say as you set off for your audition, competition, or performance is, "Enjoy it!" However, it is not easy for you to enjoy performing if you are worried, upset, or negative about any part of your personal life or what you are about to do. Yet enjoying your involvement in the performance is a crucial part of confidence, because most of the time *enjoyment and confidence go hand in hand*. It is very difficult to feel positive about the performance if you are not enjoying it.

If you can, you should enjoy all aspects of your singing. Your voice lessons and coachings will go much more easily and you will feel that you have achieved far more if you enjoy them. Try to think about that wonderful light and luminous color that seems to surround you when you are singing just for enjoyment. Have fun with your singing. Enjoy the satisfaction of being able to sing so well. Enjoy doing it. Talk to yourself positively and with confidence. How? Like this:

- Enjoy yourself during your practicing as well as your performing.
- Always walk and talk in a positive way.
- Enjoy the challenge of singing even when things are not going well. Practice this skill. The more you practice it, the easier it becomes, and soon things won't seem so bad at all.
- Smile! It is amazing how much better you feel if you can manage to smile more often. It is said that it takes less energy to smile than it does to scowl or frown. You need all the energy you can summon up for your performance!

When you have managed to energize yourself in these ways (especially on a "not so good" day), you need to know *how* you did it so that you can keep doing it. True, not every session can be super, but you can make most of them into good sessions. At the very least, you can make them better than they would otherwise have been.

Making a Confidence List

Finally, it is important that you not confuse unshakable self-confidence with cockiness or arrogance. Conceit and self-importance usually act as smoke screens hiding the fears, the lack of self-belief, the technical deficiencies, the doubts, and the insecurity in the performance arena. It is a good idea for you to take an occasional close look at confidence and ask yourself what specific components make up confidence for you.

After thinking carefully, write down all the factors that contribute to your feelings of confidence. (You may use figure 8-2 to do this.) If you think it will be helpful to you, this can be done for each aria or song that you sing, for your personal self or your performing self.

Do not be surprised by what appears on your list. It may include some things that you would not initially have thought belonged with confidence, such things as feeling a particular kind of physical well-being, the type of local venue, sunshine, real support from your management or teachers, and sleeping well. These all sound fairly general, but if you have written them down, they clearly have some importance for you. You will also be aware of emotional factors like

Date: _____		
Aria or song	Personal self	Performing self

Figure 8-2. Confidence components sheet.

serenity, a relaxed state, enjoyment, and being focused, in control, and well prepared. Tom Kubistant (1986) notes that very few of these components are likely to appear on the list of a cocky performer.

Take your confidence list to your performances with you. It is a valuable tool for you because it is up-to-date information. True, it is only a list of words, but these words can have a tremendous impact on your confidence and, subsequently, the performance itself.

Your way of thinking about yourself will reflect, first, the degree of your self-confidence and, ultimately, your behavior in practice and performance. Belief in yourself gives you the freedom to draw from all the potential, all the talents, that you possess. You can do only what you *think* you can do.

Summary

All performers who do consistently well and live up to their potential also think consistently well. They think positively about what they can do (their strengths, abilities, and skills) and work to them in their performance. This consistency of thinking begins with *feeling* positive and *being* positive about what you can do and about what you are saying and thinking to yourself—especially during performance. Begin with learning and practicing some skills that will develop your positive self. As outlined in this chapter, they are:

1. Positive self-talk and positive affirmations of three kinds: general, performance achievement, and triggers, or process affirmations

2. Becoming a positive listener
3. Thought stopping
4. Accepting mistakes
5. Reviewing your performance
6. Enjoying your performance
7. Making a confidence list.

These skills in turn give you the self-confidence you require in order to perform consistently well under pressure. Even when things do not go as planned, you can remain positive and confident.

Further information:

1. On remaining positive about yourself and your singing, see chapter 5, "The Self and Performance: You, the Person; You, the Performer."
2. On when you practice in the performance mode, see chapter 14, "The Coach's Place in Singers' Preperformance Work."
3. On trying to create an image of yourself doing this performance, see chapter 12, "Imagery in Performance."

9 The Art of Concentrating

Before you begin reading this chapter, do the following exercises.

Exercise 1. Goals

Think of a piece you are going to work on in your next voice lesson. Write down two things you want to achieve in the piece during that lesson. The goals can be anything to do with the piece, just so long as they are key points for you. The goal could be a high note, a run, an interlude, the beginning, some aspect of meaning, and so forth.

Exercise 2. How and What?

Look at these goals and write down *how* you are going to achieve them. *What* will you do to achieve these goals?

Exercise 3. Where?

Where in the piece are the two points about which you constructed your two goals?

Exercise 4. Focus, Attention, Awareness

In order for you to be successful in achieving these two goals, to perform them well, what will you focus on? Where will your attention be? What will you be aware of?

Now put these exercises aside and continue to read.

Concentration could be deemed the "name of the game" of performance. Why? In order to apply your skills and experiences and expand your performance boundaries, you must concentrate.

Proficiency at concentrating can be learned, and your present ability to concentrate can be improved upon. This is because concentration is a skill. You probably have some level of competency already and are probably somewhat able to change your focus in order to stay with the most important facets of your performance. But even if this is the case, your performances will benefit from heightened concentration skills.

Concentration can be used in different ways. It can be very highly tuned for a short time, or it can be extended for long periods of time. Whatever the length of time it is used for, your concentration should be directed, flexible, and multipurpose. It can then deal with a variety of demands in many different situations, especially those demands put upon it during performance.

According to Kubistant, there are three components of concentration that are unique but can at times overlap: intensity, focusing, and attention and awareness.

Intensity

Intensity of concentration is about your ability to be smarter, not about trying harder. (Don't confuse effort with skill.) It is about being able to use your existing energy in a much more focused way. Ideally, your energy should not be generated by external sources, such as parents, audition panels, wife, husband, partner, but should originate from within *you.*

Kubistant (1986, p. 104) equates this intensity to directing the heat of the sun through a magnifying glass in order to set grass or paper alight. The glass concentrates the energy of the sun to intensify its effect. And just like the sun's rays through the glass, high achievers use this idea of intensity to ignite their performances. When, on the other hand, as Kubistant goes on to say, "you try harder, you have no magnifying glass, and you are [reduced to] trying to find *seven more suns* to start the fire."

Focusing

The next component of concentration is focusing, which allows you to lock your concentration on the task in hand. The execution of a sharp focus is the key component in controlling your performance. When you have become competent at recognizing your own intensity, you can then direct it at something through focusing. It's not really possible to focus too clearly, but your focus should not be so rigid that it turns into tunnel vision, which is very difficult to unlock. Focusing on something, you narrow your field of vision and pinpoint the objective of your efforts. However, because your focus should be adaptable to the changes going on about you, you must also learn to adjust and refocus as you work and perform. Your concentration then becomes a dynamic process that is constantly tuning in to different things around you. In order to do this, you must also learn to take in the larger context of concentration.

Attention and Awareness

An interplay between attention and awareness, both indispensable parts of concentration, is necessary for effective concentration to take place. For example, you may be aware of all the other people on the stage with you, but your attention is with the tenor. Your *awareness* takes in the bigger picture, but you pay *attention* to one thing, one object, one person. You must remember the specifics of your piece (attention), but you must also be sensitive to and blend in with the other singers, the orchestra, and the conductor (awareness).

When all of these components come together and your concentration is good, it can be a wonderful feeling. According to the British golfer Tony Jacklin, his concentration was good when he felt as though he were in a cocoon. If he could put himself into this cocoon, stay fully in the present and be totally engaged in what he was doing, he would remain concentrated. If however, he had to declare to himself, "Today I must concentrate," it would not work.

Concentration, then, is an interrelated process, involving intensity, focusing, and attention and awareness. The more you practice, the more you refine. The more you refine, the better control you will have and the more energy you will channel into the performance. "Concentration is control, and control is the conductor to better performances" (Kubistant, 1986, p. 113).

Now go back to the exercises you did before you read this section. Review them in relation to what has been said. The goals you set *intensify* your energy. They tell you what to *focus* on. Your focus is then on the two key points you wish to deal with, and you *attend* to them. But you are still *aware* of all the parts, phrases, lines, and other components of the piece. This is concentration. Practice and you can make it more efficient.

External-Internal and Broad-Narrow Dimensions of Concentration

When you concentrate, you are inclined to work in two major dimensions. One is external-internal; the other is broad-narrow.

Within the external-internal dimension, maintaining an external focus denotes a concentration on things outside yourself, such as noisy fans or other people. An internal focus means that you are focusing on yourself, your thoughts, your feelings, your emotions, your sensations.

The broad-narrow dimension indicates that you can have either a focus that takes in a broad expanse, such as part of a stage, three or four phrases of the piece, or movements of colleagues onstage, or a narrow focus, within which you pay attention to very small details: only one note, the conductor, the slight feeling of tension in the left shoulder, or the one note you must sing in the wings before your entrance.

As a performer, you constantly switch from one focus to the other during your lessons, practices, auditions, and performances. However, a determination of how concentrated you are will depend on your ability to accommodate and harmonize your physical, technical, and mental areas of performance to the task in hand *at that moment.* David Craig (1993, p. 11), author of *A Performer Prepares*, says: "Remember: Songs are always sung in the present, at the time and in the place in which they are sung."

It is important to keep an awareness of all the information relating to your performance. Since this information is constantly changing, however, you must try to allow only the relevant information to come to the fore and disregard all the rest. This way, you can react immediately to any changes and achieve what you set out to do, giving a good performance.

Working at your concentration will help you know where your focus is and the reasons for that focus. Ultimately, good focusing skills will give you control of your performance. You will learn to deal with all those distractions that have bedeviled your performances in the past, and you will cease to worry about all the things that are actually outside your control.

How to Begin a Concentration Training Program

Your answers to the following questions are a list of challenges and form for you the basis of any concentration training plan.

Exercise
___

Take a moment to think carefully about the piece you are currently working on. Ask yourself the following questions:

- Where are the critical moments in this piece?
- Exactly when must I deal with each of those factors?

- On what do I need to focus at those times?
- How good am I, right now, at focusing on those crucial moments to the exclusion of all distractions—both those that came before and those that will come up?

The key words in concentration work are *where?*, *when?*, and *what?*

Where is my focus?
When do I need to focus on certain key factors in the piece?
What do I need to focus on?

In concentration, as with all your other mental skills, it is most unwise to wait until you perform to begin considering the extent of your ability. The skill of concentration will not just magically materialize! The answer: Always practice your focusing when you practice your music—in voice lessons, coachings, individual practice sessions, and rehearsals. In this way you will learn to focus on the relevant cues. Maintaining your focus throughout your performance is no easy task; it takes some practice.

You must discover how your own concentration works and what works best for you under specific circumstances. Concentration practice trains you to stay connected—despite constantly changing demands—to what you are doing, to your vocal ability, and to your body and its feelings, not allowing any distracting thoughts to interfere with the practice. You can trust your voice and body to do what they have been trained to do; you don't always have to force your focus on them.

Training Your Concentration

To help make your concentration skills more consistent, adopt some of the following practices, which have been adapted from Terry Orlick's book, *In Pursuit of Excellence* (1990). Make sure that you always set your goals before you begin your practice, so that you know what you're aiming for. (Some examples of goals might be: perfecting the timing of that high B♭ attack, learning the exact forward tongue position for that [e] with the *accent aigu* in the French song, and not only raising your musical accuracy in that piece written in 7/8 time but also becoming so comfortable with the 7/8 signature that the cleverness of the piece will not be submerged in your nervousness and worry.)

If you practice the following guidelines, the best focus will surface:

1. When practicing your vocal skills and techniques, try to focus totally on how those skills feel; be completely connected to them.

2. Try to execute your vocal skills in your imagination. Become totally immersed by using all your senses. Then actually *do* the vocal skill that you have been imaging. Allow it to happen naturally, without even thinking about it.

3. During your practice sessions, let yourself sing your piece without any evaluation. Just *allow* the performance to happen and realize how that feels. Use your instincts; free yourself to sing quite naturally. See what happens.

4. Re-create those mental and physical conditions that allow you to experience a focus comparable to the one you used during the best of your performances. Do this in relation to the key words that describe your focus: *Where? When? What?*

5. When you have created this condition, work on holding it for short periods of time; then increase the time during which you are fully focused. Your final goal is to be able to hold that focus for as long as necessary in order to give a good performance. You must remain totally connected throughout the intensity fluctuations and other variations within the piece. Do this in as much detail as possible every step of the way: every breath, every note, every phrase.

Finding a Relaxed Focus

Theoretically, once you have trained your voice, body, and nervous system to sing the notes you want, you should be able to do this at will. Very often what prevents you is your lack of focus or a focus on the wrong thing. Not only must you program your brain to perform the vocal skill flawlessly so that you can do it without thinking, but you also have the challenge of freeing the body and mind to connect totally with what you are trying to achieve. This demands a relaxed focus, which does not indicate a lack of intensity but rather a mind that is clear of irrelevant thoughts and a body that is free from the wrong tension, everything geared to executing the vocal skills as well as possible. A relaxed focus denotes a body that is *at ease but ready* and a mind that is *calm but focused*. However widely your concentration may vary in intensity and duration, you must remain alert and relaxed throughout.

Exercises

Learn to have a relaxed focus by trying any of the following general exercises that grasp your interest:

1. Sit quietly and allow yourself to relax. Focus on something in the room; anything will do: a flower, a texture, a color, a piece of fruit, your hand, et cetera. Really focus on it and take in all the details. See how unique it is. Remain totally absorbed in it.

2. Sit quietly and allow yourself to relax. Become aware of the whole room, train compartment, or office in which you are sitting. Take in all the detail you can without moving your head. Now switch your focus to an object very close to you. Focus down onto the one article. Take in all its detail. Keep doing this until all other objects in the background are blurred. Really connect with the object you have chosen. Try to repeat this exercise by switching from one external focus to an internal focus. The ability to switch focus is a vital skill for performers; it is, in fact, a lifesaver. Do not get bogged down in a middle zone; be focused either externally or internally and aware of what you are doing. Staying with the wrong focus gives the performance every chance of sinking out of sight. If you can switch, it means two things: that you the performer have recognized the need to refocus or change focus and that you have the ability to do so. You can practice this switching skill anywhere, walking in the park, in a restaurant, and even in the office.

3. Relax. Focus your attention on a particular thought; any will do. Let your mind and thoughts wander; then refocus on the original thought.

4. When you feel distracted, practice clearing the distraction from your mind by zooming in on what you must do in that moment in order to perform well. Nothing else is important in that moment.

5. Stand quietly. Relax. Think about a particular piece you are working on. Imagine how you will make that very first all-important entrance. Feel it; see it in the correct sequence; note how wonderful it sounds and feels. Clear your mind. Then perform the first entrance naturally and automatically.

6. Relax. Prepare yourself to focus on one note, one phrase, one thing at a time, putting the past and the future out of your mind. Then remember how you did this and practice it every day.

7. Relax. Focus on your body. Determine where tension lies and what feels good. Switch to a particular piece or part of a piece and focus on doing it well. Switch back to your body. Check it out. Is there tension? Are there good feel-

ings? Switch back to your piece. Practice this every day, changing the piece regularly.

8. Use cue words or triggers to keep your focus on the task in hand. Some cue words could be *slow*, *smooth*, *glide*, and *zap*. Some triggers could be physical: clenching a fist, stamping a foot, pressing down hard into the floor with one foot, and taking a very small step in any direction. These all help you to get into your best focus for the performance.

As you have learned in your drama work, it is also important to plan where to focus during the times when you are not actually singing, either within the piece itself (introductions, interludes, postludes) or between pieces. This is especially important in auditions and competitions, when the individual pieces may have no connection to each other. Your nonsinging performance time can be very dangerous if you are not able to keep your focus, switch your focus, or refocus when you find your attention on the wrong things. The performance must be kept alive during the nonsinging moments. If, for some reason, you are relieved when a certain piece is finished or dreading what you are about to sing, the performance itself will probably drop.

A related element—the amount of effort and skill required to deal with real mistakes during the performance—is also worth considering. "The mental effort required to obviate mistakes demands so much concentration that other factors, such as expression, are bound to suffer," says M. N. H'Doubler (1968, p. 90), author of *Dance: A Creative Art Experience*. When this happens to you, it will require more energy to get the performance back to where it was before you stopped singing. Don't waste your energy on such efforts! You will need it later in the performance.

Learning to improve your performance during the nonsinging music means that you have to be efficient in the following areas:

1. *Your ability to relax and to recover, however short the time.* The abilities to relax your muscles, lower your heartbeat through breathing, and recover from emotional turmoil are all important to your performance.
2. *Your ability to become aroused and full of energy in preparation for the next note, phrase, or piece, no matter what the situation.* This ability to generate positive energy is crucial to your work in nonsinging moments.
3. *Your ability to image and plan what you are going to do next and how you intend to do it.* Do not imagine what you don't want to do. Don't think about missing the first pianissimo of the next piece or flubbing the last high note. Your focus must remain on positive information only!

In order to enhance your concentration (especially during the nonsinging pauses), adopt some of the following suggestions when preparing for a performance:

- Think positively about what you are about to do. Credit your strengths. Even when you feel negative, try to project an image of confidence and positiveness.
- Establish a pace for yourself between pieces. This is particularly important if you are feeling angry or nervous and attempting to gain control. When you feel out of control, you will almost certainly do everything more quickly.
- Practice some deep breathing between pieces and, if the nonsinging interlude in question is long enough, during the piece also. This helps you to relax and feel more in control.
- Work at some of the imagery that you have planned. It could be imagery in the piece itself, imagery to give you confidence, or imagery of you beginning the next piece in the way you wish to do it.
- Possibly establish some rituals between pieces. Rituals help you to remain focused, in control, and relaxed—dealing with pressure more effectively. If you can stick to a well--rehearsed and defined ritual, you are more likely not to rush into the next piece. You are also likely to make fewer mistakes. After singing a piece, your ritual might include something like:
  1. *A positive physical response.* This response could be a relaxation, some type of breathing, or a positive image of some kind.
  2. *A positive preparation.* Know exactly how you wish to begin the next piece. Use positive imagery to help you. Talk positively to yourself about your strengths in the next piece.
  3. *A positive ritual.* Focus on your enjoyment of singing. There should be no technical focus at this point. Use your imagery skills to rehearse mentally how you want the first two or three notes to go. No self-talk at this point. Just do it!
  4. *An avoidance of any negative self-talk.* This type of self-talk will only add to a poor performance.
  5. *Enjoyment of the challenge of the occasion.* Don't feel threatened or frightened, especially when things are not going well. Try to project a confident, winning image all the time.

Once you are really able to focus and concentrate well, which you have achieved through a good deal of practice and a vast amount of self-discipline, you will feel as though everything is easy, effort-less. As the illustrious dancer Martha Graham said, "To me, this acquirement of nervous, physical and emotional concentration is the one element possessed to the highest degree by the truly great dancers of the world. Its acquirement is the result of discipline, of energy in the deep sense. That is why there are so few great danc-ers" (Graham, 1974, p. 137).

Does this apply to singers? Probably. If, through self-discipline and hard work, you can identify the relevant cues you need in your performance, figure out how you will access them, and then, based on this information, work hard at acquiring your focusing skills, you will give yourself a good chance of achieving that elu-sive thing called concentration—the fine-tuning needed for out-standing performance.

Formulating Refocusing Plans

When you do lose your focus, a plan for refocusing will prove ex-tremely useful at helping you get back on track as soon as possible. Try to prepare some refocusing plans before your performances. Follow these steps:

1. Go over your pieces in detail. Ask yourself, "If I were to lose concentration in this piece, where would it be likely to occur and why?"

2. Then work out a very short refocusing plan to get you back on track. It might include the use of:

- *Key words*   Such as *calm, golden, control.*
- *Imagery*   Use some image that allows you to return to the feelings you want. Watch and feel yourself perform. If you can't watch yourself, use the "as if" technique. Choose to be like another artist whom you admire. Use the qualities of that person as the basis of your imagery.
- *Physical response*   Choose one that will make you feel good: breathing, scanning the body to release tension, clenching a fist, readjusting your weight.
- *Any combination of the preceding three methods*   Example: Say to yourself: "calm; relax." See yourself: loose, smiling, full of confidence. Physically: feel your weight; feel light on your feet; relax.

Most important is to prepare some refocusing plans before your performance and practice them during practice hours, lessons, and coachings. You might not need them during the actual performance if everything goes as planned, but if there is a problem or even a fluctuation in focus you will certainly need a refocusing plan. Without such preparation you cannot hope to use your refocusing plans in performance. In addition, such a detailed preparation gives you a feeling of security, of confidence, and of being in control. Whatever happens, you've got it covered!

Summary

Often considered the most potent of the mental performance skills, concentration has three important components: intensity, focusing, and attention and awareness.

Concentration has two major dimensions: external-internal and broad-narrow. The key words to use are: *Where*? *When*? *What*?

Always have a refocusing plan for those key spots in your pieces. You can train your concentration:

> Learn how to feel
> Become relaxed
> Use your imagery skills
> Remain positive
> Enjoy your work.

Further information:

1. On the ability to relax your muscles and to lower your heartbeat through breathing, see chapter 6, "Physical Well-Being and Relaxation."
2. On practicing some deep breathing between pieces, see chapter 6, "Physical Well-Being and Relaxation."
3. On working at some imagery, see chapter 12, "Imagery in Performance."

10 Distractions

One of the key areas of concentration and focus control is that of dealing with all distractions in the performance, along with adapting to what is happening and refocusing while under pressure. This skill is probably the one that separates the singers at the top from all the others. If you have confidence in your ability to deal appropriately with distractions, by all means skip this chapter. If not, read on.

As with other mental skills, the vital skill of controlling distractions must be practiced regularly if you are to perform well consistently. Holding your focus even when distracted and refocusing when necessary are essential performance skills. When *what you are doing* is the same as *what you are thinking,* you have the right focus.

Young children have an amazing ability to focus on what interests them—a favorite toy, a television program, or a picture they are painting. What, then, happens to adults when they come under pressure, in an audition or a competition for example? They seem to lose this focusing skill, this direct connection to the activity they are pursuing in that moment in time.

In a performance situation there are many things that can act as distractions. To deal with these distractions it is of paramount importance to focus appropriately in all moments of pressure. The level at which you are performing makes not the slightest difference. Distractions are an integral part of all performance situations. They will always be a part of the game.

When we're performing well, there's an amazingly effective and complex interplay between these two levels of mental functioning [thinking and doing]. However, there are times when we get frightened, "ner-

vous," and tense up, when the conscious mind over-
analyses and overreacts to incoming messages, when
we think too much, say negative things to ourselves
and interrupt the smooth flow of input to output. There
are times when we try too hard, ignore our intuition
and worry about the things going wrong instead of
focusing on being effective and enjoying the moment.

Saul Miller,
Performance under Pressure

Awareness

Awareness is a key skill because you must first identify what you need to focus on in order to perform well. Having identified your focus, you should then keep that focus under control amid the distractions.

According to Terry Orlick, an eminent Canadian sport psychologist, distractions come from a variety of causes—family members, partners, teachers, coaches, other singers, audition panels, the media, changes in the performing environment, changes within your own performance, your own expectations, and those of other people, and changes in your patterns of routines and your own thinking before, during, and after the performance itself.

These things only become distractions if you allow them to distract you. Under the normal circumstances of your life, such things would be just a part of your everyday functioning. However, under pressure, you may choose to become distracted. Yet if someone offers a negative remark about your performance, you do not have to respond by feeling that you are a poor performer. If one of your friends says or does something that offends you, you are not compelled to get angry. Neither do you have to react with panic before the audition panel when you think they are not listening to you. You can just as easily let the distraction go without getting embroiled in it. You need not choose to let those things distract you. When you choose to pay attention to these distractions, what have you done? You have not lost your real singing skills, but you have lost the focus that allows you to perform well.

This section aims to encourage you to become aware of what tends to distract you while performing. Awareness of your needs in three areas of distraction is crucial to the control of your performances. If you feel that you need help with distractions, become attuned to the following elements:

1. Your physical environment
2. The body and its internal reactions
3. Other people present.

When singers are asked to identify the type of distraction that causes them the biggest problem, their initial response is frequently: "*All* of them!" Although this is a normal reaction, after some calm and logical analysis, the two major problem categories most often cited remain distractions caused by (2) the body and its internal reactions and (3) other people present.

Internal and External Distractions

Internal distractions include such things as fear, anxiety, and expectations (yours and others') that are set too high. External distractions include the audition panel, the voice teacher, fellow singers, and partner or parents in the audience (which can result in a performance geared to these listeners rather than a performance for yourself). If you allow yourself to continue in your distracted state rather than to recognize this behavior, then your performance is likely to be on a lower level than that which you are capable of, regardless of how well prepared you are vocally and physically.

Awareness requires that you focus your attention on the task at hand, moment by moment *in* the moment, not on anything else. Of course this means practice, but not the practice of technical skills, rather practice in the performance mode. (To practice in the performance mode, during either lessons or solitary practice, is to simulate the actual performance as far as possible, using all the skills—mental, technical, and physical—that you would use in your real performance.) This awareness and attuning is the mental equivalent of a physical warm-up, except that this process allows you to achieve the mental state and emotional mood that will be conducive to focusing upon the task. The process involves judging how appropriate your thoughts and feelings are to the task at hand—the audition, the concert, the competition, or the performance. If some distractions do exist, the next stage is to recognize them and deal with them appropriately. Dealing with your distractions in an objective manner rather than on an emotional level will cause many of them to appear insignificant. You will then resolve them very quickly.

You should consider each of the distractions in turn. Either let it go if it presents no problem or deal with it if it does indeed cause difficulties.

How Do You Develop Awareness and Learn to Attune and Focus?

Doing the following exercise first will help you to determine what actually does cause you to become distracted. If you agree that identifying your distractions will be of help, complete the exercise grid in figure 10-1 by asking yourself what the things are that distract

PRE-PERFORMANCE Environmental	Body/Emotions	People

PERFORMANCE Environmental	Body/Emotions	People

POST-PERFORMANCE Environmental	Body/Emotions	People

Figure 10-1. Discovering what distracts you.

you during the performance cycle. No matter how insignificant something seems, write it down. You can always amend it later. Next, take a very objective look at what you have written and make a decision: which distractions give you the most problems. Deal only with those distractions at first.

Let us consider each of the three major distraction categories in turn.

Your Physical Environment

The environment or place in which you are performing can act as a distraction, it can be neutral, or it can actually help you. If it is a place where you have sung before, there is less probability that it will cause any distractions. It may even feel comfortable to you (especially if you note the reactions of other singers to whom the place is new). Certainly distractions within the environment tend to diminish with time, particularly if you use the venue frequently. However, you probably do not have the time to wait for distractions to fade gradually. Clearly some of you may need help in speeding up the process. The overall effect of environment or place varies. An indoor environment is affected by many things, such as floor surface, lighting, size and height of the space, airiness, or temperature. The following list contains a few of the environmental distractions that singers have noted:

Noise: the whirl of fans, the humming of air conditioners or furnace

Confined space: too small a room in which to present oneself well

Lack of feedback: caused, for example, by a sound-inhibiting carpet on the floor of the audition space

Large space: so large that the singer feels dwarfed and vulnerable

Distance: an audition area so far from the panel of listeners that contact seems difficult to make

Atmosphere: a very dusty room, worrisome and dangerous to those with allergies

Temperature: too cold or too hot a room

Acoustics: so bad an acoustical environment that sound is either muffled or echoed

Architectural anomalies: for example, huge columns that destroy concentration and threaten to cut off sight lines to the auditioning panel

Illumination: too dark a room, for example, one with a lone lightbulb casting dreadful shadows on your face

The following procedures may help you remain "connected" with and focused on what you are doing by becoming attuned to the environment/place more quickly and by choosing not to become distracted by environmental factors.

- *Arrive early.* When the performance venue is unknown to you, try to arrive early on the audition day, if that is at all possible. You might even try to gain access to the room at another, earlier time to check it out for the audition. In this way you can become accustomed to the place, eliminating any distractions.
- *Build distractions into your preperformance practice.* If you know the venue well, you can easily build whatever distractions it might cause into the practice of the performance during your preperformance rehearsals via the skill of imagery. Sing "as if" the performance were actually taking place in the performing venue.
- *Discuss distractions with teachers, friends, and other performers.* There will be times when, although you do not know the performing venue well, you are unable to arrive early and have not been able to view it at another time. Perhaps you suspect that you may become distracted by certain things in the environment. Try to get as much information as possible about the proposed place from friends who have performed there previously. If this is not possible, then imagine yourself singing in the environment where you always sing well. This could be your own studio or that of your teacher or your favorite venue. As you do this, you also need to know that you can perform consistently well in any environment, that you can focus on doing what will help you to be positive and stay in control, and that you can look for all the advantages in the environment even if you don't know it well. Do only what you can do and what you can control.

The Body and Its Internal Reactions

This category appears to cause the biggest problem for singers. On a day-to-day basis, thoughts and feelings tend to vary much more than do physical sensations. Many ordinary things can cause this emotional swing, including:

An argument at home
A minor driving accident
An illness in the family
Worry about a child left with a baby-sitter

A difference of opinion with voice teacher or coach
Uncertainty about the suitability of the chosen audition
    clothing, hairdo, or makeup

Such everyday concerns drain you of energy. As a consequence, your focus of attention can be poor.

Inner feelings and thoughts before or during the actual performance may also cause you to become distracted, such thoughts as:

Concern about the high register or pianissimo sections
Worry that the aria or song is not sufficiently routined (a
    singer's term, meaning repetition in context so often that
    a difficult spot becomes a part of the routine)
Realization that you have not yet sung the piece the way
    you want to in performance mode (i.e., simulating
    performance)
A persistent feeling of being "not really ready"
Worry that the audition or competition may have far too
    high standards for your present state of development
Lack of confidence in your present abilities or your
    overall personal talent and skill
Feeling of inability to manage fear, anxiety, and tension
Focus on mistakes and shortcomings

Unfortunately, the performance may not have all the mental energy required when your focus is wandering elsewhere. It is important that you become habituated to checking constantly how and what you are feeling. Consider the inner feelings, become aware of them, and deal with them if they are becoming a distraction.

... one moment of physical quietness allows the background noise of thoughts and feelings to be heard, and often to quieten down.

John Syer and Christopher Connolly,
Sporting Body, Sporting Mind

To repeat, in dealing with any form of distraction, key skills are:

- The ability to become aware of the distraction
- The ability to then relax
- The ability to cope by switching focus away from the distraction.

Ignoring your body and your inner feelings and thoughts can be detrimental to performance. Don't waste energy bemoaning these problems. Switch and refocus. The following methods will help you to become attuned to your body, your thoughts, and your feelings:

- *Massage.* Some performers suffer badly from physical tension. One way of helping this is to have a gentle massage, allowing the body to be eased into a state of relaxation. Ideally, you should then be relaxed but feeling alert and ready for performance. When to have a massage should depend upon the individual and upon how long the positive effects may last. The day before or the day of the performance/audition may not be the most appropriate time because it could make you too relaxed for good performance. After or between performances massage can prove to be very beneficial. It will make you feel great. (A word of warning: Not all massage therapists are licensed and registered. Some could do more harm than good. A personal recommendation is safest.)
- *Individual physical stretching.* All singers, no matter whether it be those who tend to be distracted by inner thoughts and feelings or those who tend to be distracted by signals in the body itself, would be well advised to establish a physical stretching program. In addition, any form of stretching, even that which is exceedingly gentle, aids in lessening tension in all areas of the body while at the same time making you feel good. Some stretching programs can be modified for use while waiting to go onstage, between acts, or while waiting to be called for the audition. Experiment and see what works for you.

Cyclic stretching and releasing promotes cell and fiber growth and strengthens all tissue, whether muscular or connective. Athletes who rely heavily on precision and range of movement (gymnasts, figure skaters, dancers) spend much time stretching joints, tendons, ligaments, and muscles.

Ingo R. Titze,
Principles of Voice Production

Massage and individual physical stretching do not have to do with physical training; they are about the relationship between mind and body. It is the quality of this relationship—its cultivation or neglect, the degree to which harmony and cooperation are maintained—that determines how well you can use your full performing potential.

- *Individual work.* It is always wise to bring to the audition or the performance something to do. This can divert focus away from any distracting thoughts or internal feelings. One way of doing this is to use some vocal technical exercise on which you can focus—a very simple one that you enjoy, one that need not have anything to do with either the present performance or the audition. Some singers bring novels to read; some listen to instrumental music or plays on their personal tape machine to help cope with distracting thoughts and feelings. Be prepared, and delays will assume their proper unimportant place. It can be a long time before the tennis player is called on court for the match. (No one knows whether the previous match will last for three, four, or five sets.) Similarly, it can be a long wait before the singer is called by the audition panel. (No one knows when or for how long the auditioners will deviate from the fixed schedule.) Arriving at your appointed time only to be hurried in to sing immediately because they are ahead of schedule is as distracting as having to wait a long time because they are running late.
- *Confidence formula.* All good mental preparation programs should include the establishment of a confidence formula. To choose these words, write down any and all words that come to mind describing the nature of confidence as you perceive it *at this moment* in your singing life. By a process of elimination cross out some of the weaker words. The few (perhaps three or four) powerful words that remain will form the personal confidence formula, as in this example:

  SMOOTH + POWERFUL + FREE = CONFIDENCE

  Write it down. Carry it with you. Keep reading it. Keep saying it. Believe it. It works, and it's yours.
- *Positive pep talk.* As with the confidence formula, this positive pep talk is derived from the exercises you do to establish your own strengths and qualities as both a person and a performer at the moment. A very powerful tool, the pep talk works because it belongs to you. Thus you are more likely to believe it. Many others—voice teachers, coaches, colleagues, family, friends—can tell you how good you are, but until you can do it for yourself it is less likely to work. Your own belief in your own ability at the time of the performance is the most potent of tools for dealing with this second group of distractions and for controlling the situation.

The following is a positive pep talk used by a mezzo-soprano in the week preceding an important audition. She wrote her pep talk in capital letters in a stream-of-consciousness style seven days before the audition and read it aloud several times a day right up to the time of the audition.

> I AM WONDERFUL, I AM A FANTASTIC SINGER, I BRING THE MUSIC TO LIFE AND I AM A SUPERB MUSICIAN, THE GREAT THINGS ABOUT MY VERSION OF "UNA VOCE POCO FA" ARE THE COLORATURA PASSAGES, THE MANNER IN WHICH I PRESENT THE DRAMA OF THE PIECE, I HAVE DONE THIS PIECE EXTREMELY WELL SO MANY TIMES THAT IT WILL BE WONDERFUL, I FEEL ENERGIZED AND EXCITED WHEN I SING THIS PIECE AS WELL AS THE *WERTHER* ARIA AND THE *ROMEO* ARIA AND THEY ARE PERFECTLY SUITED TO MY VOICE WHICH IS VERY SPECIAL, I HAVE DONE WELL IN EVERY OPERA PRODUCTION THIS YEAR AND PEOPLE HAVE NOTICED THE WAY I PRESENT MYSELF ONSTAGE, THE EMOTIONAL ASPECT OF MY SINGING IS VERY SPECIAL YET DOES NOT INTERFERE WITH THE TECHNICAL SIDE, I HAVE ALL THE PIECES UP TO ABOUT 95% PERFECT AND THAT IS ALL ANYONE CAN ASK OF ME, NO ONE IS PERFECT AND NOT MEANT TO BE, I AM DOING MY VERY BEST AND IT IS SENSATIONAL, MY CONFIDENCE LEVEL WILL BE AS HIGH AS IT HAS EVER BEEN BECAUSE I'M WELL PREPARED AND FOCUSED AND I CONCENTRATE ONLY ON THINGS IN MY CONTROL BECAUSE THERE IS NOTHING I CAN DO ABOUT THINGS OUT OF MY CONTROL, I'M EXCITED TO BE SINGING THIS PIECE AND I'M DOING IT BECAUSE I LOVE TO SING AND I SING WELL AND THERE IS NOTHING TO LOSE BECAUSE I AM ALREADY THE BEST SINGER IN THE CHORUS AND AM CAPABLE OF DOING MORE.

(The audition went very well.)

- *Imagery.* It has been stated in this book that imagery is one of the most, if not the most, powerful performance tools that you should have. In this instance, you use the skill of imagery to help you deal with distractions, so as to control the performing situation. The following three exercises all utilize the skill of imagery. Try them all; then continue to use those that contribute to your performance.

Exercise 1. The Magic Box

By the skilled use of imagination, you will put whatever is distracting you into what is called the Magic Box. The exercise functions in this way.

Sit quietly. Close your eyes. Take a deep breath. Allow yourself to settle into your chair as you breathe slowly. Imagine yourself sitting at a desk in front of a window. Look out. Notice what you see, what the weather is like, what movement there may be. Then look down at the desk and see a blank sheet of paper and a pen. Pick up the pen and write down whatever is worrying you or exciting you, anything you identify as a distraction. If you find it easier, you can draw a picture to represent the distractions or your distracted mood. When you have finished, put down the pen; fold up the piece of paper. There is a box on the desk in front of you. Notice how large it is, what color it is, whether it is in the light or the shadow. Open the lid. Then put the folded piece of paper inside the box and close the lid. Put your hand on the box and say, "I will deal with you later."

Having done this, you can readily interact with those around you and perform. It is important that once your performance is over you again close your eyes and go back to the imaginary desk, open the box, get out the piece of paper, unfold it, and look to see what you wrote or drew. Sometimes this will no longer be of interest. That's fine. Or you may need to continue with the distraction. But if the exercise is to continue to work and become increasingly effective with time, the part of you that has been promised attention later on must learn to trust that it will get that attention.

This exercise may appear ineffectual at first reading, but it is anything but weak. It works; it's empowering; it can give you the satisfaction of dealing with difficult distractions; it can give you a sense of control. It is used widely in top-level athletics, and singers who now have it as part of their mental program wonder how they ever managed without it. The feeling of well-being that comes as a result of this skill can be very telling. At the least you will feel that it is all right to deal with the distraction later. Putting off facing the problem is not the same as ignoring distractions by sustaining a hope that they will go away by themselves (for they will not).

An American opera singer who was performing in Paris once telephoned in great anxiety. She was reveling in the freedom that this Magic Box exercise gave her. (Her previous performances had always been hindered by distractions.) She continued to trust the skill, and it was working well for her. "But," said she, "the pieces of paper won't stay in the box." She kept getting images of pieces of paper coming out of the box. I inquired whether or not, following the performance, she was taking care to go back to deal with whatever she had put into the box. "No," she said. She had been so thrilled and elated by the way the skill worked that she was forgetting to go back in her imagination and continue the process of dealing with the distractions. She wasn't completing the cycle, and her mental processes were reminding her of that fact. That's how powerful and helpful this skill can be for all performers.

Alma Thomas, 1993,
personal communication

A male opera singer, whose performance had once been so hindered by distractions that he literally became rigid with fear, reported to me that he kept getting images of all of his Magic Boxes. Apparently he had gleefully piled them one on top of another in his imagination and now they were "oozing green slime." What did this mean? he asked. He had put everything that gave him a performance problem into a series of Magic Boxes. He had done this over a long period of time because of the "freedom" it gave him to do so. After some debate, we decided that he actually didn't need the skill at the moment. The process was unnecessary because he himself and his performances were now so much more in control. In time he was convinced that it was all right to trust himself, that he need not continue to use the Magic Boxes as performance trash cans.

Alma Thomas, 1994,
personal communication

A very powerful skill indeed.

Exercise 2. Imagining Yourself Performing Well

Another way of using imagery to help you to refocus after distraction is to imagine yourself performing well. Watch yourself walking and acting confidently, hear the glorious sound you make, and feel your joy in the performance. Allow the power of your imagination to tap into all your performing potential and away from those negative thoughts and feelings.

Exercise 3. The Quiet Place

The Quiet Place is another example of how imagery can aid in the controlling and managing of distractions in performance. The exercise works in this way:

When learning the Quiet Place technique, you must find a place where you can sit undisturbed for five minutes. Close your eyes; take a couple of deep breaths, letting them out slowly. Allow yourself to relax from the head downward, feeling your body sink more into the chair as you do so. After completing your relaxation, allow a moment or two of silence. Then visualize yourself alone in a place that is peaceful, where there is no likelihood of being disturbed. It can be anywhere: in a field by the river, a place in the mountains, somewhere deep in a forest or by the seashore. If more than one place comes to mind, hold on to the first and allow the other impressions to fade. This is your favorite place, so linger and find your ideal spot. Notice what clothing you are wearing and what position you are in. If you are lying down or sitting, let yourself relax in that position, noticing the things around you—the objects, the colors, the line of the horizon, any faint movement in the distance. Then look down at the ground. What color is the ground? What sort of ground is it? Reach out and touch the ground. Feel whether it is rough or smooth, warm or cool, damp or dry. Rub your fingers harder on the ground before lifting them to your nose and seeing if there is an odor.

Continue this process by looking to your right and left. Notice the play of the light and shadow. Be aware of the season, the time of day, the weather. Can you feel the warmth of the sunshine? The breath of a wind? The dampness of mist?

Become aware of the sounds that belong to this place—the hum of insects, the calling of birds, the sounds of running water or wind in the trees, or children calling in the distance. . . .

Let yourself be aware of how it feels to be in this place, this place where you can relax completely. Notice all that is peaceful around you. Allow yourself to stay there a little longer. . . .

Now let the scene fade for a moment. Without opening your eyes, become aware again of your body on the chair in this room. Become particularly aware of your hands. Now take the thumb of your left hand in the fingers of the right and squeeze your thumb with a gentle pressure. As you feel this pressure, let yourself drift back to your quiet place. . . .

See yourself there. Notice the clothing you are wearing, if you are wearing clothes. Notice the position you are in. If you are lying down, sit up. Then let yourself be in that position, looking out at the horizon if you are outdoors.

Continue the process as before. When you have looked all around again, settle back into your original position. Eventually decide to come back to the room. Let go of your thumb as you do so, before opening your eyes.

Holding your thumb as you go into the imagined quiet place can be developed with practice into a "trigger" technique, eventually helping you instantly to feel yourself in that restful situation. It may take a little time for the connection to be learned, and you may find that you can easily return to your imagery without using the trigger. Ultimately, the technique will allow you to reach your quiet place instantly, for just the moment you need it during a break in your performance. The trigger, holding your thumb, can be especially useful in a tense situation, when you realize that your anxiety or arousal level has gone far too high.

Singers who use this skill with great effect report using the Quiet Place technique regularly before and during auditions, especially while awaiting their turn to sing. Others use it regularly during intermissions of their performances. It gives them just enough time and space to calm down, collect themselves for the next act, and feel relaxed and good about themselves.

You, too, can utilize this skill not only in your performances but also in your life outside of performance. It is especially valuable if you are feeling extremely nervous, if both your body and thoughts appear to have a life of their own. These conditions are major distractions in themselves. The Quiet Place skill will help to vanquish all such little gremlins inside you, to switch your focus away from them and their debilitating effects.

If you believe that you have the kinds of inner distraction problems discussed in this section, it is important to remember the process: First, you must recognize what is happening; second, accept the fact; third, do something about it. Try the exercises outlined previously. Don't let those destructive inner feelings continue without acting upon them. Left alone, they will only worsen. If you let them go on without interference, there will be no point of return. It will be too late to recover the performance.

To ignore the problem is a complete sabotage of your performance. It's your choice, because you can

- Commit yourself to being and remaining positive
- Allow yourself to get into a positive state of mind before the performance and remain there during the performance, letting it happen
- Know that you can perform well, whatever the feelings in the body
- Practice refocusing quickly and positively.

Other People Present

On the second song of my recital, I was slowly scanning the audience when I happened to focus in on a friend in the back of the audience, a marvelous soprano I knew. I had already noticed her there, but this time we made eye contact and she smiled supportively.

In that instant my mental picture gave way completely
to one of her standing on that same stage. I could see
what she was wearing, hear what she was singing, and
was, in fact, mentally reliving a specific performance of
hers. It all flashed in just a few seconds, but that was all
it took for me almost to lose my nerve. All I could think
was, "She should be up here singing, and I should be
sitting in the audience." Concentration shattered, and
with it, all support. When I had to catch a quick breath
in a terrible place (just before the last note of the phrase),
self-preservation finally kicked in. My brain said, "Stop
looking at her!" I did exactly that for the rest of the
program and was fortunately able to recover.

R.M., technically well trained soprano,
ready to move into a performing life

This area of distraction tends to cause problems for singers during auditions, competitions, and recitals that are used as part of
the examination system. In point of fact, it is not those persons
present who precipitate the problem. In actuality, the root cause of
the difficulty lies in your attitude toward the people present. In
other words, you actually choose to let people distract you.

There are three major groups of people who tend to observe
performances:

1. The first group is comprised of those who are there in the
   room or within hearing, who have simply happened along.
   (A bit like someone who, while walking the dog in the
   park, stops to observe the Little League baseball game going
   on, such a person is merely "present.") This group tends
   simply to look on with interest, nothing more.
2. The second group of observers are those who are there to
   make judgments, to evaluate the performance and the performer. Because such people tend to have a musical and
   technical background, they are seen to be "knowledgeable"
   observers. The audition panel, the judging panel for a competition, the professors, teachers, and coaches who form
   the panel to judge the degree recital in schools, some critics, other singers, conductors, and agents—the list is long.
   Nonprofessional audience members can also be designated
   as: those who came because they were persuaded by someone else, those who came to hear the singer regardless of
   the program, those who came to hear the repertoire and
   couldn't care less who the singer is, and those who came
   to scoff or criticize for some personal reason.
3. The third group is made up of professional colleagues who
   are members of a performing team, be it an opera, musical

comedy, or oratorio cast. The responsibility of giving a good performance is shared among all. Often the behavior of some individuals within the group can act as a distraction.

How you think about yourself in relationship to other people makes a great difference in the resulting performance. Perhaps you worry about the presence of people whom you believe to be evaluating judgmentally. Sometimes these people are not evaluating at all, and very often they are not even sufficiently knowledgeable to make a considered judgment. On the whole, most audition panels, most competition judges, and most audiences want you to do well, to succeed, to perform to the best of your ability. In actuality, it is your own inappropriate attitude toward evaluative and judgmental others that inhibits your performance.

Bedeviled by this attitude, you expend a great deal of valuable energy singing for others, instead of singing just for yourself. The more you do this, the more your performances will continue to drop in quality. These evaluative situations are a fact of life for you; if you want to be a performer, they will never disappear. Only when you are world-famous and internationally acclaimed will you no longer need to audition, and it might well be necessary even then. If submitting to the miseries of being formally judged is an area of distraction for you, your best (and only) course of action is to learn to deal with it.

Why Is It So Important That You Deal with the Presence of Others during Performance?

It is vital that you be able to draw from your own mental energy rather than being distracted by that of other people. Tune in to your own strengths and confidence. Use that energy as a key to good, consistent performance. If you allow them to do so, others can drain your vital energy. You must be able to reinforce your own intuitive anticipation of the upcoming performance. Your capacity to feel excited and to anticipate the performance with glee and joy is highly important. Do not be tempted to yield your own energy to other people, no matter who they are!

Do you find yourself regularly saying such things as these?

> The panel didn't appear to be paying attention.
> He sat clicking on his laptop all the time I was singing.
> They didn't like me. I just know they didn't.
> I sang my heart out for him, and all I wanted was for
>   him to listen to me.
> My voice teacher was at the performance. That makes
>   me so nervous! I just know she'll be making notes of
>   all the mistakes I made.

The auditioners were chatting, not listening.
I hate it when you're at the performance because I know
    you see and hear everything.
I could see what they were thinking—they didn't like it.
She actually ate a sandwich instead of watching me
    while I sang!

If you do say such things frequently, you are demonstrating a classic example of giving your energy (and therefore your performance) into the hands of others, either before you began or during your performance. Most of these things are negative. Apart from wasting energy, you are also further damaging your self-concept, degrading yourself, and lowering your self-worth.

To repeat, a thorough preparation is one of the best ways of dealing with the disturbing presence of others. After the four skills—vocal, musical, dramatic, and linguistic—are at a high level, make sure that you practice your pieces *in the performance mode* many times until the problems are all ironed out and you really believe in your own ability to perform them well. High technical proficiency alone does not guarantee a peak performance—as all of us have witnessed many times. The knowledge of your own worth as a singer is especially vital when you are distracted by other people.

Research tells us that the presence of others can cause problems *especially if technical skills are not honed to a high level.* The more complex the skill to be kept under command, the more devastating can be the effect of such distraction in the performance. And singing is a very, very complex skill. (Even vocal research scientists readily admit that the more they understand the complexities of technical singing skills—which are governed by the laws of physics and biomechanics—the less they can comprehend how anyone ever manages to sing well.)

What Else Can You Do to Help Yourself with the Problem of "Others?"

Exercise 1

Make friends with "those present." Learn to say to yourself, *I know that you people are there, and it's all right with me.* Give yourself permission to use your own energy (not theirs) for performance.

Exercise 2

Build "those others" into your imagery practice. Practice with those distracting people present in your imagination. Because this technique works well, they then will not cause you such a problem. Turn them into a challenge rather than a threat.

Exercice 3

Have a dialogue with "those others." All you need for this technique is two or three chairs and the ability to act a little (but you're already good at that, aren't you? or you wouldn't be a singer).

Call once more upon your imagery skills. Sit in one chair and face the others. Relax. Now imagine that those who are causing the distraction are sitting in the opposite chairs. Notice their mannerisms, their body language, their clothes, and so forth. Begin to have a conversation with them, just as if they were really there. Tell them what you yourself expect from them, what you expect to do, what it is about them that causes you the concern. Once you have completed this conversation, get up, walk across to the other chair, sit down, and become one of the "other persons." Think and act as they do and answer your own questions, accusations, demands about their behavior, and so forth. Acting as the auditioners, say why you (the auditioners) behave as you do, what you want from the performer. Ask how you (the auditioners) may have let the performer down.

Return to your own chair. Give some thought to the answers. Talk as the performer to the "others." Answer the queries and questions. Keep moving back and forth to the different chairs until you begin to appreciate both sides of the dialogue.

Finally, return to your own chair and make a decision about how you will behave and what you will do in the performance.

Exercises such as the preceding ones help you understand how much your attitude toward others is hindering your performance.

Exercise 4. The Magic Box

This skill, outlined earlier in this chapter, can also be very effective when the distraction is other people. Put the distracting people into the Magic Box and deal with them later. What a feeling of power, daring to give yourself permission to acknowledge the distracting people and deal with them at your own convenience! Magic!

Exercise 5. The Quiet Place

Don't let yourself consider the judgment about to be rendered by the audition panel; instead, use the Quiet Place, outlined earlier in this chapter. Deny that disapproving colleague access to your thoughts; go into the Quiet Place instead. Give yourself a break from the other cast members during an intermission; use the Quiet Place. Remove your thoughts from the former voice teacher who's at the competition; enter the Quiet Place before your turn to sing. Going to your own Quiet Place whenever you choose is a wonderful feeling. It can put you in control of your own performance.

There may come a time when you find yourself working in a group situation—a vocal group, an instrumental ensemble with whom you are singing, a mixed group of actors, dancers, singers, and instrumentalists, or part of a cast production. Within a group dynamic like this, other people's behavior can cause a distraction problem.

> An opera singer once telephoned on her way to rehearsal to explain that she simply couldn't face going to the rehearsal at all. During rehearsals the leading man never arrived on time and, in her opinion, never gave of his best. She felt that this was affecting her performance and that of the other singers to such an extent that there was a very unpleasant atmosphere within the group whenever the leading man was present. As a consequence, the other cast members were not able to concentrate on their staging and musical skills, and their performances were degenerating.
>
> Alma Thomas, 1993,
> personal communication

In the situation described it was quite clear that the group allowed one man's behavior to cause problems that severely affected the behavior and performance of everyone else in the cast. Within a sports team there will be the same effect. The team must pool its resources of strengths and superior qualities if the overall performance is to be of a high standard. If one member of the team doesn't pull his or her weight, then it jeopardizes the whole team's performance. Individuals become angry and frustrated and will begin to absent themselves, just as the singer wanted to do in the preceding anecdote.

As a participant in a group performance you must be able to tune in to the group spirit, its strengths and energy—if you wish the group to perform at the ultimate level. The following procedures could be of help in the event of cooperation problems within the team/group:

- *Group discussion.* If possible, try to involve everyone in a small discussion, the subject not important. (Be sure to include the individual or individuals causing the problem.) You may say that you personally do not understand what is expected of you at a certain moment in the production and ask for suggestions. You may try to organize something social after a rehearsal and involve all in the discussion. Even a discussion about some earth-shattering international news might be all that's required to pull everyone together.

- *Group skills.* Another way of getting people together to share ideas is to talk about something required of you as a group in the performance—some part of the blocking, cleaning up entrances or exits, anything that involves the entire group.
- *Pep talk.* If all else fails, you may need to have the leader (director, conductor, manager, teacher, or coach) give the whole group a pep talk. This is not to admonish group members. It is, rather, a confidence talk to remind the group of its strengths and good qualities, to say that they all must remember their group responsibilities as well as their own individual roles in order to produce a high-level performance. (In athletics, this reminder is done regularly to help develop the "*we*" feeling rather than the "*I*" and "*you*" syndrome, which keeps the members of the group separate from each other.) And remember: Expect people to behave differently at major auditions, and performances. Don't take the responsibility for their behavior and thoughts, but draw upon *your own* strengths. Make the effort to remain positive no matter who is there and what their behavior. Turn your thoughts and moods from bad into good and take control.

Case Study

D.P. is a lovely young dramatic soprano with a phenomenal voice, still studying, not yet under management. She is a very timid performer and suffers much from anxiety. She has such low self-esteem that she worries constantly about what other people think of her. We asked her to write this story of her early training to show how an intelligent singer blessed with this wonderful vocal endowment could come to have so many problems with performance.

I am a lyric soprano based in Washington, D.C. As a young singer I won a two-year scholarship to a prestigious music school. I was filled with excitement and joy. All day, every day, I was going to be able to do what I loved most—learn how to sing correctly. I was actually on my way!

My joy was short-lived. Evidently I wasn't able to do anything correctly. Repeatedly I was told that in no aspect of the training—vocal, dramatic, musical, linguistic—was I up to the correct standard. Following my performances I was bombarded with negatives. Did I really ever think that I could become an opera singer?

As a consequence, I became very unhappy in the academy. Where had all the joy of singing gone? Voice lessons, acting workshops and language sessions became nightmares that testified to my total inadequacy. Singing for the faculty and my peers was unbearable. What they thought of me and my singing caused the greatest anxiety and dread. I couldn't understand how anyone had found me worthy in the first place. Why was I given the scholarship if I was so lacking in ability?

After one year I left the academy and found a day job. My feelings of inadequacy permeated everything I did. Of course I did not sing. In fact, I didn't sing again for eighteen months.

My old voice teacher eventually inquired why I wasn't singing. Why was I wasting such a talent? Naturally, convinced of my ineptitude, I didn't believe her words. She then recommended another voice teacher who worked in a very sympathetic and supportive manner. Slowly I began to enjoy my voice again. Soon I was able to think about auditioning.

Auditions proved to be moments of hell for me. Not only was I still lacking self-confidence, but I found that I was totally distracted by everything. If it was there, I was distracted by it. Of all the distractions, the thing that gave me the biggest problem, I discovered, was the people present, especially the other singers and the audition panels. (Shades of the academy!)

It was very difficult for me to shake off the fear sparked by what I believed those people thought of me and my singing. However, I worked at the skills of dealing with people as distractions. Slowly but surely auditions became much more bearable, and soon I even began to enjoy them!

Eventually I became a finalist in the Pavarotti Competition for young singers. The day of the finale arrived, and I believed that I was as prepared as I could be. Imagine how I felt when I saw in the audience three of the faculty members who had taught me at the vocal academy. My world fell apart. I knew what they thought about my vocal skills and other abilities. After all of my hard work, why did they have to turn up on the most important day in my life so far?

Naturally, my first reaction was panic. Then I remembered all the work I had done on dealing with distractions and the skills I had learned that let me control my performance. After all, they were just people, weren't they? Come to think about it, I was much better than they had ever given me credit for. All I had to do today was sing to my own level as of now.

Gladly I put all three teachers into my Magic Box. I locked it with a key that I took with me. (All in my imagination, of course.) While waiting to go on stage, I returned over and over again to my Quiet Place. While there, I sang short gospel songs to myself. I love gospel! These songs had nothing to do with my repertoire for the competition, but they filled me with joy and focused my attention on what I enjoy most—singing.

Well, I didn't win the competition, but I did enjoy myself. I knew that I had sung to the best of my ability as of that day. Also, I was overjoyed by the response of the competition panel. The feedback made me feel wonderful.

What happened to the ogres at the vocal academy who were in the audience, you ask? I can't think why they ever bothered me in the first place!

Summary

A key area of concentration and focus control, an integral part of performance, distractions come from a variety of sources. The main ones are your physical environment, the body and its internal reactions, other people present.

Awareness is an important skill in learning to note and deal with distractions. There is a different mental skill for each source of distraction. Some of the most important skills in distraction work are:

> Confidence
> Positive pep talk
> Imagery
> Focusing on self (it's *your* performance)

Further information:

1. On the skill of imagery, see chapter 12, "Imagery in Performance."
2. On positive pep talks, see chapter 5, "The Self and Performance: You, the Person; You, the Performer."
3. On massage making you too relaxed for good performance, see chapter 11, "Dealing with Anxiety."
4. On imagery as one of the most powerful performance tools, see chapter 12, "Imagery in Performance."
5. On lowering your self-worth, see chapter 5, "The Self and Performance: You, the Person; You, the Performer."
6. On building those "others" into your imagery practice, see chapter 12, "Imagery in Performance."

11 Dealing with Anxiety

Sure it was important to me, but to who [sic] else? The sun will be out tomorrow and the stars and the moon will be out tonight. It was only a race.

Michael Johnson, U.S. sprinter, after failing to qualify for the 200-meter finals in the 1992 Olympics when he was favored to win the event

To the performance psychologist, anxiety is a complex emotional state. To the general public, anxiety is synonymous with worry, fear, and forebodings. To the singer, it is public enemy number one! When a singer freezes or commits a blunder in a big performance moment, anxiety is either the root cause or the outcome.

Performance, by its very nature, places stress on performers and makes demands on their mental and physical energy. But it also offers the participants a challenge, great opportunities, and a chance to push back their own personal boundaries, all of which can be very liberating. Performance does, however, produce some uncertainty, some doubts—how will it go? You could consider anxiety to be a reflection of uncertainty. This powerful combination of stress and uncertainty is the villain, although it is a kind of villain that could turn out to be either a blessing or a threat.

What Kinds of Anxiety Beset You?

Whenever an audition, competition, or stage performance is imminent, do thoughts run through your mind about how important it is, how much it means to you, and the probable consequences of the outcome? Perhaps you say certain things to yourself—positive or negative—about how you will perform? Perhaps you even venture some thoughts about what might happen in that performance and what that would mean for your career?

Certainly you will have some doubts. The emotional response to anxiety, characterized by worry and tension (not limited to singers), is the very demon in the human mind that causes you problems during your performance. These thoughts, these doubts, will either cause you to be anxious or free you from anxiety, will either add to your confidence or crush it. How you perceive any performance and what you say to yourself about that performance trigger your emotional reaction to the event. If, however, you were able to change your way of thinking about what the performance means to you, to change your way of viewing the belief you have in your own ability, or to deal with the situation in a positive way, then you could transform your emotional responses. Once you have done that, the only change would be in your self-perception or in your interpretation of the performance. This slight change in your way of thinking, in your way of perceiving the event and yourself, could be the means to free yourself from fear and anxiety.

Anxiety Is Internal

When you consider the amount of pressure on today's singers to perform well—the "this is it" syndrome—you might believe that anxiety is inevitable and external to the singer. Some singers have described it as being like a runaway train: Once it's in motion, there's no way of stopping it. Clearly, however, singers do manage to perform in these uncertain situations, staying confident and focused without becoming too anxious. Uninhibited by any form of anxiety, they perform well. It *is* possible! And it is possible because anxiety is not some evil ogre waiting out there for you, waiting to grab you from behind. To the contrary, anxiety is internal.

It does not exist outside your thoughts, outside your own head!

Stress that results from anxiety is not imposed by other people or by the situation. You may *feel* anxious regarding certain circumstances, but it is not mandatory that you *become* anxious in such circumstances. It is not the situation that is anxious; it's you! If you recognize that a situation is more difficult than your abilities are able to cope with, then you feel anxious, you yourself having foisted that anxiety upon yourself. Other people and events may contribute to it, but ultimately, anxiety is always under your own control.

To put it another way, anxiety results from your perception of an imbalance between what is demanded of you and your feelings regarding your own capability to achieve what is being demanded. An example: If you view an audition as very important and if, at the same time, you do not believe that the repertoire you are offering is "perfect" enough or you are convinced that it cannot reach the required level, then the imbalance, the difference between the two, causes you to be anxious. Therefore, you feel stressed. To remain in control of your anxiety you must keep the two sides in balance—that is, you must balance your perception of the performance situation and your belief in your own ability to handle that situation.

You do require a certain level of anxiety to perform well, but too much anxiety can influence your performance in a negative way. (It's OK to feel anxious, but it's not OK to be unable to manage or control this anxiety.)

Part of the challenge is to be frightened before you go on, face it, and then go on.

Elaine Paige,
starring in *Sunset Boulevard*, 1996

To perform in an ideal way you need some anxiety, just enough to make you feel excited and ready for the performance. The ability to perform at your optimal level of anxiety (or arousal) at each performance is a skill that certainly doesn't come easily. Yet the controlling and managing of unwanted anxiety is an important part of your ability to perform consistently. If you manage anxiety well, each of your performances will be achieved in a consistent manner. If not, then most, if not all, of your performances will fail to be as good as you want them to be.

The Two Kinds of Anxiety

There is a relationship between performance and your arousal level; it is the result of the interaction between two kinds of anxiety, known as cognitive anxiety and somatic anxiety.

Cognitive anxiety, more simply described as mental anxiety, results from your concerns and worries about the demands of the situation, which make you feel a lack of confidence, a lack of self-belief, and an inability to concentrate. As a rule, this type of anxiety manifests itself well before the start of your performance, often days or weeks beforehand.

Somatic anxiety, more readily understood as physical anxiety, results from the information given you by your body, such things as butterflies in the stomach, sweaty palms, frequent visits to the bathroom, and muscle tension—all symptoms of physical anxiety. This type of anxiety manifests itself at a time much closer to the beginning of the performance and may disappear soon after that.

Mental and physical anxiety management is even more important than originally thought. According to the "Catastrophe Model of Performance in Sport," devised by a British psychologist (Hardy, 1990), performance depends on a complex interaction between your physical anxiety level and your mental anxiety level. Given a relatively high physical anxiety but little mental anxiety (worry), your performance can have a steady decline. Given a high level of mental *and* physical anxiety, then your arousal will reach an optimal level, after which the bottom will drop out of the performance— hence the title word *catastrophe*: "In conditions of high worry, once over-arousal and the catastrophe occur, performance deteriorates dramatically." This has a very different effect from that of a steady decline in performance, because recovery from catastrophe takes longer: "The performer must completely relax to reach again the optimal level of functioning" (Hardy, 1990, pp. 81–106).

The term *arousal* describes the result of an interaction between these two types of anxiety, producing either a state of emotional readiness or one of instability. At one end of the arousal scale you will be highly charged and really "psyched up," perhaps even becoming aggressive, while at the other end of the scale you will be calm and very relaxed.

However, *there is no standard ideal level of arousal for everyone*. Each person requires a specific arousal level of his/her own in order to perform well. Take as an example a linebacker. Compare his need for a high level of arousal with that of a singer, who requires no such high level of arousal to perform well. Those whose profession features gross motor activity, such as the football player, not only require higher levels of arousal to do well but also are able to withstand much more arousal before it begins to interfere with their performance. The singer, whose activity involves fine manipulative skills of smaller muscle groups, requires lower levels of arousal and is not able to withstand much more arousal without hindering his or her performance.

The first thing you should do is identify your own *ideal level of arousal*. Naturally, this could vary, depending on the nature of the performance. Being in the finals of the competition may matter more and feel different from being in the first or second rounds. Or you may feel unintimidated about being in an audition with relatively unknown singers, but the addition of a couple of well-known singers might torment you! The critics' night or the opening night performance may hold much more threat for you than does the eighth performance. For this reason you will probably need to vary your arousal level on a regular basis.

Your Ideal Zone of Arousal

Inside the parameters of arousal there is a band within which you will give your best performance as a singer. If your arousal is above or below this level, your performance will deteriorate. This band within which you perform to your best is known as the *zone of optimal functioning*. When you are in the zone, good performances are more likely to occur. It is therefore imperative that you be able to recognize and identify the symptoms or signs that indicate for you that you are indeed in the zone.

Being able to read the body/mind signals becomes even more important when you consider how mental and physical anxiety interact and the resulting effect they have on your performance. Most of you have been in a situation where you were feeling great, everything in the performance was going along very well indeed, and then suddenly you could do nothing right at all. It could be compared to the experience of riding along in a car, thoroughly enjoying the scenery, everything wonderful, when suddenly the wheel comes off the car. Your journey that was going so well has suddenly fallen apart. This is exactly the experience in performance when there is a sudden and great decrease in the performance. In sports this is called falling off the performance cliff. It is quite likely that the performance will not return gradually to its former position after such a drop, but that you will require a significant period during which you can calm down before the performance begins to improve again (Hardy, 1990, pp. 81–106). You then have an even more compelling reason to get your level of arousal correct, learning to manage and control it before the performance, during the performance, and after the performance.

Learning to Manage and Control Anxiety and Arousal

All the skills outlined here will be divided into mental strategies and physical strategies. This makes sense because each type of excessive anxiety requires its own skill. The first three skills—self-awareness, managing mental anxiety, and reducing physical anxiety—are designed to help you with your anxiety during *preparation* for performance.

Self-Awareness

Before you can devise any strategies that will help you to manage and control anxiety, it is important that you be able to *recognize* the symptoms of both physical and mental anxiety. The objective of the four self-awareness exercises here, adapted from Martens, 1987, is to help you become aware of your own pattern of anxiety and the symptoms that accompany it. Take your time; this is an important step for you. Only after uncovering this pattern can you recognize which of the skills you must learn. At that point, you can begin to plan an arousal program that will help you to stay in your optimal zone, which can be built into your performance routine.

Exercise 1

On the following arousal scale write down where you think you usually are in these three time frames: before performance, during performance, and after performance.

High/psyched up ————————————— totally calm/laid-back

| 10 | 9 | 8 | 7 | 6 | 5 | 4 | 3 | 2 | 1 |

Exercise 2

Write down just how anxious a person you are. Are you a real worrier? Do you worry only a little? Are you very calm, laid-back? Or do you sit somewhere in the middle? Make some notes about your symptoms of anxiety as you go along.

Exercise 3

Think back to an ideal performance of yours, one that you would like to repeat, one in which you performed very well. Think of all the things you did before your performance, including eating, drinking, sleeping, vocalizing, physical warm-up, and traveling. Note how you felt and what you were focusing on at the time. Also recall how you felt during the performance. Work in as much detail as you can. Not only does this form your ideal arousal zone, but it also will give you some idea of how you achieved this ideal zone. Now all you have to do is learn the skills of managing and controlling anxiety. Then you will be able to repeat this pattern of getting in the zone time after time.

Exercise 4. Recognizing Your Symptoms

The symptoms shown in the chart accompanying this exercise are some of those that performers have recognized as present when they feel either physical or mental anxiety. Use this chart as a reference to help you recognize your own symptoms of anxiety. As you can see, many are very obvious. Indeed, *not all somatic symptoms are negative*. Pounding heart, increased respiration, and increased adrenaline need not be negative signs. However, the presence of other physical symptoms together with mental symptoms may mean that your level of arousal has gone too high. You should then take some action to lower the level so that it does not interfere with your performance.

Check to see which of these symptoms you may or may not have; then double-check to see whether you *do* need to take some action about your anxiety (adapted from Martens, 1987, p. 112).

Cognitive (Mental)	*Somatic (Physical)*
Indecisiveness	Pounding heart
Worry	Profuse sweating
Feeling of being overwhelmed	Increased respiration
Inability to concentrate	Decreased blood flow to the skin
Feeling out of control	Increased muscle tension
Narrowing of attention	Dry mouth
Loss of confidence	Trembling and twitching
Forgetfulness	Frequent urination
Fear	Nausea
Irritability	Loss of appetite
	Sleeplessness
	Increased adrenaline

Managing Mental Anxiety

Identifying the Causes of Mental Anxiety

What kinds of things cause you to be mentally anxious? Often it is worries about the demands you perceive being made on you, probably by others:

> I really wanted to do well in this audition, but someone from my management is here to listen, and that always throws me off.
> Look at all those good singers here! They work constantly, and I don't. What makes me think I can equal them?
> This is a really big opera company; they've heard the best. What's the point of *my* singing for them?

Also, worries about your own ability, unfounded or not:

> I just can't imagine that I could measure up to the others here today.
> There's no way I can sing well in front of such an imposing audition panel.
> I've never hit all three of those low chest-voice Cs in practice. I've always missed one of them. How can I possibly do them right here?
> Whatever made me think I should do this competition? I'm just not qualified.

Worries about the consequences of the performance:

> If I don't perform well today, I may never get another chance.

My voice teacher went way out on a limb to recommend
me for this competition. What if I fail him?
I've sung for this company before; I just hope they think
that I've improved enough.

Obviously this kind of negative thinking only results in anxiety,
and, as a consequence, your performance suffers. Since there is a
direct relationship between a successful performance and positive
thinking, one of the best methods for reducing your anxiety is to be
as confident about your abilities and strengths in your singing as
possible. Learn the following skills outlined in chapter 8, and apply
them to anxiety. Train yourself to be more confident by positive
self-talk and positive affirmations. Make lists that pertain both to
your self and to your performance achievements.

Keep repeating the specific positive self-statements relative to
your problems with anxiety. This can be done quite easily anywhere you happen to be, on the train, in a traffic jam, in the shower,
or even during a lull while you are at work. The aim of this type of
practice is to train your mind to respond to the challenge of the
performance, not the threat. By doing this, you will soon learn to
be in control of your mental anxiety, to be excited rather than fearful.

Here is the way that you re-appraise or refocus upon the demands of the situation, your own ability and skill to deal with that
situation, and the eventual consequences: Put all the words and
phrases describing these issues into a positive frame of reference
on which you can focus. Some examples follow:

Demands of the situation:

I know this is a tough audition, but I also know I'm
really well prepared.
Just because this is the Belvedere Competition doesn't
make the challenge any different. It's just a competition.
These other singers have to lose sometime; today's my day.

Your own ability:

I know what I'm good at in my pieces. I'm going to give
them something terrific to listen to.
You're doing what you know well. Relax. This is going
to be fun.
Sure, this is a tough audience, but don't worry. Stick to
your performance plan. You know it works.

Consequences:

This is my performance, and I'm doing it for me!
I know I can control my performance. I'm just going to do it!
You're good. Do it now. Never mind next week.

Compare these preceding sentences with the ones at the beginning of this exercise and see how much more positive the later statements are. This kind of talk can and will help to reduce your mental anxiety. You are simply refocusing on the positive and re-appraising the demands, the consequences, and your own ability. Try to keep things in perspective. As Boris Becker said after losing in the second round at Wimbledon in 1987, "I haven't lost a war. No one got killed. I just lost a tennis match."

Using Imagery to Reduce Mental Anxiety

(Before using imagery for the reduction of mental anxiety, you should read chapter 12, which deals in detail with the skill of imagery.)

Imagery also is a potent method for coping with mental anxiety. Recalling a very good performance and watching yourself in your imagination, performing as well as you can, is a very effective way of reducing mental anxiety. It is called mental rehearsal, and it is exactly that. Try to practice this as often as you can. It will constantly remind you of how you feel and look when you are performing *well*. You can use this skill in a quiet time just before your audition or competition performance, between the acts of a stage performance, or between groups in a recital. You can watch yourself performing the next aria in the audition or executing your next entrance and your coming aria in the stage performance. You can also practice your pieces while sitting on the train or in the car or even walking in the street, through the use of imagery. The more you use imagery as a skill for reducing anxiety, the more you will be able to perform while controlling and managing your arousal. Always see yourself as being positive and confident in your performance. If, while preparing for the performance or even during the performance, you begin to feel a little worried, all you do is check into your own positive picture show to remind you how well you can do.

Another way to use imagery for mental anxiety reduction is to think about any images that make you feel very calm and relaxed. These images could be anything. Some singers use images such as running water, which makes them feel that the tension and anxiety are running out of them. Or they see the face of their dear grandmother, a calm person, very supportive of their work. This allows them to feel calm, and it also reinforces the belief that they can do it! One very successful and illustrious singer uses the image of balloons that he has tied to his wrists! He watches them rise up away from his arms, and he uses this wonderful feeling of lifting, rising with ease, to help reduce his mental anxiety. Some singers even use color to reduce their mental anxiety. If you have a color you like that makes you feel very calm, cool, and relaxed or even helps you to focus more efficiently, use that color as an image to induce calmness. Another use of imagery to reduce your worry about part or all of your performance is to go to your "Quiet Place" and relax.

Positive imagery will help you to cope with the challenges of performance. Just find a place—anywhere you can be alone and quiet—and do it.

Breathing as a Means of Reducing Mental Anxiety

All the breathing skills outlined in chapter 6, "Physical Well-Being and Relaxation" can be used to help you to cope with mental anxiety. You should just apply them specifically for the reduction of mental anxiety.

Taking a couple of deep breaths is a tried and true way of reducing anxiety, both mental and physical, but if you have little time to really work at your physical anxiety, then the following types of breathing exercises work for most singers:

Exercise 1. Even Breathing

Inhale evenly through the nose, taking four or five long, deep breaths. Exhale to the same count through the mouth. While exhaling, focus on your relaxed hands. Repeat the process, but this time, on the exhalation, focus on your relaxed shoulders, jaw, or neck. You can repeat this process for as long as you want, depending on the amount of time you have. When you become very good at it, one or two breaths will do the job for you. This means, of course, that you do have to practice this routine as often as you can. Only in this way will it work when you need it!

Exercise 2. Ratio Breathing

Inhale deeply through your nose to the count of 5. Exhale through the mouth to the count of 10. During the exhalation, focus on watching yourself perform well, beginning with a bang, singing a small part of your aria very well indeed, or even making an entrance. This type of breathing is termed *ratio*, because the length of the exhalation should always be double that of the inhalation, for example, 3:6, 4:8, 5:10, 6:12, et cetera. Ratio breathing combines relaxation and concentration. On the exhalation you can focus on anything that will help you to feel good and reduce your anxiety. Ratio breathing has been used very effectively both before and during performance.

Exercise 3. Power Breathing

This section is adapted from Saul Miller, *Performance under Pressure*, 1992. This method of breathing asks you to focus during both the inhalation and the exhalation. As you inhale, you focus on *breathing in your own power*. Think: *This is my own power I am inhaling.* As you exhale, use your power to focus on feeling good, calm, and in control. Say to yourself: *This is my performance; I am well prepared.* While you practice this skill, you should get accustomed to the feelings associated with being in control of your mental anxiety. The more you practice, the more you will be able to use these skills when you want to, either before or during performance.

Reducing Physical Anxiety

Although most researchers believe that physical anxiety manifests itself more powerfully in the time immediately before the performance rather than far in advance, some performers do exhibit physical anxiety for an extended time previous to the actual performance. Because of this, it is recommended that all performers have a method of deep relaxation for reducing their physical anxiety in the days preceding the performance. Any method of deep relaxation can be useful following a difficult performance. It will also serve as an aid to your refocusing before the next one.

The choice of a deep relaxation method is purely individual. One method may be more suited to you than another. Some singers use yoga, while others prefer meditation or some form of deep massage, all of which allow for relaxation. In addition, any of these methods is an effective remedy for excess tension. Try out different forms of deep relaxation so that you have one reliable method that suits you, but remember that whatever method you use will take some practice before it will be effective for you. Be careful; don't go too far. Once you have reached your "ideal arousal state," any further relaxation could make you too mild and gentle for good performance.

In chapter 6, "Physical Well-Being and Relaxation," you will find outlined an adaptation of a form of deep relaxation developed by Dr. Edmund Jacobson (1974). It is known as progressive muscular relaxation. As the name implies, this form of deep relaxation advocates progressing from one muscle group to another. If you make use of this method of deep relaxation, you will find that it has many benefits apart from the ones outlined previously. It helps you recognize where the tensions in your body reside; by relaxing those contractions you will automatically release the tension.

Do you find yourself becoming very tense immediately before your performance or during your performance? If so, you may find it beneficial to use one of the momentary methods of relaxation outlined in chapter 6. It is recommended that you become skilled in the use of both methods—deep and momentary—as both of them help the performance to become tension-free. They also allow you to enjoy confidence in your physical anxiety management methods, so that you can maintain your "ideal level of arousal" throughout your performance, whatever else may be going on.

It cannot be overemphasized how important it is for you to practice these relaxation skills thoroughly. They take some time, but once you have them as part of your mental skills repertoire, you will always be able to deal with physical anxiety.

Some telltale signs associated with your physical anxiety and the higher level of arousal—butterflies in the tummy, sweaty palms, the pounding of your heart—are hard to get rid of. A practical way of dealing with these symptoms is to re-interpret the feelings you are having, that is, to view them as positive (an enhancement of your performance) rather than negative (detrimental to your performance). Instead of construing these signs as fearsome and worrying, regard them as signals that your body is ready to perform.

The symptoms are telling you that you are eager to perform, so reuse your energy in a positive way. Your stomach butterflies can fly in formation. Watch them. See their colors and buoyancy. Your pounding heart can remind you that you are alert and eager. Such a change of focus away from the negative toward the positive will help you to control your anxiety, to use all the energy you have. Because anxiety is energy, it can, if used positively, *aid* the performance rather than hinder it. In this plan you are using some very positive self-talk together with your re-interpretation of the anxiety signals to achieve an ideal performing state.

By experimenting with these methods you will find what works for you in particular circumstances.

Dealing with Too Low an Arousal Level

Most singers believe that it is very bad to have a high level of anxiety. They wish that they could be like their very calm friends who worry about nothing. But it is not necessarily a good thing to be excessively serene when it comes to preparing for performance. If you are the kind of singer who needs to work at lifting your arousal level rather than lowering it, then the following suggestions may be of help:

1. Do a short physical workout with relatively quick exercises like walking or fast running in place. This will raise your heartbeat so that you can feel an appropriate level of excitement in readiness for performance.

2. Use inspirational music to make yourself feel ready for performance, as all kinds of athletes do, unless music annoys you at such a time. The selection of music is an individual choice, but it should make you feel "up." Some singers like to hear anything other than their audition pieces. Listen to your selection on your personal cassette or CD player in the cab going to the audition or in your dressing room before your stage performance. If you find a piece that works for you, keep it always at hand. Use it to get the adrenaline going and to lift your excitement level.

3. Utilize strong verbal cues to lift your energy level. There are many such words. If you are the kind of singer who thoroughly enjoys any pressure situation but needs to get more excited, then work out some strong verbal phrases to help you. For example:

> This is a tough audition. I love it when it's hard!
> I thrive on this pressure. Let's go. Focus.
> I'm pitting myself against this impossible situation,
>   and I'll bet on me!
> I'm ready. Let it come!

Summary

The two kinds of anxiety—mental and physical—interact together to cause a state of arousal. Becoming aware of anxiety symptoms caused by arousal (anxiety-managing skills can help with this discovery), learning those skills, and finally using the skills in performance—this is the path to achieving control. Learning to manage your arousal level is done in the following stages:

1. Begin with your awareness of self in order to recognize your symptoms of anxiety: when they begin, how they manifest themselves before and during performance.
2. Isolate the skills that will help you to control your arousal levels, and then learn them.
3. Try the new skills before and during performance. When you have them, keep practicing them so that they become a permanent part of your mental skills repertoire.
4. Keep things in perspective. Focus on the *process* of your singing, rather than the *outcome*.
5. Use your imagery skills in a creative way.
6. Develop some well-honed relaxation skills, both deep and momentary.
7. Re-interpret your physical symptoms of anxiety into a means of being alert, ready for performance.

8. Use trigger words or phrases and meaningful music to ac-
tivate your arousal level.

Anxiety is an inner demon, not a monster waiting on the outside to attack you. You can control your anxiety levels if you choose
to. You are allowed to be anxious, but you should learn to manage
and control your anxiety if you want to perform consistently well.

Further information:

1. On getting your level of arousal correct, see chapter 11, "Dealing with Anxiety."
2. On being as confident as possible about your abilities and
strengths, see chapter 8, "Developing Self-Confidence through
Positive Thinking."
3. On the "Quiet Place," see chapter 10, "Distractions."

12 Imagery in Performance

Imagination is more important than knowledge.
Albert Einstein

Imagination is a key to all learning and problem solving—and to your performance as well. Imaging is a magical skill. It allows you to think in a very creative way while enhancing your performance. Creative imagination has sparked some of the greatest minds in the world. Einstein arrived at his scientific conclusions about time and space by mentally projecting himself out among the planets, where he rode around on moonbeams! In large part, this ability to maintain a childlike attitude helped him to become a giant among intellectuals. In the same way, your ability to use your imagination in a childlike fashion can be a tremendous advantage for you as a performer.

Whenever you remember some experience from the past, whenever you think of a loved one, whenever you daydream, you are using imagery. A picture or an object or a smell has helped you to remember and recall. Using imagery is a natural activity, but many singers have not realized that it can also help them to learn a new piece, remember difficult lines and phrases, or simply enhance their performance.

Exercise your imagination, just as you exercise your body when you work out. The more you use your imagination, the more it will help you. As we grow older, we do not use our imagination nearly as much as we can or should. The effectiveness with which you created your imaged picture can determine how easily you recall information and how well you manage to relax your body and mind. Both are valuable assets for you as a singer.

When used by a singer, imagery is a conscious utilization of the senses to create impressions that will aid the performance. Imagery differs from dreaming only in its *conscious* and *deliberate* use.

161

Imagery differs from visions and hallucinations in its choosing of time, place, and means. Imagery is also a very creative way of thinking and solving problems. When you use imagery to think about enhancing your performance or to learn a new piece quickly, you think in a completely different way.

As a mental skill, imagery refers to the process of reproducing the imagined situation as realistically as possible with complete sensory input. Nor is imagery limited to seeing. Hence our preference for the word *imagery* over the word *visualization*. Imagery is about using all the senses, not just sight but also sound, taste, smell, touch, and kinesthetic sense (physical sense of the body). With a developed skill of imagery you can see beyond the character or the scene. You can let yourself go, use all your senses, and, incidentally, have a lot of fun, especially when you get to the performance phase of your pieces.

It's quite exciting to see individual singers learn to have fun with their senses while singing. They discover all manner of things about themselves and about their senses other than sight, things that they can use creatively in performance. One singer learned that she had a great sense of taste. When she used this to enhance her performance, others were amazed at the difference in quality before and after she used the imagery. Her images led her to reality. Perhaps you are already able to use one or two of your senses when imaging. The process of learning to use your other senses is well worth the effort and time.

Imagery will permit you to get the best out of yourself in the practice room, the voice lesson, or the performance itself. Young singers who make good progress and singers who are successful make comprehensive and daily use of imagery. With experience and creative thought, they develop the skill until they draw on all their senses to help them with their performance. Top-class athletes, too, use their extremely well developed imagery skills daily. With imagery they prepare themselves, first, to get exactly what they want out of their training and practice and, second, to see themselves as successful while developing a high sense of self-belief. Imagery has become highly refined and sophisticated; instead of relying on your wishes and hopes, you can use imagery very precisely in your performance. Without an ability to image, expression in performance can be extremely limited.

Why Use Imagery in Performance?

The following important issues concerning the use of imagery are adapted from the concepts of John Syer and Christopher Connolly (1984) as described in their book, *Sporting Body, Sporting Mind.*

Imagery Affects the Way You Function Physically

Imagery uses the language of the body. "Verbal language is only a symbolic representation of the experiences which occur at the level of the senses," Syer and Connolly tell us. For example, as you imagine yourself moving, the groups of muscles involved in that action will move on a subliminal level.

Imagery Helps Accelerate Your Learning Process

When you image a new technical skill or part of a new piece of music, the appropriate nerve impulses and pathways are used in the same way as they would be used in the actual performance. The brain does not distinguish between your imaging of the new skill and your actually executing it. In both activities, the information received by the brain is exactly the same! Therefore, if you combine the mental skill of imagery with the actual physical practice, you will accelerate the rate at which you learn.

Two weeks before Ms. H. was scheduled to sing Juliette in Gounod's *Romeo et Juliette* she came down with a very serious respiratory infection that prevented her from seeing her teacher regarding the "poison aria," which the opera company had restored to the score. Because the infection had hung on until the day before the run-through, the young soprano was forced to sing only parts of the opera, marking the rest during the run-through. With one day between the run-through and the dress rehearsal, she was forced to rest for those twenty-four hours. Still no time to work on the "poison aria" with her teacher. At the dress rehearsal H. held back, making sure that her calculations about her vocal strength were correct and would take her safely to the end of the opera.

After the dress rehearsal her teacher asked that they have at least one hour together before the coming performance, H.'s first Juliette with this company. The teacher wished to instruct H. in a high-sternum breath support technique that they both thought would be of help in a few difficult spots. Still wary about the stamina of her vocal health, H. was loath to sing during their meeting. Therefore, except for some actual movement in the sternum region, all the work was done without actually singing.

While the two debated the advisability of putting this new facet of H.'s support technique into play for the first time, her teacher reminded her that the brain does not know the difference between real singing and the mental image of singing. H. practiced the new technique silently through imagery. At the performance she felt capable of using the new ideas in two or three prescribed places. The performance was a smashing success, and her voice was fresh.

♦

TEACHING POINT: See #8, appendix 2.

Imagery Uses a Language Understood by the Body

TEACHING
POINT:
See #9,
appendix 2.

How did you learn your vocal skills? Your teacher could probably write page after page of detailed description of how to acquire vocal skills. However, as most voice teachers can testify, teaching the learning of a vocal skill through verbal means can be a very frustrating process for the teacher and the student. Singing is a physical skill. The signals received by the body are best received in a language that the body understands. Body sensations such as feeling, sight, hearing, smell, taste, distinguishing color and movement, and so forth are the main vocabulary of this language.

How Imagery Can Be Used in Performance

The diagram here illustrates the advantages to be derived from the use of imagery, a vital tool in your vocal toolbox:

How Imagery helps
in Preperformance
- Self-Concept/Confidence
- Relaxation
- Anxiety
- Learning
- Mental Rehearsal
- Mental Rehabilitation after Injury
- Relaxation

How Imagery helps
in Performance
- Anxiety
- Mental Rehearsal
- Concentration/Distractions
- Enhancement

How Imagery helps
in Postperformance
- Forward Planning
- Time-Out/Relaxation
- Mental Rehearsal
- Mental Rehabilitation

There are nine simple guidelines that you should follow before you begin the series of exercises at the end of this section. These guidelines will help you to improve the quality and efficiency of your exercising.

Always Start with Relaxation

Imagery asks your brain and your body to have a dialogue. Tension will inhibit the passage of the correct messages to the brain. As a consequence, when tension is present the communication channels will become blocked. This conversation between brain and body will be much more efficient if you are relaxed. To begin your imagery practice use any of your own relaxation methods or use some of those outlined in this book.

Always Stay Alert

To image successfully you must relax but also concentrate. Concentration makes the images stronger; that is, the longer you can hold a vivid image, the more successful your imagery will be. Determine just how long you can concentrate; then, in the beginning, do not make your imagery sessions any longer than that amount of time. If you can concentrate well for three minutes, then when you first begin practice your imagery for three minutes only. Another method of helping your imagery is alternating three minutes of imagery with three minutes of relaxation. As you become more efficient at concentrating, you can extend your imagery sessions longer, but not more than ten minutes at a time. If your concentration keeps fading and you are distracted, end the session completely, and do it for a shorter time at your next session.

When you practice your imagery, be in a sitting position, where you will stay more alert. Lying down, you may well go to sleep!

Always Stay in the Present

Performance happens in the present, not in the future. When you stand up to perform, wherever that may be, you will do so in the present. For this reason, your imagery sessions should always take place in the present tense, "as if" you are doing the performance *now*.

TEACHING POINT: See #10, appendix 2.

Always Set Goals for Your Imagery Work

Take two things into account when setting goals for your imagery practice.

1. *Your goals should be realistic.* It might be wonderful to imagine yourself as one of the world's greatest tenors, but you should really set only goals that you know are within your reach at this time. Your imagery goals should be attainable but not too easy. As your vocal skills improve, so will the performance that you image. Always imagine yourself performing well.

2. *Your goals should be specific.* Before you embark on an imagery session you should know exactly what you are going to work at, and the goals that you set for the session should match the vocal or performance skills you are honing. Choose carefully from the work you are doing, making the goal very specific. For example, "In my five-minute

imagery session I will work on Rigoletto's triplets just at the end of the duet before 'Caro Nome.' " The more specific the image, the more effective it will be. In this way you can make a judgment about your progress, your competency, what needs further work, and what doesn't. If you happen to discover that your skill level has dropped, setting specific goals for imaging a very good performance will help you to recover your ability and once again gain confidence in the required skills.

Become Efficient at Using All Your Senses

As you may have discovered already, you are much better at using some of your senses rather than others. Individuals express their experiences in different ways. You may find that you can see an image very clearly but have problems feeling what is happening in the body. On the other hand, you may be a performer for whom colors are very vivid but imagined sounds are indistinguishable. Of the main senses—seeing, hearing, and feeling—what are your strongest? Identify them. Probably you have one main sense that you use all the time and two lesser ones. Find out what appears to be your major sense when recalling the performance or experience and begin to work with that sense. Give yourself permission to use all your senses in your mental imagery work, no matter how esoteric this process may seem in the initial stages. Work in as much detail as you can when recalling any performance or experience. Create sensory images that are as full and realistic as possible. When you begin to go over a past performance or experience and allow your senses to work for you, you will know how good you are at mental imagery.

Image in Two Ways

There are two valid ways in which to image. Perhaps, when asked to watch yourself performing, you will do so as if you are watching yourself on a video or on television, outside of your performance looking in. Or perhaps you see yourself as a singer/performer looking out. Both methods need to be practiced. Both methods are important, but initially you may be stronger at one than the other. If you can include the kinesthetic sense in your imagery work, you will be creating a sensory picture and impression that is closest to the way you feel when you are actually singing and performing.

Always Image at the Correct Speed

Imagery can only improve your performance if you do it at the correct speed. Practice your imagery at the same speed that you would actually perform. As an example, for an audition your imagery should replicate the performance, under the same conditions, at the same audition venue, wearing the same clothes, at the same time of day, following the same warm-up, speaking the same introduction of yourself, singing your pieces exactly as you would actually do them. Remember: The information you give to the brain is important! If you slow things down in the imagery, then you will tend to slow things down in the actual performance. The brain doesn't distinguish, so give it the correct information right from the beginning.

There are, however, two occasions when it would be suitable to slow the image down. One is when the skill is extremely complex and/or difficult. This might be an intricate vocal point in the piece or even a difficult bit of blocking in a performance. First, go over this slowly and in detail with your teacher or coach while you image and rehearse it. Then, as soon as you have the detail correct, do the actual piece at the correct speed. Such a plan is very helpful and can be used effectively when you are learning a new vocal skill.

The other time to slow down your imagery is when you are trying to break a bad habit or change your vocal technique in some other way. Slowing down the image allows you to isolate what is wrong. Take the "faulty" part out of the piece, slow it down, and practice it until you have got it right, or even change it if required. Finally, put it back into the full piece/phrase and sing it at the correct speed.

When you are working on this kind of correction and slowing down your imagery it is very important to always finish your session with that image at correct speed. Never practice your imagery at a faster speed than the actual performance.

Practice Imagery Regularly

Imagery is a skill that improves quickly if you do regular, short practices. Three five-minute sessions daily for five days is much better than one weekly session of thirty minutes. Thirty minutes one day, none the following day, and five minutes the next—on/off patchy practice—would be of little value to you. In order to become accustomed to regular practice, it is a good idea to begin with about one or two minutes of imagery. Then take time out, relax, and continue with your work. As with all skills, honing your imagery takes time and practice. Don't give up; it's worth the effort. If you can't find the time for these regular minutes of practice in a comfortable place where you can relax and be quiet, then do it on the subway, on the bus, sitting in a traffic jam, or standing in line in the store. This is infinitely better than not doing your practice at all.

Enjoy Imagery

There is nothing worse for your vocal practice than boredom, frustration, or anger. These emotions can have a disastrous effect on your imagery practice. The quality of your work will be low; you will not learn; you will not retain any of the work you do; you will be wasting your time. Only when you feel relaxed and free from tension will you be positive about yourself and your work. It's your choice. Don't subject yourself to negative feelings and thoughts when you don't have to. It is really senseless to introduce any negativity into your practice when it's unnecessary. It will almost certainly spill over into your actual performance and affect it badly. If you find yourself not enjoying your imagery work, you should stop and do something very different, then come back. (This is also a good plan for your normal vocal practice.) By enjoying your imagery work you will give yourself more chance of really enjoying your performances.

TEACHING POINT: See #11, appendix 2.

How to Begin

The initial exercises are very easy. They simply help you to judge your own sensory ability at the moment. Try out some of the following exercises, using all your senses. (Focus on one sense at a time.)

After closing your eyes, get yourself relaxed and quiet before you begin. If you have problems relaxing, perhaps some of the following images will help, or you can invent your own.

- Ice melting
- Water flowing easily, gently, over the stones in a clear brook
- Harsh lights changing to soft hues of peach or apricot
- The warmth of the sunlight coming in your window
- Rocking in a hammock
- Lying under a tree in dappled sunlight on a wonderfully warm day.

Exercise 1. Sight

Sit comfortably, close your eyes, and allow yourself to imagine:

- A famous performer in your fach (vocal category)
- The bright orange sunset over the ocean
- Your favorite opera house with you on the stage gazing out at the splendor
- A bright yellow circle. See it in full bright color; then watch the circle change its color to black. Keeping an eye on the circle, change its shape to square. Allow this black square

to become a long black line that disappears into the distance. Make the line come back to you, and watch it change into a wonderful green triangle.

How vivid were the images? Could you see quite clearly the shapes, sizes, bright colors? How long were you able to hold onto each image before it faded?

Exercise 2. Sound

Relax. Allow your mind to imagine the following sounds:

- The silence of a thick fog, a wall of gray mist
- Church bells ringing in the distance
- The voice of your favorite singer
- The wind whistling in the trees
- A telephone ringing
- A dog barking quite close to you. Allow the dog to move away from you, but still hear it barking in the distance.

Create your own sounds, for example, the ocean, your favorite piece of music, a child's laughter, et cetera.

Exercise 3. Touch

Relax. Imagine that you are not able to see or hear; touching and feeling are all you can do. Allow yourself to feel the following things:

- The warmth of the sun on your face
- The softness of silk next to your skin
- The deep textured bark of a tree trunk under your hands
- The richness of deep velvet
- The seat on which you are sitting. See a book on the table in front of you. Pick up the book. Feel its cover, the texture of the pages. Put the book down and pick up the round marble ornament from the table. Allow the ornament to roll around in your hands. Feel its cool, smooth surface and its weight.
- Warm, coarse sand. Bend down, pick it up, and allow it to run through your fingers.

Exercise 4. Taste

Relax. Close down all your senses except taste. Imagine the following tastes:

- The sharp, sour, tart taste of a lemon
- The sweet taste of something that you like such as sugar or chocolate or honey

- The burning sensation in your mouth caused by a hot chili dish and the cooling down of your tongue by ice cream
- The juicy, sweet taste of a piece of your favorite fresh fruit.

Imagine all your favorite tastes. Eat part of your favorite meal. Enjoy the taste, the texture, and the luxurious, satisfying feel of good food.

Exercise 5. Smell

Relax. Using only your sense of smell, imagine the following:

- Wood burning in the countryside
- Roast turkey cooking in the kitchen
- Freshly baked bread
- Newly painted woodwork
- Your favorite perfume.

Enter the world of smell, exploring all your favorite and not-so-favorite smells from your life. Go back to your childhood and explore the smells that remind you of happy moments.

Having done the preceding exercises, you will be in a position to evaluate how well you got on. As you will have discovered, some senses are easy to access, while others require you to work at it very hard. You may have found that you were unable to hold onto two senses at once—for example, the dappled sunlight *and* the warmth. Know which sense was the stronger and then which others followed.

If you would like to explore more ideas on this subject, consult *Visualization for Change*, by Patrick Fanning (1988).

Learning to Use Your Senses to Help Practice Your Performance

Any form of imagery will supplement your physical practice of a new vocal skill, will improve it, will increase your learning speed, and will aid your consistency. All imagery work can enhance your performance in some way, if only by developing a higher level of self-confidence. When you are injured or suffering through a bad cold, you can still practice by using imagery. This works because both your vocal technique and your performing consistency are predominantly dependent upon precise mental coordination. Thus, even if you are physically unable to sing, your nervous system still remains tuned to your vocal skills through the use of imagery. You can then return to physical vocal work and regain your old level very quickly.

Using Imagery to Practice Specific Vocal and Performance Skills

Before you begin, it is important to know what imagery you are going to do and why you are doing it. Write it down as a very short-term goal. In this way you will not forget, you can evaluate your success, and you will also have a record of what you have been practicing.

Try to create as real a situation for yourself as possible. Imagine yourself in the venue where you want to improve a vocal skill that you already have, where you are practicing a new vocal skill that you are learning, or where you are trying to restructure a bad habit—it may be your own studio or that of your voice teacher or coach. See the room in detail; know what you are wearing; feel the textures; see the bright colors. Are there any sounds? What is the atmosphere like in the room? Use your senses to get as much detail as you possibly can.

Watch yourself prepare to practice this skill. What are you doing? Are you holding a piece of music? Do you put it on the music stand? Do you put a tape in the machine to record your session?

Now begin to practice the vocal skill you want to work at. Take particular notice of the significant factors in the skill you are trying to improve. Watch yourself perform the skill very well. Notice how you look, how you stand, how relaxed you are, and so forth.

Relax. Then begin the practice once more, but this time watch yourself only for a short time. Switch then to how the skill feels when it works so well, paying special attention to the important elements of the skill. Let's take as an example a particular high note that must be attacked after a dominant seventh chord and a pause. What exact shade of vowel are you singing? How open is your mouth? When do you breathe—*as* the chord is played or *after* it is played? Are you trying to attack directly on the pitch or coming from below? Where do you feel the breath: Ribs? Abdominals? Exactly how long are you holding it?

At this point your focus may be only on certain parts of the vocal skill or on a short fragment that you want to get right. Repeat the practice, and make sure that you are always successful. It looks great. It feels great!

Relax again. Repeat the practice. This time try to be aware of all the sensations in the body, in the voice, in the sound: its shape, its color, and its texture. Once you have this, repeat this wonderful performance again and again in very short bursts of time, for example, three minutes followed by one minute of relaxation, followed by a three-minute practice, followed by one-minute relaxation, and so on, for about ten or fifteen minutes, no longer. Enjoy the whole sensation of performing the skill well in every possible way.

Finally, put the skill back into the phrase or put the fragment into the whole piece. Really enjoy the way you integrate all your senses, how successfully you have learned the new skill or difficult phrase. Pay attention to how the end product flows from all the sensations entailed in performing the skill efficiently, that is, with ease and with high quality.

Imagery and Your "Ideal Model of Performance"

This method of imagery is used by performers in all areas of performance: sports, performing arts, the boardroom, and even school and college examinations.

Ask yourself the following questions: "Which singer performs very well either the skills I am working at or the piece I am practicing? If I could, would I want to sing it just like that particular performer?" (Be sure to pick an artist whose vocal category is the same as yours. What is it about this particular singer that you idealize? Pay attention to everything, mental as well as technical and physical. This is a performance!)

Now relax, and allow yourself to go back to your practice place, which you know well by now. But instead of watching yourself perform this piece, watch your "ideal model." As the performance begins, take notice of how your ideal model performs the skill or the piece. Notice the stance, the relaxed body, the ease, the enjoyment, everything about this singer. Relax for a moment and return to your ideal performer, but this time try to *become* that model. Are the feelings different now? Take note, so that you begin to acquire that artist's confidence, ease, and enjoyment in performing so well.

This is a very effective means of gaining access to the sensations that accompany successful and confident performing. You will be sending some very positive messages to the brain about skillful performance.

Your Best Performance and Imagery

Your ability to access your very best performances through your use of imagery will prove very useful to you.

Relax. Continue with the following process:

- Think back to one of your very best performances. Where was it? What was the occasion (an audition, a concert, a recital, a stage performance, or even one aria in a staged performance)?

- Allow your memory to go back over this performance in detail. What were you wearing? What color was it? What did it look like? How did you look? Take in all the details of how you looked and how positive your body language was. Watch yourself for some time so that you can tap into the senses of sight and feeling in the body. Note how good it looks and feels.

- Now begin to take notice of what you were singing. Allow yourself to go over again that wonderful sound, the rich quality, the ease with which you sang some of the very difficult parts of the pieces. Tap into all the other senses that you are capable of, and use them to recall your very best performance. Allow these messages to filter through to all areas of your body, so that the brain recalls how you did it. Run the performance again and enjoy again and again what you have done. Sometimes watch yourself from the audience's point of view; then change your position and watch yourself from the wings. Now become the singer, looking out at your audience. Focus on the key elements of your performance and notice with great care how it feels to perform in this manner.

- Instead of recalling a whole piece, you can use this skill to recall part of the piece or even small fragments, such as a high note, a run, a phrasing. The process is the same as the preceding one. Try to complete your imagery session by putting your technical skill or your part of the piece back into the whole, performing it all very well.

This use of imagery is not designed for improving a skill or a piece of music but rather for permitting yourself to go back to performing very well. It is possible to experience being very down or feeling that you will never perform well again. Use this method to help to recall that, in fact, your skills have not deserted you!

Imagery Used to Substitute Skills

There are occasions when you are unable to image yourself doing a skill very well. Perhaps you are focusing on the negatives rather than the positives. Actually, you could be focusing on the very mistakes you are trying to eliminate. If this is happening to you:

- Relax. Go back over a different skill or piece that you know you do very well and access those feelings of performing to the best of your ability.

- When you have this feeling, gradually try to image yourself until, eventually, you are watching and feeling yourself performing the problem skill or the part of the piece that is giving you the trouble. The transition should be gradual. Don't force the image. It will come if you allow yourself to infuse the feelings from the best skill into the problem skill on which you are working.

- The feelings are important, so spend some time luxuriating in them. Experience the good feelings before going back to the problem skill.
- Once again run the image from many viewpoints: the audience's, a side view, within yourself. Relax in between to give yourself time to recover and rest.

For both these last two exercises write down what the feelings were, how you looked, how it sounded, the vividness of the color, the texture and quality of the piece, and the positive body language and enjoyment.

The "As If" Technique

The "as if" technique is an imagery skill that can be utilized immediately before or during performance because it doesn't require you to close your eyes, but rather to become someone or something else, acting a part "as if" you were emphasizing those qualities from the image you have chosen.

All kinds of sports furnish us examples of this skill. Nicknames, symbols, and images all conjure up feelings of qualities that are associated with them. For example, Jack Nicklaus was called "the Golden Bear." This sobriquet immediately conjures up a picture of a quiet, blond, gentle giant with a good deal of strength. Muhammad Ali's self-descriptive phrase "float like a butterfly, sting like a bee," while not winning any literary prize, does immediately invoke his lightness of movement and the suddenness of his punching in attack. Used constantly are phrases such as "performs effortlessly, just like water running over shallow rocks in a pool"; "his movement, so quick around the court, is just like a panther: strong, alert, and effortless"; "they sing like angels, pure clear and sweet"; and "the sound of his voice was like the wonderful rich taste of very expensive chocolate, smooth, rich, and silky."

Once, in a certain soprano's session with Pavarotti, she was told by the great man himself, "No, you are singing this phrase too red; try to make it bluer, like a lovely blue silk." Blue is cooler than red; silk is lightweight and floating. These were the qualities Pavarotti was after. Other singers have used such images as babbling brooks, crystal glass, soaring birds, bright red fading to a wonderful soft pink, the richness of royal purple velvet. These are typical examples of the use of imagery as an "as if" technique. With work of this nature, you aim to absorb the qualities of the image with which you are working.

If you find yourself unable to tap into particular qualities from within yourself, you can have access to those qualities by using other images that are like the qualities you want to emulate. You then use that "as if" image to gain the qualities you want. The images may sound stupid or simple, but they do work. Never be surprised at any image that comes to you. You can use anything you want. What it is doesn't really matter. If it works for you, then use it. To everyone else you are simply singing beautifully.

To become accustomed to using this skill, follow these steps:

- Relax. Then take some time to think carefully about which qualities you want to develop, either in yourself or in your piece of music. It can be a quality you wish to attain for the whole piece or for just a part of it.
- Once you have isolated the quality, begin to think about people who have this quality or inanimate objects that have this quality, such as light, color, water, sunshine, animals, and all kinds of objects. Use whatever comes to mind.
- Close your eyes and allow your chosen image to become very clear. What is this image like? What does it feel like? Feel it and know it in all your senses.
- Now take the piece or part of the piece with which you are working. Watch yourself. Feel yourself singing it well. This time try to focus on your chosen image while singing. Use the image while singing the piece. Do not revert to technical thoughts. Allow yourself to put the image out there in front of you. Use it "as if" your piece were that image. Notice how different it feels, how much more at ease the performance is, and how much its quality and your confidence have improved.

Imagery can also be used for the following:

- Improving your confidence and positive thinking
- Helping you to deal more efficiently with your anxiety and arousal control
- Reviewing your preperformance and performance routines.

Summary

Remember that you think in images rather than in words, which are merely symbolic representations of your images. Drawing from your many experiences in life will help you to improve and enhance your singing. Imagery is a very powerful tool for use in your performance and in your preparation. Do not underestimate its worth to you as a performance skill, but rather be open enough to use it thoroughly and to its full. Enjoy the freedom that comes from playing with and using your images. They are yours!

Further information:

1. On the areas listed on the diagram, see all chapters of part II, "Preperformance," as well as chapter 22, "Mental Rehabilitation following Vocal Injury or Illness."
2. On always starting with relaxation, see chapter 6, "Physical Well-Being and Relaxation."
3. On always staying alert, see chapter 9, "The Art of Concentrating."
4. On keeping your goals specific, see chapter 7, "Setting Goals."
5. On practicing even though injured or suffering by using imagery, see chapter 22, "Mental Rehabilitation following Vocal Injury or Illness."

13 Memory

Memory is an important part of your performances. Perhaps you often worry about whether your memory will cope, realizing as you do that you have not only the music and the words to remember but the blocking as well, if your performance is staged. The human mind remembers almost everything that happens to it, but sometimes the information cannot be recalled. When you say, "I can't remember," you actually mean that your memory is (temporarily) blocked. You will be pleased to know that it is rare for human beings to forget information altogether and even more pleased to be told that, like any other mental skill, memory can be enhanced in two ways:

1. *By linking it to the learning methods that suit you best* (you do have your own personal way of learning—visually, kinesthetically, verbally, or any combination of these).
2. *By knowing how to deal with memory blocks.*

Remembering does not take place instantly or haphazardly. The efficiency of retrieval—the final stage of the memory system, when information is recalled from storage—is dependent on the efficiency of the whole system. If you behave sympathetically toward your memory throughout the process, you will be surprised at just how easy it is to recall quite large sections of your performance without too much effort.

The Four Stages of Memory

1. The *perception* stage, when you receive information through the senses

2. The *encoding* stage, when you begin the process of trying to understand, while selecting, organizing, and storing the information in your short-term memory
3. The *storage* stage, when you understand the information and "groove" it into your memory paths through learning, repetition, and familiarization and, finally, store it in your long-term memory
4. The *retrieval* stage, when you recall the meaningful information that you have stored in your long-term memory.

Useful Strategies to Help Improve Your Memory

There are some useful strategies that you can use to help you improve your memory. At the perception stage, when you are actually receiving information through the senses (this may be when you first hear the music or read through the music, when you first see the written words of the text, or when you first read about the character you will play), the information received is stored in four separate memories: verbal, visual, motor skill, and factual. To receive this information and store it easily, you should be

- Relaxed (this makes the reception of information much easier)
- Intent on remembering (this will deliberately signal the system, deliberately setting the mind to remember)
- Focused on the information without becoming distracted.

Although this sounds fairly straightforward, there are certain occasions when you are tired, frustrated, angry, busy, or feeling put upon or hassled. These feelings will cause difficulties with your memory process at a time when you are beginning a new piece or receiving new information about a piece you're working on. You've probably rushed to your voice lesson/coaching from work or from another appointment. Without taking a few minutes to relax you are less likely to receive information very efficiently. This is recommended: If you know you are going to begin a new piece, try to plan this for a time when you are not under real pressure, when you can take at least a little more time.

You will want to make the next stage, encoding, as efficient as you can. To receive and store the information in such a way that you will be able to recall it in the future, you should

- *Be selective about how much of the information you need.* Not everything needs to be remembered.
- *Organize the information into logical patterns, groups, links, and associations.* Use such devices as mnemonics,

active recall, live reading and singing, live testing, musical tape, and the use of "what if" cards.

- *Feed information in digestible quantities.* Try to divide into manageable pieces the material to be learned and remembered. Do not set yourself expectations that are too high and then fail to meet them. When you do that, you will soon start telling yourself how bad your memory is.
- *Work on the material in short blocks, just as you do with all mental skills.* Short sessions done frequently are much better than declaring, "I will spend the next *three* hours learning and remembering the words of my first *six* recital songs." Try to divide your sessions into thirty-five or forty-minute blocks. In this way you will learn and remember more.

When you store information and then transfer it from your short-term to your long-term memory, it has to be done quite deliberately so that it is "grooved" strongly into your memory paths. To do this you should:

- *Read, sing, and familiarize yourself with the words and music as often as possible.*
- *Use all your senses to familiarize yourself with the material.* Try to use all those separate memories—sight, sound, and feelings—to reinforce the grooving.
- *Rehearse the meaning of the information regularly.* Don't just read or sing; do it with understanding and meaning. This way you will remember it better while, at the same time, you are working on other mental skills as well.
- *Use association to help you remember the information.* As an example, images can quite easily help to remind you of certain things in songs. Deliberately plan these images. They will always be there to help you if you come under pressure at any time during your performances.
- *Get enough sleep.* Sleep is an important part of your memory strategy. If you want to learn and remember something, try to get to sleep early. It is also useful to read or sing the piece the last thing before going to sleep. Incorporate this strategy into your imagery work as well. You tend to remember things better if you do them the last thing at night.

Probably most of these strategies are somewhat familiar to you. In addition, try to treat yourself with care, to be kind to yourself, while in the process of learning or memorizing. If you try to force it, it will not happen at all. Provided that the preceding process was done thoughtfully, your recall/retrieval of the information should be relatively easy.

Your motto is:

There is nothing wrong with my memory.

If you think calmly, you will realize that you can remember all kinds of things with very little difficulty. When you forget something and are trying to remember it, don't bludgeon your memory. Be sympathetic and positive. Focus on the images associated with the piece of information. This will help your memory and perhaps unlock the information. Another bit of "old wisdom" that might help is to recite the letters of the alphabet until the information is unlocked, the first letter of the item being used to trigger the recall.

Summary

Memorizing is an important mental skill for you because you do have a tremendous amount of different kinds of information to learn, store, and recall. Your memory will not fail you, but you can help it along the way by doing some of the skills outlined in this chapter. You can enhance your memory skills. Link them together by means of the same learning methods that you now use and by knowing how to deal with memory blocks.

There are four stages of memory: perception, encoding, storage, and retrieval. Treat your memory with care. Don't push it too far for too long with too much information. Learn to relax and to associate things together so that you will recall information exactly when you need it.

Remember: Be positive. There is nothing wrong with your memory.

Note: This chapter on memorizing and memory has been adapted from *The Exam Game*, by Mike Williams and Alma Thomas (1994). Used by permission.

14 The Coach's Place in Singers' Preperformance Work

Nonsingers, even musicians who are not singers, are sometimes perplexed by the mere existence of a singer's coach, not to mention the exact parameters of his or her occupation. A flutist doesn't have a coach; a pianist doesn't have a coach. (In both instances the teacher acts as a coach as well as a technical adviser.) Why must a singer have a coach in addition to a voice teacher?

Why a Coach?

As a singer, even you might ask this question: What purpose does a coach serve?

The coach's place in the vocal scheme of things is dictated by two facts:

1. Singers, for all practical purposes, never sing unaccompanied.
2. When they do sing, they must always sing from memory (and most frequently in a language that is not their own).

Even singers may often fail to recognize that only solo instrumentalists are required to play from memory. In a song recital, you are accompanied by a piano or a chamber group of instruments, each player using written music. In an opera or orchestra concert, you are accompanied by an orchestra whose members and whose conductor do not memorize but use written music.

What does this have to do with the time you spend with a coach?

You need a practice time that is specifically reserved for familiarizing yourself with the sounds of the musical accompaniment, whatever they may be, and for becoming accustomed to the ensemble problems posed by the interplay between you and the accompanying instrument(s). You also require a kind of practice time specifically designed for routining your memorization of the music and for accomplishing all the subtle and not-so-subtle linguistic requirements of the foreign language in which you are singing. Why don't you take care of all this during the voice lesson? For one reason, the time you spend with your voice teacher is too short, as it is, for the vocal technical work that must be done, partly because a voice cannot begin its technical training until the body has matured, which puts a singer years behind other musicians. Furthermore, few voice teachers have the skill to play as well as a professional accompanist, nor do they usually have sufficient pianistic skill to permit them to add to the accompaniment all those cues sung by the other operatic characters or played by the orchestral instruments. Suppose your voice teacher *could* do all the preceding tasks at the piano, how helpful would it be? More than likely, the more your teacher did at the keyboard, the less he or she would be able to achieve with your voice and your singing. It is doubtful that a voice teacher can be simultaneously a great teacher and a great accompanist. There are too many things going on for one person to catch them all, with the possible exception of a very few true geniuses.

In addition, speaking financially, the bottom line is this: Your voice teacher is probably the most expensive member of your team. Why use your teacher for musical/linguistic work when you could do it at a much lower cost with a *répétiteur* (literally, a "repeater")? Many of the tasks you accomplish while just repeating do not require an experienced coach at the piano. Having on your team a coach and a *répétiteur* would not be just a convenience for you; it would also benefit a pianist/coach-in-training, who would do well to spend several years just listening and learning vocal truths while familiarizing him- or herself with the literature before he or she hangs out a "coach" shingle. At the same time, the prohibitive costs that you must bear during your early singing years would be lessened by dividing your work outside voice lessons between a (presumably more expensive) coach and a *répétiteur.*

Added to the problems caused by the very joining of language to music (constantly changing vowels and consonants add further technical burdens beyond the emission of beautiful tone at varying dynamic levels), music with words tends to limit and define more strictly than music without words. Because you sing words, you are perforce playing a part at all times and, to be effective, you must always appear to be in the grip of whatever emotional condition the words and music define. This in turn means that, as a singer, you cannot beat time with your body—no elbows lifting and falling, no head wagging, no foot tapping—for that would dilute the dramatic image. It also means that you cannot appear to being doing something difficult, revealed by facial grimaces and body tensions (as some instrumentalists feel free to do), for that would belie the audience's dramatic understanding. Like dancers but unlike other performers such as athletes (with the exception of figure skaters, divers, and gymnasts), you are required by the nature of your art to make your efforts look easy. Singers and dancers must appear not to be singing or dancing but just *being* in whatever emotional state the music and words dictate. (As the old theatrical maxim goes: Nothing requires so many rehearsals as spontaneity.) When singers have vocal and musical mastery, it is just the beginning of their work.

There is another very important peculiarity that distinguishes you, as a singer, from instrumentalists but not from dancers or athletes: Singers' instruments are their bodies. However, unlike dancers, singers find that almost every physical skill that is a part of their technique is hidden from view. For you, just as for dancers, muscle memory, or what we regard as muscle memory, is the one and only way to acquire a dependable technique. Your only recourse is to turn inward, to listen, to feel, and to remember your kinesthetic responses so that you can repeat them at will. At the very same time, you are called upon to surrender to the dramatic and emotional qualities of the music and text, to relate openly to the audience, to project outward—all of which distracts your attention away from technical skills. What a puzzle!

The consequence of these facts is this: You must possess, finally, a physical control of your body that permits only the dramatic elements to be seen but none of the natural vicissitudes of making the music (except possibly the functions of your breath support, parts of which may be quite obvious). To do this, you must practice in a different way from other musicians, in what might be called layers of responsibility, which are achieved one at a time, almost all of them dependent upon muscle memory. Some of this work can be done in privacy or in the voice studio, but much of it must take place in a pianist's or coach's studio. It is quite clear that your performing abilities as a singer cannot be measured only by musical and vocal technical expertise. Drama and language, with all that those elements entail, must be equal players in performance. The audience must find themselves involved in the dramatic truth of the words and music.

TEACHING POINT: See #12, appendix 2.

What Is the Coach's Job?

Here is the bill of particulars that the coach fills: He or she, a superb pianist by definition, is also the appointed overseer of accuracy in musical and linguistic skills. A coach is the designated arbiter of stylistic matters, often having been trained as a conductor. But the coach wears yet another hat: that of the one who should be helping you to arrive at performance state. You, no one else, must decide when you have arrived at that point. You must distinguish for yourself between a good rehearsal state and a fully prepared performance state. You should persevere until a performance state of technical skills (musical, vocal, linguistic, and dramatic) has been reached.

It is important that you find a *répétiteur* (or a coach) who, understanding a singer's challenges, is willing to repeat accompaniments endlessly. Perhaps you have found a coach who understands better than you the necessity for repetitions; if so, take care not to lose this coach. But perhaps your coach is (understandably) bored by the ad nauseam repetitions you request. Once you have done the piece correctly a few times, some coaches believe the job done, but you cannot afford to believe that. *In order to achieve the correct mind-set for your performance, this repetition is vital.* In reaching a standard of excellence in performance the old motto "practice [and repetition] makes perfect" is only half the story. It should be amended to "practice and repetition that are correct make it perfect." The only way that you can feel sufficiently confident in your technical command is to repeat so often that you trust the piece to be permanently lodged in your nervous system and more likely to be retrievable under stress in performance.

How the Coach Assists You in Achieving Excellence

In the preperformance work, then, the coach should aid you in achieving the many layers of excellence. You must be able to:

1. Surmount the musical difficulties
2. Recognize vocal, orchestral, and piano cues
3. Accomplish linguistic authority and flair
4. Routine vocal problem spots until most are on automatic pilot
5. Acquire physical control of the dramatic elements
6. Make your memorization reliable
7. Let go of obsessive concern with technical accuracy by means of performance mode practice.

Let us consider these requirements individually.

Surmounting the Musical Difficulties

Many singers are not trained to find their own answers to perplexing musical problems. Possibly this stems from the fact that most sight-reading and ear-training courses are, in point of fact, taught by T(eacher's) A(ssistant) graduate student instrumentalists, who have little or no understanding of the practical difficulties of reading music with an instrument that lacks geographical pitch points—no frets, no valves, no black and white keys. Or possibly singers' difficulties stem from the fact that many of them discover their voices only after puberty. Consequently, many have missed the opportunity to learn an instrument in their earlier years. In any case, singers quickly form a habit for letting *someone else* tell them in what ways they are musically deficient and how the music should go. ,

This dependence on others who you presume are more musical stultifies your musical creativity. Under these circumstances solving musical problems represents a terrible chore that inspires fear of inaccuracy instead of fostering the joyful and confidence-building experience of finding a workable solution.

Lucky the singer who finds a coach willing to be a liberator of his or her singer's musicality instead of a musical commander in chief. It is not part of the coach's job description, but if he or she takes time to teach musical principles during the cleaning up of problems, you will blossom artistically at the same time that you become musically accurate. The fact that some of you who started musical studies late in life may not be good musicians does not guarantee that you are not musical.

I was a pianist before I was a singer. During all those years when I was a pianist, no one ever questioned my intelligence, but the minute I became a singer, my intelligence was called into question constantly. Why should this be? I was the same person with the same mind.

J. L., mezzo-soprano, under management but just beginning a career, 1996

As the only singer in the jazz ensemble at school, I was treated really badly. I was so upset by the instrumentalists constantly putting me down that I gave up singing with the group and took up the trumpet. The minute I started playing trumpet, I was welcomed as a friend and colleague again.

C. G., college senior, 1996

On the other hand, singers have a responsibility, too: to make it clear to the coach that improving musicianship in general and growing musical creativity in particular are things that you want to achieve.

There are, of course, myriad ways to learn complex music, and no one way will work best for all. A good coach will have several answers to offer, watching to see which one is best for *you*. Here is one example of a comparatively unorthodox but creative method for conquering difficult music: Learning contemporary music will often go much faster and much more efficiently if the coach will teach you how to make linear, not harmonic, chords out of the melodic line, rather than trying to get you to learn each interval for its own sake against the chords actually written in the instrumental accompaniment. For several sessions the coach can play only the chords outlined by your melodic line, while you learn first to hear and then to sing the written notes as chords accompanied by melodic nonchord tones. When you are accurate and confident, that is the time for the coach to sketch in the real chords written underneath, a few at a time, until you can accurately sing your line unswayed by the real chords. Eventually the real chords will be amalgamated into your hearing, the combination will make sense to you, and accuracy will be achieved. Singers usually tend to learn melodically, but, with patience on the part of the coach, you can be taught to hear and fit into the music vertically, harmonically.

A beautiful example is afforded by Britten's *Les Illuminations* for high voice and orchestra. The rhythms of this piece are matched in difficulty by the pitches. Whether you decide to learn the rhythms first (usually a good idea) or not, when you do get to the pitches you will subtract many hours and much insecurity from the process if you learn them at first with chords that are made by the horizontal melody and then, later, add the correct instrumental vertical chords as written.

Recognizing Vocal, Orchestral, and Piano Cues

There are two basic types of cues to be learned, melodic and rhythmic, plus several variations on each and combinations of both. (Linguistic cues, a third type, are best learned attached to the rhythm at first and then to the melody.) Many singers have not been taught to listen for preceding tunes in the accompaniment or sung by others, cues that bring them into their own line, to count rhythmic and melodic repetitions so as to enter correctly, or even to decide which is the better method for attacking a particular problem. These are commonsense solutions, but they are not taught in any course in school. One of your primary teachers must point them out to you. A patient coach can not only give you accuracy and ease but also improve your actual efficiency at learning difficult music and raise your musical consciousness at the same time.

Patience and goodwill on the part of the coach are essential, as is the knowledge that your coach approves of you. Singers spend so much of their lives being criticized that it is no wonder many have a fragile and insecure nature. The broad scope of duties to be performed is staggering, especially for an opera singer. To get up before a large audience, watch the conductor while pretending not to, cope with the vagaries of props and sets, interrelate with singing colleagues in a realistic way, remember all details of the blocking, use costumes with naturalistic ease, sing in awkward physical positions, sing ever from memory in a foreign language, not to forget the technical difficulties of vocalism—such duties and tasks could very well produce a continuous nervous state that impinges upon the instrument. (Your responsibility is to try to take control of your own thinking, to remain as positive and objective as possible while learning. Whatever your level of vocal accomplishment, you can always do something well, while the learning process continues. Accept and believe in what you can do, step-by-step.)

Singers do depend on their coaches and must believe that it is safe and productive to do so. The coach's kindly, patient, musically generous, and constructively critical attitude can make a better singer and a better musician. An impatient, unfeeling, disdainful, or unremittingly critical manner can literally destroy a career. Bottom line: If your coach isn't helping you, keep looking for one who will. (Surround yourself with positive people. Constant negative feedback is injurious. You need as much help as you can get—positively!)

Accomplishing Linguistic Authority and Flair

Most singers visit a language coach from time to time, usually when starting a new piece or when essaying a new foreign language. Nevertheless, they depend on their musical coaches to do the day-to-day overseeing of the memorized words, the correct pronunciation, the authority with which they are uttered, and the validity of the accent. Especially when a singer is learning a new piece, the constant vigilance and, yes, kindly nit-picking of the coach are invaluable. Once the brain has memorized a bad linguistic habit, it is twice as hard to eradicate it.

Routining Vocal Problem Spots Until Most Are on Automatic Pilot

Once again, we have arrived at the necessity for repetition. At the voice lesson, you and your teacher work until you believe you have found the solution for a problem spot. But you have other work to do, and the whole voice lesson cannot be spent on that one spot. A few repetitions must suffice. It is during your coaching hours that repetition can either (1) solidify the muscular solution or (2) prove that the method you and your voice teacher found is not going to be good enough. If your present coach is not willing to repeat enough, you have two choices. Find another one who will (perhaps a *répétiteur*), or work with more than one coach, doing certain things (lieder, perhaps?) with one coach and certain things (*Don Carlo*? early music repertoire?) with another. And don't forget the newest technology, such as computerized pianos, which will play your pieces over and over, as many times as you need. If you view this as a destroyer of artistry, consider the opposing view: What destroys artistry is a reliance on last-minute inspiration rather than the confidence that comes through endless repetition.

Acquiring Physical Control of the Dramatic Elements

Components of your dramatic art are best thought out and planned alone or with a drama coach. Eventually, however, you must routine them with the music; this means with the pianist/coach. Music exists in time. If you must show a dramatic change of heart, and therefore a change of facial expression (perhaps even physical position), between two phrases, then you must learn to time this visible change to the existing music. Unlike an actor, a singer cannot experience dramatic elements in natural time. They must happen at specific moments in the music. Thus working on them while hearing and singing the music is a requirement. Again we have returned to the necessity for repetition. There is no other way to acquire the control that gives an *impression* of ease and spontaneity on the stage. (*True* spontaneity can be achieved only *after* you have become knowledgeable, skilled, and crafted in all areas of your art—physical, technical, and mental. These attributes, in turn, demand hours of repetition and an eye for a very detailed approach to your work.)

Making Your Memorization Reliable

Most of the tedious work of memorizing must be done alone, on your own. But there are many helpful hints that the coach can give to a singer about this process. There are other methods and some shortcuts that are actually more efficient and result in greater security than the basic tried-and-true ways. Here are two examples:

1. Many singers have formed a habit of depending upon counting the number of beats whenever there is an introduction or interlude before their entrance, whereas often it is more efficient simply to learn the salient feature of the accompaniment instead—a tune, or a rhythmic pat-

tern that repeats a certain number of times. Let your coach help you find the most efficient method.

2. Many singers have not learned to use mnemonic devices when (à la mode de Schubert) they are faced with four verses of the same melody whose texts are different but repetitive, often using some of the same words. Yes, mnemonic devices are somewhat mechanical, but they do avoid that terrible moment when you find yourself repeating verse one instead of singing verse four. (It is no picnic for the pianist either to figure out where you are at such a moment! This is a great recipe for chaos on the recital or audition platform.) Memorizing by means of the sense of the text does not always preclude errors, particularly when the poetry is arcane or repetitive, as in lyric, contemplative, or philosophical writing. Therefore, the best, most productive practice is probably asking the coach and the voice teacher for help in this area before beginning the memorization process by yourself. Try some new ways and new combinations of ways. Be creative.

Letting Go of Obsessive Concern with Technical Accuracy by Means of Performance Mode Practice

It is truly unfortunate that most singers, having started their technical training a good ten years after most instrumentalists and dancers begin theirs, acquire a mistaken and unshakable belief that technical musical and vocal skills matter most. Before long, singers are obsessing about technical expertise, and this gets in the way of performing. It is true that nothing takes the place of technical skill, but we all recognize the difference between one who sings well and one who also performs well. We usually ascribe performing ability to an accident of birth or to flair. This book takes another view: One can also *learn* to be a good performer. That's a good thing, too, because the truth is this: Most of those who come out on top in an audition are employed by conductors, stage directors, and administrators, who expect to hear competent singing and good musicianship and therefore give the job to the singer who *also* has charisma and performing ability.

As a consequence, you must factor into your preperformance preparation the need for a type of practice that ensures performance skill and freedom. Most singers practice technical musical, vocal, and linguistic skills right up to the last minute. Then they devote one or two repetitions of the piece to "going straight through it." It is not an exaggeration to say that, under this system, it is almost always too late. Letting go of compulsive left-brain analytical monitoring cannot be done by wishing it so. A decision to "perform *this* time" will not make it happen. You must *practice* throwing away your vocal worries. And you must practice it a lot.

When and how are you going to practice? Here are some suggestions for a performance practice program:

1. Some performance skills, such as positive thinking and concentration, should be ongoing from the very beginning of your repertoire study, and you want to be in performance mode as soon as it is feasible (but you can't do anything until you know the notes and rhythms). That is, the very minute that you and the voice teacher have concurred that vocal elements of your piece are sufficiently under technical control, the earliest moment when you and your coach have decided that you are adequately in command of the musical, linguistic, and stylistic components of your piece, as soon as you have uncovered the true meaning of the text for you—then, at the earliest possible moment in the preparation process when you will be able to handle it, that is the time to start practicing in performance mode. (But remember that you cannot substitute great performing skills for technical control. You need both.)

2. Treat your coaching as an audition. Before you leave your house do your work on relaxation, confidence, concentration, anxiety, self-talk, and so forth, as part of your preperformance routine, described in chapters 5, 6, 7, and 9, just as you would for an audition.

3. Take a tape recorder to your coaching (not only for those sessions when you wish to practice in the performance mode but *all the time*; you are wasting your money when you don't remember the things your coach told you the last time). Tell your coach that you are going to do a practice performance and wish to wait for the end of the piece before discussing any details that may have gone wrong. Sing a *performance* of your piece, not analyzing your vocal work as you sing, not worrying about musical inaccuracies, not concerning yourself with your Italian double consonants or German umlauts, just performing with as much dramatic truth and personal involvement as you can summon up. No stopping for any reason.

4. After your first "performance," make—aloud—notes of what needs to be adjusted vocally, musically, linguistically, and dramatically. Then ask the coach to give his or her corrections. Keep the tape rolling. Do the same routine for each of the three performances. Then use the rest of the session for other work.

5. At home, listen to the tape and make your conclusions. There are only two reasons for the things that went wrong, especially those that went wrong every time. Either you didn't routine that problem spot sufficiently before trying to perform the piece or you haven't yet found the right technical solution for it. Before attempting another performance-mode practice, work more on the spots that failed, or return to the teacher and find a better technical solution—if you have time. (Beware of attempting new technical solutions close to the actual performance. There will be no time for things to become automatic. As a consequence, there is almost a complete certainty that these new techniques will fail under performance pressure.)

6. If nothing much went wrong, but the performance was a little lame, just continue the practice. This is the time to practice your performance routine again and again. However, it will still need focus, which you can provide by setting two very simple goals for each run-through. This directs your attention and raises the quality of your work. When you are finally at the stage when nothing would deter you in an actual public performance—with all that entails—repeat until you feel at ease and satisfied with what you have done. It takes much longer than you think. Short of this point, you are not really ready to sing that selection publicly, nor can you reasonably expect that your performance would be a good one.

The Coach's Place on Your "Team"

In the triumvirate of singer, voice teacher, and coach, your coach is properly the "ear." Both you and your teacher must depend upon his or her conclusions about the worth of your singing, your musical decisions, your linguistic command, and your dramatic impact. Possibly the coach's most important function is to be a supportive but vigilant watchdog: Has that vowel that was once too far back and woofy now transmuted into a vowel that is too far front and shrill? Has that dramatic personality that was once too shy become too brash? Has that body that was once frenetic and lacking in serenity now transformed itself into a somnolent being that exudes boredom? Have those low notes that were once nonexistent now become bastions of raucous chest voice in unsuitable places? No doubt the coach has noticed, even if you and your teacher have not.

With all this, the coach is not your voice teacher. It is quite understandable that coaches, wanting desperately to be of help when hearing problems that are not being solved as quickly as one might wish, cannot resist trying a few folk remedies of their own. The facts to be remembered here are two:

1. Voice training may seem hit-or-miss or overly conceptual and not concrete enough to a pianist whose training has been based on *seeing* fingers, hands, wrists, and elbows and discussing them with the piano teacher, but most voice teachers know what they are doing and will, in time, finish the job creditably.
2. Coaches may *hear* what is wrong, but their ideas of *how to fix* the problem are, at best, based solely upon their intuition, gathered from all the singing they have heard, not on technical truths that are within the realm of their experience. It is interesting to note that pianists who are accompanying instrumentalists virtually never offer technical advice to them.

The voice teacher surely wants to be in constant touch with the coach, to hear everything that the coach has to say, to discuss ways in which the coach can help sustain an effort that the teacher has initiated in the voice lessons—to make the coach a full-fledged partner in the triumvirate. It is in the singer's best interest, however, that the coach not try to correct when finding a technical problem that is not yet solved. It will only cause confusion and set the progress back. Better that the coach use this sentence: "Take this to your teacher and get back to me." On occasion, the coach may have a good idea on how to improve something. It is *your* responsibility to check out his/her suggestion with your teacher.

TEACHING POINT: See #13, appendix 2.

Summary

You need a coach whose ear you trust and whose judgment you wish to use as your performance criterion. You need a coach whose expertise includes high pianistic, musical, and linguistic skills. You need a coach who is willing to repeat as much as you deem necessary to accomplish the seven means of achieving excellence discussed in this chapter. You need a coach who approves of you and of your work, who does not make you prove yourself or "audition" for him or her each new hour that you study together. You need a coach whose attitude echoes yours: *We are collaborating to find the best solution for this piece.* You need a coach who will remain totally objective while giving you constant positive feedback about the continuing work. You need a coach who doesn't try to teach you how to sing but is willing to cede that right to the voice teacher. You need a coach who, recognizing that vocal study is a process and cannot be hurried, is willing to take the responsibility for helping you at whatever stage you currently find yourself. This indispensable member of the team may be one or more persons.

Further information:

1. On the general subject of memorization, see chapter 13, "Memory."
2. On letting go of compulsive left-brain analytical monitoring, see chapter 15, "Exploring and Planning 'Meaning' for Performance."

III PERFORMANCE

Performance excellence rests primarily upon how singers have taught themselves to *think*. Think correctly and positively, and the appropriate action will result. There is no more important time to think well than during the actual performance.

Performance thinking is a real skill. The fact that internal belief, external technique, communication, and expression are fundamental aspects of voice performance is well-known. It is not the separation of belief and technique that is at issue but their marriage within the performance. Though there are different types of vocal performance, most of the principles of mental preparation skills and synthesis apply to them all: the audition, the competition, the song recital, and the staged performance. There are, however, a few differences in preparation for any of these performances, which the singer must take into account.

All performance occurs in the present. It is perhaps one of the few moments when a human being lives totally in the moment. It is *now*. Even when singers practice, it is a performance. It is *now*. Only in this way can singers experience the performance, becoming aware of everything required in it, repeating the performance as many times as possible so that it becomes "grooved" into the memory.

The epitome of a singer's performance is the communication of the meaning and expression, because without meaning and expression the performance is nil. Singers must trust the vocal training, allowing it to take over during the performance so that they can use their mental energy wisely, thus liberating themselves to communicate the meaning as well as to enjoy the wonderful feeling of singing. All singers crave that feeling and want to be able to experience it consistently. With relaxation they will be able to achieve and maintain such consistency, and it, in turn, will give the performance a chance to move onto a higher plane. As they adjust and attend to the ever-changing demands of performance, singers extend themselves, but not without a physical and mental price.

Achieving a maximum performance is not without risk, but performance itself is a risk. This is why singers perform: They have ability; they work extremely hard; they aim to synthesize all they know and finally unleash it. Yes, the performance is a risk. It is the playing field on which singers must prove just how much they can push themselves.

Despite the many long years of instruction, study, practice, and training that most athletes put in, they generally do not act consciously when they make outstanding plays. The conscious knowledge of correct and incorrect moves serves as kindling and logs to a fire, but in the white heat of the event they are burnt to nonexistence, as the reality of the flame takes over— flames originating in a source beyond conscious knowledge, melting athlete, experience, and play into a single event.

M. Murphy and R. White,
The Psychic Side of Sports

15 Exploring and Planning "Meaning" for Performance

Thousands of words have been written purporting to help you explore the meaning in your musical repertoire. As a singer, you are nearly always caught up in the technical demands of your vocal production, so much so that the ideas, actions, and meanings behind the words, as many of you report, tend to be tacked on at the end. Obviously, the music itself has meaning, and if you were a flutist or a violinist, this might be enough. But in an opera or recital, where words expand or narrow the meaning, it certainly is not enough.

Ethan Mordden (1984, p. 7) describes opera this way: "At one level, it is the volatile public, a collection of ruthless factions. It is exposure at the highest level, with no quarter given . . . the most collaborative possibility in the arts." Discussing the recital, *The Art of the Song Recital* (Emmons and Sonntag, 1979) refers to the beauty, the excitement, and the personal and artistic gratification with which the recital repays those who master its provocative form.

True, opera is a difficult art form. You have to learn, become expert at, and synthesize many things and then perform "as if" you are not thinking of any of them. Most of you will spend many hours in acting classes, learning how to deal with the words you are singing. Unlike the instrumentalist, you are a language instrument. The moment words are used, you become a character: complicated, articulate, a person doing something, somewhere, for a reason, with a background, an inner life, and the need to communicate with words. And when you perform song repertoire you must be able to do all the above and, in addition, encapsulate it in a minidrama probably of only three minutes' duration, without the help of costumes, sets, or props.

Let's explore this a bit more. Singing is significant to you; most likely you cannot imagine your life without it. You learn to explore the meaning of what you are saying, with help from your acting classes, and often you do it very well. However, mere delivery of the words will not do in opera or recital. You have to do more than just "speak" the words. Yes, you do actually know the literal meaning of the words, but that alone is not sufficient in your art form.

We see many performances—in workshops and auditions and on the stage—that stay exactly at the "fact" stage, with words only. Alternatively, we see performances that stay only with the meaning inherent in the music. You need to have both, of course. Most of you are very good at the meaning in the music; this is what you love and enjoy. To really enhance your performance you need to incorporate the meaning that the music has for you with the meaning achieved through the words and what is beneath the words *for you*.

If the meaning of the words is overwhelmed by the meaning of the music, then you have to find dimensions of thought and action equivalent to the size, sweep, and grandeur of the music. Or, if the music is odd and dissonant, perhaps you must find odd and dissonant ideas and actions. (Great composers, of course, express their ideas about the meaning of the text by means of the music, and they do this with enormous care and subtlety.) Learn to fuse music and text, synthesize it, and you are on the road to knowing how to achieve meaning in your work as well. This process of synthesizing the whole also allows you to tap into your reservoir of potential.

In chapter 5, "The Self and Performance: You, the Person; You, the Performer," you were introduced to the concept of attitudes. That is, you were told about how you attach meaning to and have a belief about certain things in life, such as culture, war, people, color, race, objects, and so forth. Then, because of this belief, you have an emotional response, which you evaluate. This is precisely the

TEACHING POINT: See #14, appendix 2.

same process through which you go to explore meaning, with one exception: You must also use your imagination boundlessly before you can experiment, experience, and evaluate on the way to a full synthesis of your performance that includes meaning.

The Process: From Meaning to Performance

This is how the process works:

Meaning
=
Beliefs and values (people, places, issues, articles, colors, culture, et cetera)
+
Knowledge (which brings conceptualization)
+

Responses (react to these things; explore ways of tapping into them)

+

Imagination (through all the senses: feel, touch, sight, sound, smell)

+

Experience (experiment; play until you begin to experience it within)

+

Synthesis (planning, practice, routine until it is synthesized through repetition)

=

Meaning

=

Performance

As you are aware, you have to be skilled in many areas before this process can take place. The process of breaking down the text is a craft that you must learn and become skillful at doing. As a musician, you may be further ahead in breaking down the music than in interpreting the words. As *The Art of the Song Recital* (Emmons and Sonntag, 1979, p. 111) reminds you, "In the end, you don't perform what *you* think Paul Verlaine meant by his poetry. You must perform what *you* think *Fauré* thought Paul Verlaine meant." And how do you know what Fauré thought Verlaine meant?

Breaking Down the Text

Breaking down the text is a skill, a tool that helps you break into and through to the possibilities of meaning *under* the words, a way to discover and experience what's going on, who your character is, and what pushes the character to speak. It is also a way to tap into the well of your own imagination, stimulated and awakened by the ideas revealed through the words of the text.

Step 1. Place

To break down the text's world, its place, you must first look at the words of your song or aria and make a list of your impressions. Write down the facts as well as any more abstract ideas that come to you.

For example, *La Bohème*:

a garret apartment	romantic
Paris in 1830	good friends
Bohemians	it's cold
a bunch of artists	they're poor
passion	they're happy

You have beliefs about these things and some knowledge, to which you react. Another example, *Valhalla*: What impressions do you have of this world? Write down anything that comes to you.

mythical	struggle
gods living on a mountain	fading power

As another example, *Carmen*:

outdoors	fate in the air
castanets	hot
brink of death	

The words you come up with must stimulate, stir you up, bring out *you*. They must make you alive to the world in which your character comes to life. If you are singing in a concert or an audition, what impressions do you have of where you are? Do you want to be in a concert hall, open space, impersonal, with an audience to deal with, or do you want to be, through the power of your imagination, in a Bohemian garret in Paris?

Step 2. Action

As you continue this breakdown process, you will begin to come up with the possibilities of action. What is your character doing? What is the nature of the action? Take, as an example, Mimì singing "Mi chiamano Mimì": Break down the possibilities of action. What is she actually doing? As you write down your impressions, come up with words that will help discover actions that will lift her to the passion of the music. Obviously, her action is to introduce herself to Rodolfo. The nature of that action is to tell him her name and that she makes artificial flowers for a living, but she longs for the real blossoms of spring that speak of love. *That's the fact, the plot, the story.*

But what is she really doing? What words can you come up with that will give her an action as powerful as the music? It is important not to be judgmental about your responses or to limit your imagination. Allow it to bubble up. What could she really be doing?

Flirting
Confessing
Risking
Revealing
Reaching for the romantic love she's always dreamed of
Giving herself totally to the thrill of the moment with
    Rodolfo
Experiencing inner explosions of burgeoning, flowering,
    growing, blooming love
Talking about artificial flowers and melting snow

Whatever action you choose from this breakdown, it has to be bigger and more passionate than merely "to introduce yourself." It will make the sweeping phrases about spring and melting snow inevitable to the action, not literal to the text, and not a surging of general emotion. Emotion is a danger. If it's *your* emotion, we don't want to see it. However, if, through a justified action, you begin to feel something of the meaning you attach to the action, then you are on the right track. This is not the same as emoting!

Step 3. Justification

The next step is to justify your actions. As you continue to work with your impressions, the reasons behind the actions will emerge. What propels your character into action? Why do you or your character do what you do? What justifies the action? The justification has to be experienced by you, through your imagination, to understand and respond to whatever it is that drives your character into action.

Why does Turandot insist on beheading her suitors? Her ancestors were ravished by invading Tartars, and she is driven to do what she does by the need to avenge such wrong. It is tribal, savage, pagan, honoring her ancestral roots. Continue to break down the word *avenge*, and it will feed and justify her action. When you discover the justification that makes you take action, you will come to life. You will experience the action because you are engaged with what makes you do it. The quality, passion, and power of your justification determine the quality, passion, and power of your action.

Step 4. Character

As you come to know the text better, you will begin to discover who and what your character is. Separate it from the plot. The plot is what happens, but to whom does it happen? While you are doing all this work, you are not, however, playing *you*. You are trying to discover and experience the place, the actions, and the justifications of your character.

If you discover that your character is shy, break down the notion of shyness. For example:

timid	removed
frightened	an outsider
self-conscious	different
inhibited	insecure
uncomfortable	

What would such impressions of shyness make you do?

withdraw	sink
hide	cower
pull back	be silent

You know who you are by what you do. Consequently, if you know that your shy character tries to withdraw and hide from life's situations, then you know how to approach the justified actions of the scene. Carmen and Mimì would never meet the men in their lives the same way!

Another example: If you are Pagliaccio and he is a type of clown, break down *clown* until it is meaningful to you, and see what you come up with. The fact that Canio is not a circus clown does not change the fact that a circus or sideshow is the closest that ordinary folk come to the atmosphere of a tent show.

We are all clowns from a certain point of view.
A clown gets caught with his pants down.
His face is a mask, half-laughing, half-crying.
He understands the unbearable, ridiculous, desperate truth of our ludicrous lives.

He's a fool. He makes us laugh!
A clown gets slapped.
A clown is a buffoon.
He makes us laugh, while he himself is crying.
His face is painted.

The whole of this process engages you in asking yourself many questions:

What am I (or my character) doing?   *Why* must it be done?
Where am I doing it?   *Who* is doing it?

Or you may ask:

Who is singing like that?   Does the sensed meaning of
To do what?   the music illuminate,
For what reason?   merge with, the inner life
Where?   of the text?

When you have the craft and the knowledge, when you work hard at the process outlined in this section, you will begin to release the meaning. Just like your detailed work on your vocal technique, discovering meaning requires the same nitpicky approach.

Meaning comes from a depth of mental energy that conceptualizes itself into a form. You then have to put it into performance mode. The way you think, how you use your information in a creative way, will determine how good a performance you give. You must use your mental energy wisely to exploit the added dimension of meaning that the words can give you.

There are many things you must do as a performing singer. You must sing, and do it well. You must act, and do it well. You must watch the conductor without seeming to do so. You must be in perfect ensemble with your accompanist without seeming to work at it. You must become the character, still singing, and yet also be part of the cast on the stage. You must remember your blocking. You must (in a staged production) accommodate all the vagaries of the important individuals such as the conductor, the director, and the producer. Most of all, wherever the performance is, you must appear *not* to be thinking about any of this detail, just communicating the meaning to your audience.

Two-Channeled Brain Activity in Performance

These tasks involve you in a particular process of thinking, which takes on board the two different channels—the right brain (the intuitive, creative, imaginative side) and the left brain (the logical, analytical, planning, strategic, critical side). Without the meaning there is no performance. During the process of developing the meaning and making it an integral part of your performance you will indeed use two types of thinking. However, for the performance you must trust your vocal art, leaving it, together with all your critical and analytical thinking, to the side. It takes great courage to stay with the kind of thinking that allows your imagination to work to its full capacity. Staying in this channel of thought, with only the very occasional visit to the other channel (analytical), you will be in the realms of a performance. Yes, it takes bravery, trust, and sometimes a little risk, but it is worth it.

This is the journey your thinking takes you on to get to that final, trusting, exciting end. Only at this level will the performance become a spontaneous activity, like play. You will be freed from the constraints and pressures mentioned previously and will be able to immerse yourself in your performance for its own sake. Performance is then magic!

In figures 15-1 and 15-2, note carefully the transitions and changes of brain activity. A process that begins with a predominance of essential logical and analytical thought patterns passes through a period when both are used and finally resolves to the creative, imaginative thought processes. (In both figure 15-1 and figure 15-2, LB denotes left brain and RB right brain. Capital letters denote a *large* amount of that thought pattern and lowercase letters denote a *small* amount of that pattern.)

Meaning will be released in all dimensions if you are willing to go through these processes, working in detail. As you can see from figures 15-1 and 15-2, whether or not the full meaning is included as an integral part of your performance relies on the nature of your thinking and where you place your focus. The nature of the perfor-

What you have to do	Nature of the Thinking Channel	Channel
Sing. Vocal production. Vocal technique.	Logical, very specific, detailed work, analytical thinking, verbal, self-instruction, critical, sequential	**LB**
Discover what meaning is embedded in the music for you and the composer.	Critical, sequential, logical, rational, plus insight, feel, touch, intuition, creativity, emotion.	**LB/RB**
Learn the craft of breaking down the meaning in the text. Gain knowledge in action and thought.	As above. Discovering the other dimension of meaning, which doesn't detract from the musical meaning.	**LB/RB**
Select what is needed for your piece, learn, practice, **maintain** by DOING.	Logical, analytical, planning, strategies, critical, verbal (some insight and intuition)	**LB/rb**
Adjust, adapt the structure.	Logical, analytical, verbal, critical, strategic thinking.	**LB**
"Routine" the meaning. Use constantly in voice lessons, coachings, private practice. **Repetition.**	Synthesis, automaticity, feel, intuition, creativity, evaluation free, positive, imagery, goal directed, simultaneous. Practice meaning, *not* just words and music.	**RB/lb**
Performance mode.	As above, with short visits to the other channel of thinking when you need to vocally, as rarely as possible. Planned.	**RB/lb**

Figure 15-1. Brain activity in audition, competition, and recital. These three types of performance all require the kinds of thinking described in the figure in order to discover the meaning in each of your pieces. There is no way out; this two-channeled thinking is necessary for a good performance. It also directs your focus!

mance thinking should be creative, imaginative, intuitive, and spontaneous, with the very occasional visit to the logical and analytical type of thinking. This itself should be planned!

To repeat: Without meaning, there is no performance. The meaning is the life, the light, and the magic in your performance. To achieve this magic, you should learn to think along *both* "channels" on your journey of discovery, but only along *one* "channel" (the creative, sensitive, imaginative, intuitive, and positive channel) when you are in performance mode. Only on a few occasions during your performance should you be logical and analytical in your thinking. Such visits are planned, are brief, and are reserved

What you have to do	Nature of the Thinking Channel	Channel
Rehearsal. Some changes, other selections made. Decisions made by others.	Thinking and focus is logical critical, sequential, detailed.	**LB**/rb
Adjust your own plan to incorporate changes and then make them yours.	As above.	**LB**/rb
Routine, repeat, until they are in performance mode.	Mainly creative, intuitive, evaluation free, positive, insightful, using imagery, kinesthetic, holistic, goal directed.	**RB**/lb

Figure 15-2. Further brain activity in staged performance.

for moments when you know you need that vocal focus. Then, and only then, do you feel the exhilaration of a completely synthesized performance.

Above all else, you should really *trust* that vocal technique you have worked so hard to achieve. It's yours. You can do it. Use it and enjoy it, but do not keep checking it or be a slave to it. Spend your time using your energy wisely with your imagination and your creativity. Just have fun. After all that work, you deserve it.

There is a vitality, a life force, a quickening that is translated through you into action . . . and because there is only one you in all time, this expression is unique. . . . It is not your business to determine how good it is, nor how valuable it is, nor how it compares with other expressions. It is your business to keep it yours clearly and directly. To keep the channel open.

Martha Graham in Agnes de Mille's *Martha*

Summary

When you begin to explore an aria or a song for meaning, both musical and verbal, try to be very aware of the nature of your thinking, about where your focus is, in addition to learning and developing the crafts required.

- Begin with the facts, the plot, the story, the basic idea.
- Explore the life under the facts. This is something that you *do*. You ask yourself the key words: *what, why, where,* and *who.*

- Explore the composer's sense of the musical meaning and your own.
- Know where the sensed meaning of the music illuminates and merges with the inner life of the words as well as the facts.
- Select what you need to do, want to do, and discover why.
- Practice, routine, repeat, repeat, until it is a part of you and your performance, until it is like a second skin.

Meaning *is* the piece. It is the *essence* of the performance. Your vocal skills, your acting skills, your crafts, are only the vehicles you use to achieve the total performance. Unless you learn to think correctly, knowing when you need to be critical and analytical and when you need to be creative, intuitive, and imaginative, you will waste energy, and the performance will be the worse for it. You can draw from all that potential that is yours, but you need to think and plan appropriately to do it. Yes, opera is a difficult art form, but when it all comes together there is nothing like it. Yes, song recital is a most complex and subtle form, but it is worth every moment of your efforts. These two musical forms are what you spent years striving to perfect. These are the jewels in the crown for you. Meaning comes from a depth of mental energy conceiving itself into form. You dance; you write; you sing; you suddenly "see." It might be the golden hues of the dawn—its form, its uniqueness, its energy, and, if you're lucky, its meaning.

Further information:

1. On breaking down the text, see "Showing the Auditioners and Judges What You Think the Piece Is All About (Sometimes Known as Communicating)," in chapter 16, "The Audition and the Competition," and chapter 17, "The Song Recital and the Staged Performance."

16 The Audition and the Competition

> I managed to get through my first aria—just. My second aria was a disaster and I didn't really get through it at all. I felt as if I was totally out of control and there was nothing I could do about it. The physical terror and horror of being "up there" is more than I can cope with at the moment. I've told my agent that there is little point in his representing me if I can't audition.
>
> Professional tenor, describing a
> Metropolitan Opera audition, 1994

A Psychological Overview of Auditions and Competitions

Auditions and competitions give singers the closest approximation to the real experience of competing in a sporting event where the competitor gets only one shot at the target. Just as in competitive sports, if you fail or are not up to the required standard you will not often get a second chance. To perform very well while coping with an audition/competition scenario makes demands on your performance thinking.

Psychologist Denis Waitley (1984, p. 15) has outlined ten qualities of a total winner. The combination of Waitley's list and the two additions *we* would make—*positive technical knowledge* and *positive performance craft*—should comprise your mind-set when you are auditioning and competing.

Positive technical knowledge	*Positive performance craft*
Positive self-awareness	Positive self-esteem
Positive self-control	Positive self-motivation
Positive self-expectancy	Positive self-image
Positive self-direction	Positive self-discipline
Positive self-dimension	Positive self-projection

It is necessary for you to have a clear understanding of what auditions and competitions mean mentally. You must realize that these performances are different from other kinds. In a competition someone always wins and someone always loses. Because you get only one chance to prove yourself in the audition and competition environment, performing consistency is of prime importance. Some of the key psychological insights linked with competing and auditioning are:

- *Be a decision maker.* Be guided by the experts, but learn to make your own decisions. Do what you know is right for you. Too much conformity to what others think is detrimental to a competitor or auditioner.
- *Base a decision for repertoire selection on strong,* positive *information regarding your strengths in all areas of the performance.* Being self-confident is the first rule in competition.
- *Be capable of showing both your person and your performer sides.* Because there will not be much time for you to accomplish this objective, self-awareness is crucial.
- *Stay in the present.* Devote your concentration to one piece at a time, then leave it behind before moving to the next composition. Don't be tempted to take feelings and emotions, good or bad, from one piece into the next. Make sure that you have specific plans to help you with this.
- *Be more performance-oriented, rather than outcome-oriented.* Of course you want to win; that's what competition is all about. Of course you want to be the one who is chosen; that's what auditions are all about. However, if you get the performance right, the outcome will look after itself. In the moment of the audition or competition, focus is crucial. Always focus on your strengths in the present piece.
- *Construct for yourself a comprehensive goal-setting program for the time period running up to the audition or competition.*
- *Provide yourself with complete knowledge of the competition's criteria and rules.* All competition is rule-bound. As a competitor you will be expected to follow the rules. Work to your own advantage within them. If you understand the exact purpose for the audition, you'll be able to behave accordingly, that is, choose your repertoire sagely, set your goals efficiently, et cetera.

A Vocal Overview of the Audition

The audition is, after all, a performance of a special kind. In an audition your vocalism is being critically analyzed for its success or failure: How well do you sing? How secure is your musicianship? What kind of musical imagination do you possess? Is your use of foreign languages authoritative? At the same time you are also being judged physically and personally: Do you suit the role vocally? Do you look right for the part? Will you be easy to work with or cause trouble with your colleagues? Do you have a look of confidence and competence? Do you present yourself well? Most important of all, do you appear to be in control of this audition event? With regard to questions about your personal qualities, you must remember that you are *seen* before you are *heard*.

Singers must audition. Auditions are a permanent fixture of your life. Do not believe those who say that auditions don't make them feel anxious. Auditions carry stress and anxiety for everyone. You may never become accustomed to auditioning, you may never enjoy it, but you can make the experience much less stressful by learning the specific mental skills to help with anxiety and with distractions.

We all know the symptoms: cotton mouth, tight throat, clammy hands, and rigor mortis of the lips. You might tremble and twitch a little, perspire profusely, have muscle spasms in your back. Worst of all is how difficult it is to concentrate. Once you are aware of your tension, it tends to be the only thing you can think about. Trying to put it out of your mind is like trying not to think of a black duck. And, of course, tension breeds tension, so the whole thing can escalate.

Ed Hook,
The Audition Book

Once you have learned to have enough confidence in yourself and your ability, you will not view the audition as such a threatening situation. You might even learn to anticipate it with some relish and enjoy the challenge.

A Vocal Overview of the Competition

Winning versus losing is the essential characteristic of a competition, but the very nature of this event impels most singers to take as gospel the following list of doubtful tenets adapted from Vernon Yenne (1996).

1. *The entire musical world shares a belief in an inflexible standard of vocal excellence.*

    Wrong. There are far too many standards for what constitutes vocal excellence. Read the review of a concert by a singer whose work you admired immensely. The review may take a totally different tack. While attending the opera, you may be applauding madly for a singer whom others are booing. Even in the Olympics, where there are concrete numbers to tell the tale (10.578 seconds wins over 10.579 seconds), individual judges' viewpoints can vary tremendously, especially in gymnastics, diving, and figure skating, where beauty and seeming effortlessness play a part. In singing competitions, there are no concrete numbers; we have the personal opinions of five or so human beings, translated into numbers by them.

2. *All judges believe in this model.*
3. *Therefore, there is only one system for judging, and it is applied consistently throughout all competitions.*
4. *All judges are well qualified to judge fairly and impartially.*
5. *Therefore, judges are always right.*

Statements 2, 3, 4, and 5 are all wrong. Judging will ever be subjective. Judges, being human beings, have divergent ideas of what constitutes great singing. One who hates the interpolation of the [h] consonant in agility passages will severely mark down a singer who does this, whereas another judge may not have a strong feeling about this element. Sometimes judges are not impartial and fair, and sometimes they are not even competent to judge, because those in charge of selecting judges have many agendas not known to us. The individual judge's strength of character varies, and so does the composition of the judging panel. In the last analysis, on an adjudication panel there will always be some whose votes are based solely on personal opinion.

6. *The only favorable outcome of a competition is winning.*

Wrong. You always win even when you lose, because singing in competition is a way to practice honing your competitive spirit and abilities and to practice learning how to handle the results, whatever they may be. The outcome isn't important!

7. *Winning a competition means that you are the best singer in that group of competitors.*

Wrong. The fact that you win a competition does not mean that you were the best singer in the group; it means only that you have won. Due to the vagaries of judges' attitudes and the comparative superiority or inferiority of the rest of the competitors, a competition is, as it has often been described, "Russian roulette." Next time, with a different set of competitors and judges, you might lose even though you sing just as well. Chance plays a part. All winning means is this: At that moment in time, in that place, with those judges, you were considered *subjectively* to be the best. (This is not the same, for example, in track-and-field competitions, where the results are totally objective and measured.) Not even the seeming impartiality of numbers guarantees what you may consider to be a fair result. Consider a competition in which there are five judges and fifteen contestants. If four judges rank a certain contestant No. 1 and the fifth judge ranks the same singer No. 14, then another singer who gets five ratings of No. 2 will win. What could persuade a judge to rank an obviously fine singer (with four rankings as No. 1) down to No. 14? Clearly the singer did something that the fifth judge found totally without merit and the others did not. Chance plays a *big* part.

8. *You cannot launch a career without winning an important competition.*

Not true. It is true that winning a competition calls you to the attention of those in high positions and lifts you out of anonymity, but you will seldom be engaged just because you won a competition. You will always have to deliver a successful audition to do that.

Winners know who they are, what they believe, the role in life they are presently filling. Their great personal potential, and the future roles and goals which will mark fulfillment of that potential. They have learned these things, and are constantly adding to their knowledge through experience, insight, feedback, and judgement. As a result, they can continuously not only "play from strength" in the game, but also avoid errors and correct weaknesses.

Denis Waitley,
The Psychology of Winning

Useful Strategies for Auditioning and Competing

Let us take in order the normal sequence of events comprising an audition or a competition and consider some procedures that will help you to make each into something that is under your control, rather than a threat from outside forces. If your goal is to be in control from the outset, there are two areas to explore: technical control and personal control. Nothing promotes technical control so much as proper preparation. As the great architect Mies van der Rohe said, "God is in the details."

In the previous chapters it has been accepted that elite performance does not really include technical analysis and left-brain activity but, rather, must be executed almost in its entirety on automatic pilot. Being able to perform with all your technical systems on automatic pilot presupposes command over *both* the technical demands and the proper performance thinking.

Assuming that you have achieved such control by working according to the principles articulated in this book, here are some areas of auditioning and competing that can be aided by taking certain strategic actions. Unless you find a separate statement for each, both audition and competition are served by the same formula.

Repertoire

For Auditioning

Do the kind of material that you do best at the moment (within the material that the auditioners have specified); if necessary, do it in several languages and styles. Contrary to the usual belief, variety in your material is not really an issue unless the auditioners have insisted upon a variety. When you are auditioning for an entry position as a professional singer, you need only show what you do better than anyone else. Let them discover you at your best. If the material requested by the auditioners does not represent you well, then perhaps you should wait for another occasion to audition.

In choosing your repertoire for the audition, be sure that you are vocally capable of singing all the pieces in any order whatsoever. As to your mental skills, if you make sure that you are very clear about *why* you chose to sing those pieces and what your strengths are in each, the order won't matter. You'll just put your preperformance routines in place. Make the important decision about which piece you will begin with only after many trials before some kind of audience. Your opening selection should show you to best advantage; it should be a fail-safe piece; it should be one that you really want the audition panel to hear. (If you are auditioning for a specific role, you have little choice—you must come prepared with all the major music from your role.) Choose repertoire much in advance of your audition date, and do not change it just before the audition. For real confidence, allow for thirty days of practice in the performance mode.

For Competing

For the two major types of competitions—those featuring either opera arias or recital literature—the requirements are perhaps more onerous in the song repertoire. For an operatic competition, a maximum number of five arias is generally stipulated and a maximum of two arias is generally heard. A song literature competition may ask for a program comprising forty-five minutes or an hour of music—possibly eighteen or twenty songs. Here competitors may sing only fifteen minutes (twenty minutes at most) of their program. Practically speaking, this probably means as many songs as can be heard in fifteen minutes.

Thus the first conclusion to be drawn is that shorter pieces are more advantageous for those who wish to show more of their abilities in the song literature competition. Putting a seven-minute, forty-second piece (e.g., the first movement of Ravel's *Shéhérazade*) on a competition program means that the contestant has effectively squandered half the allotted time on one piece that shows all it is going to show during the first two pages.

The second conclusion is that every piece on the program must be a "winner," since the contestant can never be sure what the judges will pick. "Winners" cannot be discovered without a lengthy process of winnowing out by means of trial-and-error scrutiny. Message: Start your preparation very early.

The third conclusion concerns the tradition that gives the choice of the first piece to the contestant. That choice must be determined by several criteria: Choose the piece that shows off your present abilities to the best advantage; choose the piece that is fail-safe for a beginning; choose the piece that would cause you the most distress if the judges were never to hear it.

Three conclusions that are *equally* applicable to both repertoires are these:

1. Contrary to widely held opinion, making a big effort to present variety in your choices of operatic arias or songs is not at all so important as doing repertoire from just one vocal category and doing that extremely well. Singing what you do best (in several languages, if that is required) is productive. If doing repertoire that appeals to you means going outside your fach, it is bound to confuse the judges and, worse, it appears amateurish and ill-considered.

2. Some thought must be given to the very strong opinions afloat in the community of judges about whether the singer ought to "act" or "stand still and deliver," even while singing operatic arias. Some reconnaissance (by way of gossip) on the opinion of those judges that you will face is perhaps the only safe way to proceed.

3. When a certain piece of music is required from all contestants, take it very seriously and prepare long and well. In a required piece you can be compared to other singers more efficiently.

On the subject of familiar rather than unusual repertoire, it is somewhat dangerous to opt for the unusual. Yes, the judges are sometimes bored by hearing "Deh, vieni, non tardar" for the umpteenth time that day, but on the other hand, some judges do not have much knowledge of repertoire and do not trust themselves to judge a singer on unfamiliar repertoire. You may have an unusual aria or song that is so smashing in its effect as you sing it that you cannot resist singing it for the competition, but, again, perhaps it is better to play it safe with an ordinary well-known piece (that shows you to be a fine singer) rather than run the risk of putting yourself at a disadvantage.

The most important advice in both repertoires is: When competing, *be absolutely ruthless about choosing the best and the most suitable music, as well as searching out brief rather than long pieces.*

As has been said, each piece must be a personal "winner." In order to choose only winners for your competition program, you must get the pieces on your list of possibilities into some version of performance mode long before you choose the final program. Only in this way can you efficiently judge which pieces are most effective in your voice and which are most telling with your dramatic and musical skills. You want to sing only what you do better than anyone else at this moment in your life. Variety is not so important as you might think, unless the competition rules mandate that. Just do (within the rules) whatever material shows off your voice and your skills to best advantage. Make sure that you do not choose your repertoire at a time too close to the competition. Also, do not change your repertoire just before the competition. Your goal should be to have the repertoire learned one month before the competition date. That leaves thirty days for rehearsals in the performance mode.

When choosing your "winners," make very sure that you can sing all the pieces in any order whatsoever. Do not assume that the judges will be considerate. Competitions are littered with the disappointed tears of failed mezzo-soprano entrants who thought that the judges would never ask for Dorabella after hearing Amneris (not that trying to sing both those ladies was too smart in the first place). Do not plan to sing anything that absolutely requires "a little rest" before singing it. Do not try to outguess the judges' selection process or try to sing what *you* think *they* want. To repeat once more, as to the decision about which piece you will use to begin, make this important decision only after having sung many trials in the performance mode before some kind of audience.

A good competitor competes only with him- or herself. The world has plenty of room for many singers of your vocal category. If you have something valuable to offer, there will be room for you. Therefore, it matters not what others are doing, even if someone is singing your piece and singing it well. Concentrate on what you must do in order to do your best.

Food and Drink before Auditioning and Competing

The ever-present bottle of designer water that accompanies a large proportion of singers in the audition or competition anteroom represents, at best, a wild fancy. The *facts* are these: Yes, your body must be hydrated vigorously in order to maintain vocal health and ease. But while drinking water up to an hour before singing hydrates the inside of your body, including your vocal cords, drinking water during singing or just previous to singing strips the mucus from your cords and makes them drier than they were before. This is the real reason that you continue to feel dry even after drinking. The general health of your vocal cords requires hydration, but the health of your vocal cords during the moments of singing requires mucus. Answer: Peel an apple and cut it up into small chunks, putting them into a plastic container or bag. Bring this with you to the audition. Eat a small chunk whenever your cords feel dry and, by all means, just before entering the stage. (The acid/carbohydrate balance of an apple is exactly the same as that of your mucus.) Drinking water makes your cords feel wet for that moment, but because an apple stimulates the flow of mucus, your cords really *are* wet when eating an apple. Keep that mucus flowing by chewing the chunks of apple. The chewing process produces smaller chunks that will also provide the extra benefit of taking some phlegm down with them. This is why apple juice will not do.

What to eat and when to eat it before singing are two questions that must be answered in a very personal way, decided by trial and error. Try out your possible solutions before voice lessons and coachings and learn what suits you best. Feedback information seems to dictate these general rules:

- Don't eat just before singing.
- Make sure to get the protein necessary for the energy required by prolonged performing, but remember that the same quantity of protein is not required for singing two or three pieces.
- Don't eat gooey sauces or sugary or highly spiced foods.
- Remember that clear soups, unadorned protein, fruit, and veggies are best.

But don't take someone else's word for it. Check out your own personal reactions by simulating many times the conditions of an audition or competition and drawing conclusions as to the best methods for you.

Vocalizing, Clothing, and Travel for Auditioning and Competing

Take nothing for granted in your preparation. Because anything that can go wrong will go wrong, the best motto is: Anything that *can* be practiced *must* be practiced. By trial and error—again using your coaching and voice lesson for this purpose—discover what is the best vocalizing routine for your program. Write it down so that you will know how to alter it when the repertoire must change.

Rehearse in the clothing and shoes that you plan to use. (Remember what Birgit Nilsson said when asked how to sing Wagnerian opera? "Get a good pair of comfortable shoes.") Discard, change, or become accustomed to that which causes discomfort or distraction. Women, take an extra pair of panty hose in your briefcase. Everyone has heard the old canard: "Never audition in a red dress (unless you are auditioning for the role of Carmen)," but no one can prove it with circumstantial evidence. If you look fine in red and it does not belie the character you are portraying, go for it.

Plan your travel method, allowing extra time for minor disasters to happen. Remember: Whatever can go wrong will go wrong! Prepare for contingencies so that you can remain calm.

Waiting for Your Turn at the Audition or Competition

To keep concentrated on your task do not chat with other singers and pianists beyond courteous greetings. Keep to yourself. Find a place where you can do your mental exercise duties without unduly disturbing others: positive self-talk, getting your energy to the optimal level, controlling your anxieties, doing your imagery work, and so forth. Remember: Imagery skills are the most potent performance helpers you have in those minutes before the audition. Mental rehearsal of you doing your pieces with total technical accuracy (vocal, musical, linguistic, and dramatic) is the best kind of practice, because the brain doesn't know the difference between you *singing* the piece and you *imaging* yourself singing the piece. Imaging will remind the brain and the automatic pilot of what you can do and will do. Then you will be free to *perform* when you enter the stage. Focus on what your strengths are and enjoy showing them off.

At an audition, part of your positive self-talk should include this realization: Results of the audition that is before you are partly out of your control, in the sense that auditioners will always prefer a certain voice type and physical type for certain roles. There is nothing you can do about the color of your voice or your height. Therefore, *Will I be hired?* is not an appropriate question. Give a good performance and go with the flow. *I love this piece, and I sing it really well* is a much better thought, and much more useful to you. Even if you are not hired for this particular engagement, they might use you for something else later, provided you have sung and performed well this time. You are not in competition with others; you are in competition with yourself.

Presentation of Self at Auditions and Competitions

When you are asking for advice on how to most effectively enter the stage at any performance, be it audition, competition, or recital, almost everyone is quick to say, "Just be yourself." But this is not so easy. *Which* self shall you be? The self that arrives at a backyard barbecue clad in blue jeans? The self that has been invited to a state dinner at the White House? The cocktail-party-guest self that is looking for an interesting person of the opposite sex? *All* these selves are you. This much is virtually certain: Trying to show some ambiguous, undefined, free-floating version of a "relaxed you" in the audition, competition, or recital situation will be impossible, or flawed at best. No one is "natural" at these times. Trying only for "naturalness" under audition or competition circumstances is close to hopeless. Perhaps it could be done in performance, but not at an audition or competition (which are much more anxiety-ridden). Which self do you wish to present on this occasion? (Check the lists you made in the early chapters for some thoughts you might have forgotten.) Once you have made that decision, it becomes a simple acting job. As you enter, play yourself with your chosen qualities. Show us what you want us to see. Is it confidence? Happiness? Assurance? Control? You've done that many times before at parties and public gatherings. And you're very good at it when it isn't on the stage. Just stop *trying* to be your "natural" self. It's a hopeless quest.

An inner dialogue as you walk in or out could be helpful to your "acting." What might that dialogue be? *Here I am. I'm really happy to be with you and to have this opportunity to show you what I can do. I'm here and I am a very good singer. You are going to enjoy what I have to sing for you. I love this piece that I'm starting with, and you will, too.*

Being in Control from the Outset at Auditions and Competitions

In an audition and a competition you and your pianist are autonomous, especially as compared to an opera, where either or both the conductor and the stage director have the power to insist that you do everything their way, even when it renders your performance "iffy." Seize the power given you by the audition and competition parameters, and do exactly what you wish to do. It is your audition. It is your competition. *You* are in charge.

Have your "what if?" list at hand, so that you can be confident that you have all possible contingencies covered. With each audition your "what if?" list will become more comprehensive. *Control only the controllables.*

Dealing with Fatigue in Auditions and Competitions

Fatigue makes cowards of us all.

Vince Lombardi,
former coach of the
Green Bay Packers football team

The first order of events is not to *allow* yourself to be in a tired state for performing. This requires constant vigilance and early planning. If you are auditioning in another city, figure out a way to get there a day in advance. Call in your chits and find someone to stay with so that an expenditure for a hotel is not necessary. In any case, arrive in town early. Make sure that a hotel room (if you must stay there) is not near the elevator or the garbage cans or the morning collection point. A no-smoking room, of course, and no fresh paint on the walls!

Singers should learn to use wax earplugs. Just as sure as you are singing the next day, horrible noises will happen outside your apartment or hotel window that night. In addition, acquire over-the-counter sleeping pills. They are very mild, just antihistamines generally, but they will allow you to get to sleep when you are nervous. (Yes, antihistamine is drying to the cords. The apple and your hydration will rectify that.) If you are against taking pills, then take several calcium tablets instead. Remember your mother's dictum that calcium-filled warm milk would make you sleep? That's what the tablets do. You want to be sleepy *early* the night before the audition. To achieve that state, stay up late the night *before* the night before the audition and get up early the next morning, the day before the audition. You will be really sleepy that night. That, plus the calcium or antihistamine pills, will do the trick. Either type of tablet will make it easy to get back to sleep when you wake between 3:00 and 4:00 A.M. with nerves, which singers almost inevitably do.

Showing the Auditioners and Judges What You Think the Piece Is All About (Sometimes Known as *Communicating*)

In an opera you play the same character and remain in the same musical style for the entire performance, but in an audition or a competition you must change character and style with each piece you offer. All the decisions you can make about the motivation of your character count for naught unless the listeners can *see* and *hear* what you believe about the piece and the character. What ways do you have to *show* the auditioners or the judges your personal insight about the characters inhabiting your audition or competition pieces?

First of all, your vocal tone color and dynamic gradations send a message. (Your decisions are: Shall this passage be loud or soft? Would a darker tone be more expressive here, with more chest in the mix?) Second, your musical decisions and the skill with which you implement them help to indicate your intentions to your listeners. (Your decisions are: Shall we make a ritard before the fermata? When does the accelerando start? Should this be a diminuendo?) Third, your use of the language and its expressive qualities also bolster the meaning behind your musical and vocal delivery. (Your tasks are: Don't forget that expressive Italian double consonant in the first bar! Be sure they can hear every element of that German consonant cluster! It transmits real meaning.) Fourth, your eyes and facial expression (whatever is left over from the parts of your face that *must* contribute to technical facility, due to the nature of the vocal demands), your gestures, and your body stance and movement all speak to your audience of what you are trying to transmit dramatically. Of these communication tools, eyes are a must, gesture is the hardest to do with seeming spontaneity, and body movement is not only the easiest but also very telling. In your dramatic delivery, do not neglect any of these elements.

Distractions

Once you have learned how to deal with whatever distractions beset you in an audition or competition, do not forget to factor into your preparation the following potentially stressful issue: Another singer may sing your chosen piece just before you come out to do it. You must believe that in no way does this matter! Your performance belongs to you. Your presentation of the piece is your own and very different. Yours is based on your strengths and on in-depth performance preparation. Just stay in the present and do well what you have planned to do.

Being judged is a fact of singers' lives, and you will have to acquire the mental toughness to deal with it. Coping with the presence of other singers, whether they be friendly or not, is another condition of auditioning that must be conquered.

After the Audition or Competition

TEACHING
POINT:
See #15,
appendix 2.

Make sure that you evaluate your audition or competition performance afterward, just as you would a full-length performance. Learn from each audition, from each competition, so that each is better than the last. Perhaps you could elect to audition or compete, just for the purpose of bringing up your skills before doing those that really matter.

Case Study

B. E. is a young dramatic soprano, not yet under management, whose voice is much bigger than her years would suggest. For some reason, this causes her difficulties in an audition situation. We asked her to write down the disheartening story of her audition for a small New York opera company with delusions of grandeur.

I was called for 10:00 A.M. and supposed to sing during the next hour. At 2:00 P.M. I was still waiting. I called my voice teacher to ask what I should do. I wasn't warmed up anymore; they wouldn't let us sing in the building; there was no place to sit and wait and we were all standing. I was tired and hungry and, worst of all, becoming more and more un–warmed up. She said, "This is an emergency. Go down to the end of the block and warm up on the sidewalk. This is New York; no one will pay any attention. They have to call you soon." But what they did was send someone down the block to tell me to stop singing because I was disturbing the auditions! When I finally got to sing, I walked up on the stage and said, "I'd like to sing 'In questa reggia' from *Turandot*." The man in charge looked up from his table and said, "I bet you would. Think you can get through it?" After all I'd been through, his rudeness was the last straw, but it did make me so angry that any nervousness I had felt disappeared. I just turned around and sang it as I never had before.

Summary

In the arduous games called auditions and competitions, preparation is your best defense against the stress. First, fight back by preparing technically, dramatically, musically, and linguistically to the best of your ability. Second, because auditions and competitions are competitive by nature, become a "winner" in your own right despite the outcome. You will do that by synthesizing all your performance skills and developing a "competitive" mind-set by focusing only on what *you* can do, never mind anyone else.

Further information:

1. On showing both your person and your performer sides, see chapter 5, "The Self and Performance: You, the Person; You, the Performer."
2. On staying in the present, see chapter 4, "The Performance Cycle: Plans and Routines."
3. On focusing on your strengths, see chapter 7, "Setting Goals."
4. On learning the specific mental skills to help with anxiety and with distractions, see chapter 11, "Dealing with Anxiety," chapter 9, "The Art of Concentrating," and chapter 10, "Distractions."
5. On executing elite performance, see chapter 2, "The Characteristics of Peak Performance," and chapter 3, "What Is Mental Toughness?"
6. On practice in the performance mode, see chapter 14, "The Coach's Place in Singers' Preperformance Work."
7. On preparing for contingencies so that you can remain calm, see "What Ifs?" in chapter 4, "The Performance Cycle: Plans and Routines."
8. On mental rehearsal of you doing your pieces, see chapter 12, "Imagery in Performance."
9. On enjoying showing off your strengths, see chapter 8, "Developing Self-Confidence through Positive Thinking."
10. On which self you wish to present, see chapter 5, "The Self and Performance: You, the Person; You, the Performer."
11. On your dramatic delivery, see chapter 15, "Exploring and Planning 'Meaning' for Performance."
12. On acquiring mental toughness, see chapter 3, "What Is Mental Toughness?"
13. On coping with the presence of other singers, see chapter 10, "Distractions."
14. On evaluating your audition or competition performance, see chapter 4, "The Performance Cycle: Plans and Routines."

17 The Song Recital and the Staged Performance

> This was a most enjoyable performance. It is the most
> prepared I've ever been. I couldn't believe the amount
> of freedom and joy it gave me during the performance.
> M.R., young heldentenor,
> under management, following a 1995 concert
> performance as Siegmund in Act I of *Die Walküre*

A Psychological Overview of the Song Recital

Because you and your pianist are autonomous in the recital—choosing the repertoire, arranging the program order, making the musical decisions—you need to work on a number of psychological skills that will help you the person, you the performer, and your performance itself. (You will see that some of these skills clearly apply also to opera performance.)

Person Skills

- A very precise assessment of who you are as a person and which of your qualities and strengths you want the audience to see
- A clear understanding of how to use your own positive body language (nonverbal communication) to prevent giving off signals of negativeness or anxiety
- A confidence in the presentation of self in all its manifestations—your body concept, your feelings of well-being, even the clothes you choose to wear.

Performer Skills

- A very clear awareness of your strengths as a performer
- An in-depth knowledge of your strengths in each piece of music and a belief in those strengths
- A confidence in your strengths as a performer and a belief

that the program as selected does show you to advantage
(not to be labeled "ego" since the audience's enjoyment is
lessened without your self-belief).

Performance Skills

- Assiduous practice of the pertinent performance skills
- Thorough practice of the performance itself *in performance mode*, complete with breaks and pauses where necessary
- Development of the necessary imagery for each piece as part of performance enhancement
- A real grasp of how you have determined the meaning in each piece and how you will communicate that to your audience.

A Vocal Overview of the Song Recital

As an aspiring recitalist, you know that you must either possess naturally or acquire through study and experience the attributes and skills expected of a polished recitalist. A list of these attributes and skills, as compiled in *The Art of the Song Recital*, may at first overwhelm, even intimidate, you by its length and comprehensiveness, although song recital aficionados would regard it as incontrovertible:

- A well-trained voice of some natural beauty, with a wide range of color and the ability to spin long phrases without inordinate effort
- Secure musicianship accompanied by dedication to the art and a sincere reverence for the composer (often the poet as well)
- The discernment to make details fit into the musical whole, with finesse in vocal, musical, and dramatic execution
- Insight and imagination permitting deep penetration of music and text
- Versatility of styles (which American singers especially cannot do without)
- A strong and attractive personality
- Musical and intellectual flexibility
- Self-confidence
- Technical acting skills with which to express personal convictions about the music (sometimes described as projection or communication)
- An ability to work simultaneously on many levels
- The capacity to seize what has been taught, then go beyond that, forging it into a personal style and presence.

This list is, to say the least, daunting. Certainly it is a list of ideals. To aspire to these standards of excellence is to live a life of happy artistic dedication. To live up to these ideals is to have the power to sway an audience, to thrill them, to give them an unforgettable experience. To go beyond these ideals is to accomplish the ultimate as a singer—command of self, control of resources (Emmons and Sonntag, 1979, p. 21).

Different Skills Required for a Song Recital and a Staged Performance

The skills required for performing a song recital—as opposed to doing an operatic role—lie mostly in a realm outside of vocalism. Aside from the necessity, because of the size of an opera house (generally larger than a recital hall) and the presence of an operatic orchestra, of using a tone that has great carrying power, the vocal demands are much the same for the song recital. Singing a single song in a recital closely resembles singing an aria, usually a fairly static lyric moment in the midst of operatic action, and performing a cycle of songs or a cantata demands much the same kind of continuous concentration on drama as does performing an operatic role.

However, the salient difference between the two forms has to do with your persona. In a song recital of twenty songs, you play twenty parts, but you must reveal yourself to the audience as a person during the time not spent in actually singing, that is, entrances, exits, and the moments between songs. In the opera, the audience sees you only as the operatic character until the curtain calls, when you show them the real you.

A Psychological Overview of the Staged Performance

As soon as you become a cast member of a staged performance or a member of any performing group, there are other important principles to consider. For a staged performance to be successful, there should be a high level of "team" spirit. You must feel comfortable in your role and be totally committed to the whole cast performance. When this is achieved, the complete group of performers can produce a performance in which all the individuals' abilities culminate. You should therefore:

- *Focus on your job as a "team" member.*
- *Make every effort to do your own job as well as you possibly can.* Whether you are a soloist, the leading man/lady, a

minor player, or even a chorus member, use all your strengths and abilities to be the best you can.

- *Feel very comfortable in your assigned role.* Everyone in the cast has his/her own role, but for a successful staged performance each cast member (including you) should be quite clear about that individual role. Ideally, when all members of the cast are happy to accept whatever roles have been given to them, there will be a successful "team" performance.
- *Try not to worry unduly about other members of the cast.* They, too, should be left to work at their own strengths.
- *Try to set some goals for your own performance.* Be open to the communication of other people in the group. They may have some good answers to your performance problems. Apart from that, open communication lends itself to happy performers, which in turn tends to lead to maximal performance onstage.
- *Not become distracted by the demands of other roles and characters in the performance.*
- *Concentrate on the successful accomplishment of your own performance skills.* Don't allow others to distract you by the things they say, the way they behave, or their looks.

Very recently a performer, who was cast in the leading role, spoke at length about the distraction caused by two other cast members. These two male performers were being so competitive with each other on stage that she found it very distracting during the performances. Each was trying to outdo the other for the audience, and outdo her as well. It wasn't until the third performance that she found a strategy to cope with this kind of behavior, and take her rightful place as the leading lady.

Alma Thomas, 1997,
personal communication

Without doubt, this kind of behavior is not conducive to a good performance, and it probably interfered with the performance of the whole cast. As an individual you must somehow have some "what if?" strategies ready. You should not allow this kind of distraction to interfere with your own performance.

- *Be aware of the individual differences of the group members and try to be sensitive to these as far as is possible.* You do want to be a part of a successful performance!

- *Make sure that you remain as positive as you possibly can.* This positive thinking should also be apparent at the group level, though it is difficult for you to take this responsibility on board. It belongs mainly to the director and/or the conductor.
- *Try to keep yourself as highly motivated as you can throughout the performance.* There are some occasions when this can be very difficult. For example, your leading lady or man may be going through a bad patch and performing very poorly. Once you start to empathize with him/her, then your performance will also begin to drop. You start giving your performance energy to that person. We know it's tough, but *you* are your responsibility. Look after yourself. Empathize with the others after the performance, not before or during. There may also be occasions during rehearsals when you feel your time is being wasted by other members on the stage. Try to keep your focus. Set yourself some very short-term goals to keep you going. Don't waste your energy on other cast members; let them use their own.
- *Control only what you can control.* The overriding responsibility for a very good team performance lies with the person who is leading the group—the director, the producer, or the conductor, for example. If that person is inattentive to or does not care about a group performance, then you must take good care of yourself. It is the leader who should try to ensure that everyone in the cast works to his/her own full level of ability.

Being a Cover

Covering a role for another performer can be very frustrating and often boring. When, as is frequently the case, it leads to feeling not part of the group at all, it is accompanied by the inevitable emotions of failure and being an outsider. If you ever find yourself in this position, try to have some of the following strategies on hand:

- *Know how committed you are to the performance.* As a cover, you may have to work a little harder to remain very confident and highly motivated. This may be even more apparent when it happens just as you think you are making your way up the ladder of success. Always remember that when your star is rising, the competition also rises.
- *Develop your self-confidence in relation to your role within the cast.* Keep an eye on your own strengths and qualities. You need them.

- *Always recognize what you can and cannot control.* Fighting issues that you cannot resolve is a waste of time and energy and may lead to feeling sorry for yourself.
- *Keep the lines of communication open with the "leaders" and also with the other members of the cast.*
- *Be ready at any time to go on.* This is why you should try to remain as positive as you possibly can, which is especially hard as performance time nears and you await the word—yes or no. Spend time with others who are positive. When you do get to go on, don't try too hard. You have nothing to prove to anyone except yourself. Do only what you are good at doing!
- *Stay in the present and reward yourself occasionally.* You hold a very responsible position within the group.

A Vocal Overview of the Staged Performances

> The creative capacity of an actor and a singer is a science. You have to study, develop it, as you do other forms of science.
>
> Constantin Stanislavski and
> Pavel Rumyantsev,
> *Stanislavski on Opera*

What is opera and what demands does it make on your mental preparation? Ethan Mordden has put it in words probably better than any other writer:

> What is opera? At one level, it is the volatile public, a collection of ruthless factions. It is exposure at the highest level, with no quarter given. . . . What is opera? Production fights composition. Glamour wheedles dedication. Fame disturbs concentration. Talent is timbre here, musicianship there, then acting, then looks, then just being famous: and becoming more famous inevitably follows. Talent is at war—with other talents, with the state of the art, with critics, with voice-wrecking "modern" composers, with audiences. . . . Opera is as much an improvisation as it is rehearsed, as perverse as gallant, the most collaborative possibility in the arts (1984, pp. 6–7).

And what has all this to do with *you?* With every passing year, the financial pressure upon opera companies grows. With every passing year, the United States at large and Washington politicians in particular enlarge their view of opera as "elitist" and undemocratic (because it is not immediately understood by everyone) and therefore unworthy of government subsidy. When the results of this view filter down to the lower ranks (meaning singers), the outcome is fewer rehearsals. Fewer rehearsals mean that you must be even more self-sufficient in your preparation—if only to protect your own reputation as a singing artist. Audiences cannot assign blame for botched productions with any accuracy. You are out there; generally the onus is upon the singer. Your only recourse is to be so well prepared that you can survive a lack of rehearsals and the attendant difficulties that impinge upon your performance. *Reliability* and *consistency* have become two of your greatest assets as a singer, far outweighing mere talent.

> When I found myself in the enviable position of having one contract and wanting to accept another one for the same time period, I asked my management to get me out of the first one. Not willing to release me, the administration of the first company did not threaten me with the usual punishments. They said (and I listened), "We will tell everyone in this city that she is *unreliable.*"
>
> S. B., young professional soprano,
> under management, 1992

Strategies for Recitals and Staged Productions

Clearly the preparation for your recital or role must be efficient and all-encompassing. While of course you will take the steps leading to command over your technical skills and your performance thinking, some other areas of dealing with the song recital and the staged performance will be aided by your taking certain strategic actions:

Repertoire

For the Song Recital

Certainly if your recital is a degree recital, then all choices must follow the departmental guidelines. Whatever the type of recital, be sure to choose repertoire that you love, because you will probably sing that better. Choose repertoire that reflects what you can do very well at this stage of your development. Remember: Every composer has written some material that is easier and some that is harder. (Britten wrote settings for folk songs as well as "Winter Words." Samuel Barber wrote "The Daisies" as well as "Nuvoletta." Ravel composed settings for the "Five Greek Folk Songs" as well as "L'Histoires Naturelles.") And every so-called minor composer has written at least one "jewel," such as "Psyché," by Paladilhe, or "Mandoline," by du Pont. Search out the pieces that are both representative of your present skills and a respected part of the glorious song literature of the world.

For the Staged Production

Clearly the choice of an operatic role is an entirely different matter. One cannot simply choose a role for love of the character and the music. Other factors must be considered: Is your voice type right for the role? Are you imposing enough or tall enough or short enough to fit the character type? Are you at least 70 percent the same type as the character, allowing for acting skills to take up the slack? Do you have the stamina to sing the role? In what size house (4,000-seat or 500-seat would you be acceptable in this role? Will anyone other than you find you suitable for the role? And so on. When you are deciding what roles are good for you, it is impossible to solicit too much advice. But, in the end, you must seriously prepare enough of the role so that *you* can judge how well it suits you. It is not unheard of for a singer to be offered a role that he or she feels unable to handle. The courage of your convictions is essential in this case, but first you must have come to your own conclusions by actually singing the role, hearing others sing it, and watching others perform it.

On the stage of a great opera house awaits the ennobling challenge of Rossini, Bellini, Donizetti, Verdi: the urgency of narrative; the instruction of character; the intent phrasing of a line, colored, loved, hurled, bent, observing itself even as it comes to life; the ideology of historical style, the responsibility to the work; and the simple bottom-line hazard of stamina, of giving what is required, forcing muscles to obey. This is highest calling and hard labor.

Ethan Mordden,
Demented

Vocalizing

Take nothing for granted in your preparation. Because anything that can go wrong *will* go wrong, the best motto is: Anything that *can* be practiced *must* be practiced. By trial and error—again using your coaching and voice lesson for this purpose—discover what is the best vocalizing routine for your recital program. Write it down so that you will know how to alter it when the repertoire changes.

Vocalizing for a stage role is slightly different. Your plan may need to include several vocalizings in the course of the production to accommodate the vocal challenges that come in various forms and in various places in the score. Perhaps your role begins with long passages in a very high tessitura but by the time of your second entrance demands a great deal of strength in the lower register. Your plan must ready your voice for both. Perhaps you are called upon to ride over chorus, orchestra, and all the principals. Plan where your voice must cut and where you sing as usual. Perhaps the role is very long and heavy. Plan how much vocalizing to do so that you don't end up with no voice for Act III. This is very personal. Kirsten Flagstad sang through Isolde's part three times before doing it the fourth time on the stage, but Birgit Nilsson reportedly used the Queen of the Night's second aria for her Isolde warm-up. Use your sessions with the coach to clarify your own needs.

Because it is possible to make very large mistakes in choosing roles, the general rule of doing lyric roles first and moving into heavier ones later is a wise one. The following amusing and trenchant excerpt from *Demented*, by opera aficionado Mordden, illustrates the point admirably:

> One reason why *Aida* is performed less often than the other very popular Verdi works is a single note, a high C at the end of Aida's third-act aria, "O patria mia." There is no avoiding the note and, because of the scale-like passage that leads up to it, it stands out even to ears that have not heard *Aida* before. There are actually first-rank and very popular divas who avoid the role because that one note creates so much tension it ruins their lives. Every time they sing a contract to sing *Aida*, the months leading up that that note make them nervous wrecks and the months after all like getting over a bad marriage (1983, p. 12).

Clothing

Your recital clothing must combine flair and practicality without making you feel ill at ease. Often formal wear has certain built-in physical stresses, so be sure to rehearse in your recital clothing and shoes well in advance until you become so accustomed to them that they feel like a bathrobe and slippers. Only then will you be able to put aside your concerns with them, whether those concerns are subliminal or overt, and concentrate on the performance. (Women, take an extra pair of stockings or panty hose along with you, for obvious reasons.)

No matter how much charm you must muster, no matter the wiles that you must practice, try to make friends with the costume

department so that you can spend a lot of time in your opera costume. It will pay off in the end. When you feel very comfortable in
your costume, you will be able to summon up the sense of living in
the historical period of the production. Then you are on your way
to a fine dramatic portrayal of your character.

Preparing the Recital Performance

Because there is so much repertoire involved in a full-length recital, it is best to prepare your music with the help of a list that
puts your duties in a linear format. Do this early on so that you
can keep track of what is done, what is almost completed, and
what must still be done. This way you will not find yourself with
something unfinished late in the process, leading naturally to
panic. As an example, let us assume that you have the usual eighteen or so pieces of music on your program. Here is an efficient
scenario:

1. Learn no. 1 musically and linguistically. When this is done,
   take it to your voice teacher.
2. Solve the vocal problems of no. 1. Learn no. 2 musically,
   linguistically.
3. Begin to work no. 1 dramatically. Take no. 2 to your voice
   teacher to begin vocal work. Learn no. 3 musically,
   linguistically.
4. Take no. 1 to coach for cleaning up style, language, and
   music. Solve the vocal problems of no. 2. Take no. 3 to
   voice teacher to begin vocal work. Learn no. 4 musically,
   linguistically.
5. Begin to work no. 1 in performance mode. Begin to work
   no. 2 dramatically. Solve the vocal problems of no. 3. Take
   no. 4 to your voice teacher to begin vocal work. Learn
   no. 5 musically and linguistically.

And so on.

When all the music is learned, when all is vocally under control
and dramatically worked out, begin to practice the entire rectial
straight through in performance mode.

As your performance date draws close, sing the entire program
before an assortment of enemies and friends. (Enemies are actually
of more use to you because they make you more anxious, but you
can capture good feelings when you do your program in a friendly
situation.) In this way you will learn where, under stress, the weaknesses are, where your control is not absolute, and which places
need more routining. So will you make it possible to do your recital without resorting only to left-brain analytical performance.

Musical Preparation of Your Role

Frequently young singers are somewhat overwhelmed by the task of learning a complete role. The longer the role, the more the task's enormity looms before them. If you have not yet had the practical experience of learning many roles (which will, of course, teach you a *personal* approach to the most efficient way to prepare your roles), the following method may be of help:

1. Count the number of pages in the entire role.
2. Divide this number by the number of days in the time available before you must start work with the coach. (E.g., 221 pages with one month of time equals approximately 7½ pages per day. If you wish to do it faster so that you can spend the rest of the month making inroads on the memorizing process, a plan of 15 pages per day would do it.)
3. Now that you have a plan and the time frame seems manageable, remember: The safest method for memorizing is to repeat ad nauseam. Walter Taussig, experienced vocal coach of the Metropolitan Opera, observes that memorizing is harder for the musically gifted than for weak musicians, contrary to what we might think. Strong musicians can make up several musical ways out of any lapse of memory; they find it so easy to read music that they have trouble buckling down and learning the specifics. Therefore, your only recourse, unless you are blessed with an infallible photographic memory (actually, a photographic memory can easily make you concentrate on the wrong things for performance), is to learn by rote, as less gifted musicians do instinctively and of necessity.

Rote learning is in the long run most efficient because, for best results during performance, the memorized material must reside in the subconscious. Singers who have memorized intellectually are put into a position during performance where they must sacrifice part of their valuable concentration in order to assure the correct notes and words. This is not only a waste of resources; it may well prevent memory from functioning at all. It is far better that the music and words be lodged in the subconscious, programmed to reissue to certain stimuli; memory must *allow* itself to be revived during performance.

More specifically, there is no doubt that persisting for too long a time or with too long a section of music is counterproductive. Strengthen your memory as you do your muscles, by frequent, short exercise. As psychologists have proven, spaced learning is better than unspaced. Thus, repeating small sections daily at first, the sections getting longer as your memory permits, is best. Above all, do not cram! Cramming is difficult and pressured. It cancels the advantage of effortless learning that would otherwise have accrued to you by osmosis between regular practices. Most important, it renders the musical experience unenjoyable. Do not leave the score too early, especially if you are a good musician. A rule of thumb might be to repeat the section daily with scrupulous accuracy until you find yourself singing the tune and words while making your bed or washing the dishes. This is a good sign that you are ready to leave the written music.

This method is probably most important in opera, where your responsibilities are so numerous that the memorizing of the music is only a way station on the road to a good performance. It is axiomatic that the things that can be made automatic must be made so. Surely your musical command can be made automatic, or nearly so. The conscious mind should be free to grapple with vocal technical skills, dramatic sincerity, and those musical ensemble issues that cannot be automatic.

Waiting before the Recital and between Groups

To keep concentrated on your task—that of providing a splendid evening of song for your audience—do your best not to chat with outside people, or even your accompanist, before the recital or during intermission. Otolaryngologists assure us that talking on cords that are in a warmed-up condition, once the singer is either ready to go or has already sung one group, is the surest way to deplete the cords' vitality and therefore their capacity to deliver well. It is true that sponsors, friends, teachers, managers, and such do not appreciate being kept out of dressing rooms, but talking before or during the recital (or, indeed, the opera) carries with it the risk of debilitating your instrument. This is not a matter of temperament. This is a medical matter. Devise a tactful way to keep silent.

During the prerecital months keep a running list of what needs to be done for each piece to be the way you want it. After each practice session or lesson the contents of the list will change, reflecting the work already done and the work still to be done. Following such a list, you will not find yourself ten days before the recital with a sudden realization that one of your songs is way behind the others in readiness. By the time the recital rolls around, your list will probably contain just one or two musical spots in each piece about which you must take care, one or two vocal problems that require vigilance, or perhaps a reminder about some dramatic timing or physical position that you want to remember.

Before group one and between groups, keep your mind concentrated by reading the list *only for the coming group*, in order to refresh your memory about your intentions *for that group.* then, once out onstage, just sing; just perform.

Presentation of Self in Your Recital

Remember that you play yourself (which self?) entering, leaving, and between songs. But you play the personage in the song when you are singing. That means you play some eighteen persons during the recital. But do not neglect to play yourself in between. Part of the audience's pleasure is in seeing you transform yourself from singer into the character in the song. Singers often overlook the fact that the audience really enjoys seeing this transformation. Do not cheat them of this experience. When you remain forever in the closed-off place belonging to the song's personage, it is truly boring for your audience. The transition from the regular "you" to the personage of the song is part of the minidrama of each song in the recital—there are eighteen of them! The more overt the changeover, the greater your listeners' pleasure.

Being in Control from the Outset

Remember that in recital you and your pianist are autonomous. You are in charge. No conductor or stage director can tell you what to do. Therefore, do *what you can control.* Take the power that the recital form gives you and go with it. Keep your "what if?" list handy so that all possibilities are covered.

In an opera you must bow to the desires of the conductor and stage director. But even with a totally controlling director or conductor, there are always tiny areas where you can do your own thing. Even if the director dictates every gesture you are to use, you can still, for example, carry your body in your own way. Even if the conductor controls every nuance and every fermata, you still own the potency of your voice. Find the area that reflects *you,* and use it. Preparation is power.

In doing a role for the first time, you would be wise to make an effort to stay one rehearsal ahead of everyone else. For example, if the blocking should be memorized by the third rehearsal, you try to do it by the second. Your efforts are appreciated by the director and you, in effect, have one extra rehearsal in which to practice the blocking or something else.

Another way to control things for your own benefit is to rehearse very hard at the beginning and then slack off just before the opening. By deliberately working hard at the beginning and letting up a bit in the days before the opening you have a level of performance to rise to, you have a plan that controls the pace and intensity, you can stay in the present, and you will be comparatively rested when it counts: for the opening. (The new practice of inviting a paid audience for dress rehearsals is insidious. If you make an enormous effort at the dress, you will probably have trouble getting yourself into an arousal state higher than that for the actual opening. If you don't make an effort at the dress but coast a bit, husbanding your resources for the opening, you run the risk of alienating the administration and/or the potential audience. Under these circumstances everyone wins but the singer. Try to protect your own interests as much as possible.)

Showing the Audience What You Think Each Song Is About

The training for a singer is almost the antithesis of the actor's training. The singer is trained to place each note in its correct place; the breathing must be precise, the pitch accurate, the rhythm and tempo exact. *Control* is the key word for the singer. But the very controls so needed for singing seem to get in the way of good acting. Ideally a singer ought to be spontaneous in his or her acting and at the same time be able to maintain necessary vocal control. Jean de Reszke, the greatest heldentenor before Lauritz Melchior and a singer famed for his acting, had a very interesting answer for this dilemma. To an adoring fan who asked him how he "became" Tristan on the stage, he answered, "My dear woman, what you see when you think I become Tristan is really me *imitating* what happened at the one rehearsal when I permitted myself to go all out and *be* Tristan. That way I can also *sing*" (Emmons, 1990, p. 148).

There is much nonverbal communication going on in both recital and staged performance. Knowing what signals you are giving off is not communicating emotion, nor does it mean that you are having an emotional experience. Construct an image of your character and take that onstage with you, not the emotion. Work the image, not the emotion. With all the current emphasis upon building a character and searching for motivations, sometimes singers forget that composers send messages *in their music* as to what they think the text means. The composer's conclusions, written in the music, are the source of your image.

In an opera, although you are playing the same character and remaining in the same musical style for the entire performance, you do have the added advantages of costumes, sets, and props that fill in background for the audience, plus other characters to play off. In a recital, all the decisions you can make about the composer's musical expression of the words and their meaning, the motivation of your character, count for naught unless the listeners can *see* and *hear* what you believe about the piece and the character. What ways do you have to show your personal insight about the characters inhabiting your recital pieces (or the inner feelings of the character in your opera aria)?

Just as a recipe, even in Julia Child's hands, can't solve every cooking problem or guarantee success—so a page of music is only a set of instructions to the singer.
Alice Parker,
choral conductor

First of all, the color of your vocal tone and the subtlety and effectiveness of your dynamic levels send a message. It can be one that carries dramatic thrust and commitment or not. ("Will a darker tone here, with more chest in the mix, make my intentions clear?" "Should I use a very heady tone that sounds younger?") The conclusions you have come to about the music, and the skill with which you adopt them for performance, help to indicate your intentions to your listeners. ("If we make a ritard rather than a sudden stop with a fermata, what effect will it have?" "On what beat does the rallentando start? If it starts this late, doesn't it change the feeling of this section?") Your sense of the linguistic expressive qualities ("Language *is* style," says coach John Wustman) also attests to your sincerity. ("Don't forget that expressive [ʃ] that starts the word *stille* in 'Nacht und Traüme'!" "Where is the stress accent in this phrase?" "I must make sure they can hear that *raddoppiamento* in 'O, Dio'!")

When a performer is successful with the arias, the situations on stage, the character and the period of the piece, it is easy to feel that everything has been done that needs to be done. This is quite misleading, because the singer also has to perform. He must play the performance. He must create an effect on the audience.
Robert Cohen,
Acting Power

Second, your eyes, your face, and your movements, together with the shifting of your body weight and your body postures, all convey to your audience what you believe to be the dramatic truth of that moment. Of these communication tools, eyes are the most important, gesture is the most difficult to achieve with naturalness, and body movement is perhaps the most effective. In your plans for the dramatic elements of your performance, be sure to include all three.

> The acting singer, once fledged, is opera's salient ele-
> ment. Truly great performances are triumphs not of
> design but of emotional imagination, and the great
> roles are more than portraits. . . . When working with
> a drudge [director], the singer is at her most exposed,
> with a master [director], she is both protected and de-
> fenseless: *by* his imagination and *against* his power.
>   Ethan Mordden,
>   *Demented*

Distractions

Losing concentration in performance nearly always has a detrimental effect on both you and your performance. Awareness of
what actually distracts you is your first duty. (Do coughing, little
children wriggling, people leaving early, garlic on your stage
partner's breath, or having to descend stairs onstage distract you?
Figure it out.) More important, you must then know how to deal
with this distraction when it occurs during your performance.
One of the better solutions is this: Always have some "What ifs?"
prepared. The more quickly you deal with the distraction, the
better.

Speaking from the Recital Platform

These days the strongest concern among recital givers and recital
promoters is the issue of accessibility. Because the song recital is
perceived as elitist and rather stern, getting an audience, especially a younger one, is often difficult. One of easiest ways to
break down those formal barriers between singer and audience is
for the artist to speak from the stage. Some people are dogmati-
cally opposed to any speaking; others may feel that talking about
your songs is a condescension on the part of the singer. There can
hardly be a rule; it resolves to a matter of taste. Naturally, your
speaking must *seem* spontaneous. If you prepare well, each of
your audiences will believe that you have made up your words at
that moment. Even as long ago as 1978, in the era of conservative
recital traditions, a New York newspaper declared that there is
more than one critical point of view with regard to speaking by
the performing artist and that most professional recitalists would
insist the audience is delighted to experience the personality and
charm of the artist as revealed through the spoken word. Since
that time, the incidence of major artists speaking spontaneously
and extemporaneously to the audience during a song recital has
increased tenfold.

Second Half/Second Act Letdown

Many singers report that they make silly mistakes at the beginning of the second half of the recital. Why? The second half of the program often contains slightly easier music; this presents a particular hazard. Suppose the first half has gone well in spite of its difficulty. During the intermission you have a feeling of justifiable satisfaction and a consequent natural relaxation of tensions. Without your being aware of it, relaxation turns into carelessness. You start the first song with a bit of lack of concentration; one careless mistake breeds a second, and panic ensues. To avert such a scenario, after a well-deserved rest at the beginning of the intermission reestablish your concentration as it was before the first half. Review your list.

At the beginning of the second half or the second act, try to create the mental mind-set of starting again. Treat each act or each song as a different performance, because it helps you to stay in the present. You cannot control what happened in the first or second half or act; you can only control what you have to do *now*. Your mental preparation should be on what you are about to do or are doing. It is wise to use the intermission as a time for mental and physical relaxation, if you need to do so, before you begin to recycle some of your preperformance routine for the next "performance." A few words about the second performance in a run: It does *not* have to be better than the first. Each performance is a separate entity. Try to think of starting again to build a new performance, not just top the last one.

After the Recital and the Staged Performance

Make sure that you evaluate your recital or staged performance. Learn from each so that each is better than the last, especially in a run of opera performances. Be assiduous about using your performance feedback sheets.

Further information:

1. On confidence in the presentation of self, see chapter 5, "The Self and Performance: You, the Person; You, the Performer."
2. On the pertinent performance skills, see chapters 6, 7, 8, 9, 10, 11, 12, and 13.
3. On practicing in the performance mode, see chapter 14, "The Coach's Place in Singers' Preperformance Work."
4. On refocusing in breaks and pauses, see chapter 4, "The Performance Cycle: Plans and Routines."
5. On development of imagery skills, see chapter 12, "Imagery in Performance."

6. On how to determine the meaning of each piece, see chapter 15, "Exploring and Planning 'Meaning' for Performance."
7. On "what if?" strategies, see chapter 4, "The Performance Cycle: Plans and Routines."
8. On how to do your recital without resorting to left-brain analysis, see chapter 1, "This Thing Called Performance."
9. On learning by rote, see chapter 13, "Memory."
10. On just singing, just performing, once onstage, see chapter 4, "The Performance Cycle: Plans and Routines."
11. On presentation of self, see chapter 14, "The Coach's Place in Singers' Preperformance Work."
12. On "what ifs?" (including a "what if" list), see chapter 4, "The Performance Cycle: Plans and Routines."
13. On distractions, see chapter 10, "Distractions."
14. On performance feedback (including performance feedback sheets), see chapter 4, "The Performance Cycle: Plans and Routines."

18 The Coach's and/or Accompanist's Place in Singers' Audition, Competition, and Performance Work

I just knew that my first Metropolitan Opera audition, scheduled for 6:00 P.M. on stage, would be shortened for lack of time in that scant half hour just before the crew began to ready the stage for that night's performance. I had agonized for weeks together with my manager, my teacher, my coaches, about what to sing in that short amount of time. We had finally agreed, and I was totally prepared to sing the two pieces we had decided upon. In the minutes just before we went out on stage my accompanist started to question whether we should stick to my decision or change the repertoire. My concentration, my confidence, and my feeling of well-being disappeared in an instant. I'll never know whether my lack of success that day was due to me and my abilities or to the upheaval that the pianist caused in my mental stability.

F.L. professional singer
in midcareer, 1994

Two Kinds of Accompanists

In public singing performances such as auditions, competitions, or recital work there are two possibilities with regard to the pianist: Either your coach is also your accompanist or your coach is not your accompanist. The first situation usually makes your work easier. The coach/accompanist is well aware of your musical habits and also your weaknesses. He or she will be able to aid your performance immeasurably by both anticipating the former and hiding the latter, when either action is necessary for the good of the performance. Neither your strengths nor your weaknesses will come as a surprise to the coach/accompanist. You can rely on a good coach's thorough knowledge of your skills.

On the other hand, if your coach is invaluable to you in many other ways but adds to your nervousness in performance, you must

241

then find a tactful method of using another pianist for public performance.

A pianist who helps you learn by his or her criticism during coaching sessions is separated by a vast chasm from a pianist who judges severely all aspects of your delivery during the performance. This issue presents a difficult transition for some coaches to make, as in coaching sessions you rely upon your coach as your teacher, while in performance the coach must be a supportive colleague. It is not only you but also your coach who must learn not to judge, evaluate, or think analytically about results during performance. The pianist also, whether he or she be your coach or your accompanist, must learn the skill of suspending judgment until later. Of course, it is probably impossible for your coach to turn off *all* evaluative listening, but this fact remains: It is not just counterproductive for the singer to sense that a verdict is being prepared during the performance; it is actually fatal. Performance, as reiterated so often in part III, must be *in the present*. The past and the future do not exist; there is no right or wrong; there is only the performance. For the good of your performance, you must be confident that your pianist or coach/accompanist believes this and will act accordingly.

If your accompanist is not your coach, then the ease of the collaboration depends upon the length of time the two of you have been working together. Only experience will tell you whether you can be compatible with this pianist. Take the time to find out whether the relationship is harmonious. Sometimes answering this question presents a dilemma in terms of tactfulness, so think ahead and plan for a trial period before embarking upon public performance with someone who may not be congenial or capable of meeting your needs. If, despite all your care, you end up in the unfortunate position of being accompanied by a pianist who is not properly supportive, then that very fact should form part of your preperformance planning.

Criteria for Judging Accompanist's Stability and Supportiveness

But regardless of whether your accompanist is your coach or not, what will be your criteria for judging his or her capacity for stability and support?

You have the right to feel utterly secure about your pianist's ability to execute the previously agreed upon musical and dramatic tactics during the audition. A great part of your peace of mind— and consequently your ability to perform well—depends upon the freedom from fretting about the parts of the performance that are controlled by the pianist.

Remember (not to make excuses but rather to set you to thinking clearly) that the pianist has the music in front of him or her, while *you* are singing from memory. Bear this in mind: As a singer you have more to remember than does any pianist (words *and* music *and* drama *and* vocal technique) and no written music on which to make notes that will refresh your memory during performance. While it is true that a strange piano is off-putting, the piano is always in reasonably good voice (if tuned and enjoying keys that function); *you* are not. Singing is perilous: A speck of dust inhaled, a blast from the air conditioner that stirs up allergic reactions—absolutely anything could be an irresistible distraction that shakes your concentration from the task at hand. At any one moment in a staged production a singer is balancing forty different psychological processes. Surely this indicates that in recital you are balancing at least twenty. If you attempt to enumerate the forty *or* the twenty, you may find that there are more than that number. The fact that few pianists have found it necessary to think about this issue (why should they, unless they intend to make accompanying their profession?) does not make it less true. On the other hand, you must keep in mind that pianists have two jobs—they must remember what *you* are going to do and must execute well their own part in addition.

At an audition, the basic and incontrovertible duty of the coach or accompanist (assuming competence at the piano) is to be supportive. You must accept the fact that you deserve unconditional support at this time. Either find a way to make this clear before the audition or suffer it through doing your best and find another accompanist later. An audition is no time for second-guessing choice of repertoire, for last-minute reminders or corrections, for interruptions to your concentration or any other part of the preparatory routine, or for any attitude other than confidence, empathy, and stability.

The same is true for your recital work. As soprano Maggie Teyte, a world-renowned recitalist, once said:

To memorize a recital of sixteen or twenty songs is a major feat of concentration, and if that is to be perfectly maintained, there must be complete accord between singer and pianist. Too late an attack or an entry that is ever so slightly too early can jar the singer out of his intense concentration and cause momentary forgetfulness of words or music, or both. . . . It takes many years of experience to learn to give and take in the making of music together. All good accompanists have to learn diplomacy.

Maggie Teyte,
Star on the Door (1958, p. 163)

Think clearly about the foregoing issues. You will find an Accompanist Criteria Sheet (chart #15) in appendix 1. If you determine that it could help you to clarify this issue, then take the time to fill out this questionnaire.

But perhaps it is *you* who have not made your performing ideals clear to your pianist colleague. What are your views? Express yourself. Neither the pianist nor the coach can read your mind. Let your accompanist know how you feel. See whether he or she agrees. You cannot lay the blame for a poor performance at the door of your accompanist if you haven't seen to it that you prepare together in an efficient manner. The efficacy of your joint preparation is your responsibility. Remember: It is your performance. You control whatever happens both in rehearsal and in performance.

There is nothing so rewarding as a fine partnership of equals sharing musical and performance ideals. In our imaginative view of this exemplary and successful ensemble partnership we are presupposing:

- Pianistic, linguistic, and musical skill on the pianist's part
- High musical, vocal, and linguistic standards on your part
- Sufficient rehearsal time
- Courteous behavior on both the singer's and pianist's part
- A concordance of spirit, musicality, and creativity.

Summary

Once you have come to understand as much as possible about all aspects of performance, then you and your accompanist will succeed together, because you will be in control. Yet in the moments of public performance you can triumph in your search for artistry as a singer only when accompanied by someone who understands and is sympathetic to the challenges peculiar to the art of singing.

Closing our summary is a direct quote from a very accomplished and responsible professional accompanist/coach:

Great accompanists will only be satisfied when you triumph; your success is their success. Don't settle for someone who merely goes through the motions and then expects to be paid! I personally feel that the reason there are so many "no-talent" fakers out there calling themselves accompanists is because singers don't know enough to demand better for themselves. In addition to teaching their students how to sing, maybe voice teachers could also teach them what to look for in an accompanist.

P. O'D.

19 Fear in Performance

Mental toughness almost guarantees a good performance, and *lack of fear* is one of the essential elements of mental toughness. Peak performance cannot exist alongside fear. But, as we all know, experiencing fear during our performances is very common for most, if not all, of us at some time. Yet Franklin D. Roosevelt's statement: "The only thing we have to fear is fear itself" is not only inspiring but also absolutely accurate. You *must* learn how to deal with your fears and use them in a positive manner, because fear is one of the biggest obstacles to successful performing.

Fear takes on a different aspect for each individual. Because all types of performance are public, your fear is also public. Your fear during an audition, competition, or performance is apparent. No one mistakes it for anything other than fear. Moreover, when you suffer from fear in a performance, there is nowhere for you to go and nowhere to hide. You are up there for all the world to see!

Therefore, it's important that you understand how fear affects you—if it does—and how you can deal with it, how you can overcome it. If you want to push the boundaries of your performance, tap into your entire potential, achieve the goals that you have set, then it is important to understand performance fears and deal with them. If, however, you are one of those fortunate performers who have conquered performance fears, you need not read further.

You Are Not Alone

The first comforting thing to say about fear is that you are not alone. Most people have been afraid at some time before or during their performances, and many continue to be fearful. (Throughout a long career in international opera companies, one twentieth-century singer regularly vomited in the wings before each entrance.) Indeed, it would be unusual to meet anyone who can say with deep conviction that he/she has never been fearful in a performance situation.

Fear creeps in surreptitiously. Even after evaluating all facets of a poor performance, you may conclude that some kind of fear was responsible. Another important point to be made about fear is this: Even though you can recognize an overall major fear (for example, being afraid to sing in front of audition panels), that may hide a much more subtle and insidious fear (rejection, for example), which you then re-interpret as indicative of poor self-esteem and lack of self-worth.

According to performance consultant Tom Kubistant (1986, pp. 65–80), there are some common sources of fear that affect all performers. They are:

- Fear of failure or success
- Fear of rejection
- Fear of change
- Fear of discomfort
- Fear of the (un)known.

Only the first three of these will be discussed in this chapter, since they appear to be the major issues for singers.

Fear of Failure or Success

Fear of Failure

One of the greatest fears a singer has to deal with is fear of failure. Some of this fear may have begun in your youth, when you were especially afraid of letting down your parents, friends, and teachers who expected much of you. The more you performed, the greater were the pressures to succeed and the more numerous were the possibilities of failure. This may have caused you to regard any failure as a failure of your self-esteem and self-worth also. That is, if you appear to fail in your performance, you may believe that you are also a failure as a person. Once such a cycle begins, you then begin to think about what will happen to you if you fail and all the reasons why the performance will fail: arriving late for your audition, having an argument with your partner before leaving home, a poor accompanist, being disliked by the auditioning panel, bad weather, forgetting the words, or even not wearing the right shoes! The fear of failure makes you envisage paralysis, rejection, embarrassment, the poor assessment of your talent being handed down by others, and letting down your mother, father, voice teacher, coach, and the audience, not to mention the rest of the cast. If you are in this type of cycle, you could be talking yourself into failure before it happens.

The more you focus on your fears and the resulting failure, the more you guarantee failure. The more you think about failure, the greater the chance of becoming anxious and tense, forgetting the words, and giving a poor performance. You may be tempted to give a "careful" performance; that is, just in case you might fail, you won't take the chance of giving everything you can. This kind of thinking may lead to frustration, anger, and further disappointments. The secret is to try to avoid this cycle, not only because of the harm it does, but also because you deserve better.

Fear of Success

The fear of success and the fear of failure are closely related, though fear of success may be more difficult to cope with. This is because when you are successful you apply pressure to yourself, feeling that you must perform successfully and well *all the time*. You may also feel that you have to perform *better* each time. Consequently, each success is transformed into the imposition of an onerous responsibility to succeed again and again. Those who fear success often try to "run away from their destiny." The major coping strategy used is one of sabotage. You may sabotage your own performance (although subconsciously) so that you will not succeed. You arrive late on purpose; you don't prepare thoroughly; you don't check the schedule; you feign illness; you don't learn your lines. You enjoy saying, "I told you I couldn't do it." Most of all, you really wish to be ordinary, one of the pack, rather than a star. In athletics such a person may actually become permanently injured so that playing is an impossibility. As Kubistant says, "They perceive comfort and acceptance in mediocrity, in that they feel they will not stand out from the crowd so much" (1986, p. 68).

How to Deal with Fear of Failure and Fear of Success

Both kinds of fear can be exceedingly harmful to you both as a performer and as a person. Both forms can have a devastating effect on your performance. They *can* be dealt with, but you should consciously *want* to effect the change.

If you have a problem with fear of failure and/or success, try the following suggestions:

1. Make sure that your goal-setting skills are good as well as efficient and that you consistently set appropriate goals in voice lessons, coachings, your own practice, and performance.

2. Focus on the *process* of the performance itself, rather than the *outcome* of the performance (winning or losing). Having the correct focus and appropriate goals will make you motivated rather than frightened. In this way you will learn that success is not frightening, but positive and productive.

3. Give yourself permission to focus on your *performance* and the *tasks* that you set yourself. Don't fight it; the outcome is not important. Built into the audition system is the fact that some of you will not succeed, some of you will be rejected, simply because not everyone can get the role. Yes, you will be judged, evaluated, and rated alongside other singers. Yes, performance can very often be lonely. Yes, it can be frightening and you can feel unprotected. These facts, sad as they are, represent something you must get used to. They will not go away. They will not change. But you can still be successful.

Fear of Rejection

Nobody enjoys being rejected, but it is important that you do not view your failure as a rejection. Mistakes do happen when you try to push the boundaries of your performance. That's the challenge. If you view such occurrences as threats, then you may be less likely to extend yourself, and your performances might become worse.

If performing becomes your whole life and your whole being, the rejection that follows an audition will be perceived as a lack of self-worth. You may view yourself as a bad singer and worthless at what you do. Perceived rejection is thus blown up out of proportion.

If you believe that you fear rejection, try some of the following techniques:

1. Try to view the performance as a challenge, rather than a threat.
2. Learn to focus on what you *can* do, on your *known* strengths.
3. Tell yourself that if you are not successful in this audition it is not a rejection and it will not make you a worse person. It simply means that on this occasion you didn't fit the bill for that audition, and that's OK.
4. Evaluate your performances objectively rather than emotionally. Learn from the mistakes and push the performance further the next time. Mistakes do not make you a failure.
5. Keep your whole life in balance. Remember that your performance is not everything in your life.

6. Remember that not being selected for the role, not winning the competition, does not mean that you are a failure as a person. It is simply the nature of performance, a minor setback, nothing more.

Fear of Change

All change involves some doubt. If you fear change, then perhaps you find the uncertainty difficult to control or the risk too much for you. You may lose the competition; you may not be accepted for the summer program—for some people this is too much to accept. It's much easier for you to stay within your little secure world, that "warm, cozy rut" you get yourself into. The unknown can be threatening and frightening, rather than exciting and wonderful, for some of you.

It may be that you have clung far too long to routines or formulas that have worked for you in the past. Even though they have been successful in the past, they still need reviewing and changing. You could be holding onto old beliefs simply because you cherish the familiar or because you feel secure within that stability. About this Kubistant says: "This mind-set is like holding on to a rock in the middle of a river. It may not be the best place in the world, but at least it represents some form of security, stability and familiarity. The problem with this strategy is that eventually other debris starts to snag on you, drag you down even farther, and make it impossible to ever let go" (1986, p. 72).

Change is a necessary part of improving your performance and of tapping all your potential for performing. When you have self-confidence, you will find it easier to deal with change. It does take awareness, courage, and a lot of trust in yourself to make the necessary changes. But if you do, you will begin to see other new, exciting alternatives ahead of you. Look for a new way forward.

If you think you fear change, try the following suggestions:

1. Develop your singing strengths and know what they are.
2. Always look for the opportunity to extend the boundaries of your performance. Never be satisfied with what you've got; it can always be better.
3. View change not as frightening but as something exciting. Even if you discover that you are going up the wrong channel, at least you have energy that you can convert into the appropriate things for yourself.
4. Have patience. Change takes time, and it takes time to get accustomed to the change. But if you do the right things, sooner or later everything will begin to go right.

5. Don't be afraid to take a risk. If you know what you are good at in your performing, then you will not be a failure.

Summary

TEACHING
POINT
See #16,
Appendix 2

Being afraid is normal, but there are things you can do about it without it destroying your performance. Some have been outlined in this chapter. Begin by trying to know what your own fears are. Learn about them. Get to know them. Then think carefully about the categories outlined here. Use them to strip away the extraneous layers with which you have camouflaged your fears. When one fear is present, it is not uncommon to find others lurking about.

While fear does limit you and your performance, it is also a source of energy. Your goal is not to rid yourself of that energy, but rather to reuse it in a positive way for the control over your performance. Do not allow the fear to control you.

You work very hard and make every effort to do well, so develop your knowledge about fear. Seek out the knowledge; don't shrink from it; apply it. Don't confuse effort with skill. Make mistakes. Learn from them and push even harder for excellence. You deserve to be outstanding at what you do. You can deal with your fears if you choose to.

Further information:

1. On poor self-esteem and lack of self-worth, see chapter 5, "The Self and Performance: You, the Person; You, the Performer."
2. On making sure that your goal-setting skills are good, see chapter 7, "Setting Goals."
3. On focusing on the process of the performance, see chapter 7, "Setting Goals."
4. On focusing on your performance and the tasks you set, see chapter 9, "The Art of Concentrating."
5. On keeping your whole life in balance, see chapter 5, "The Self and Performance: You, the Person; You, the Performer."

IV POSTPERFORMANCE

So now it's over. The performance came and went, very quickly. Was it really worth all the time, effort, and money lavished on it? Of course it was, but the job is not over. Because singers extend themselves during their performances, they must take time out to rest, recuperate, and make the most of the postperformance period for it doesn't last long. Performance demands progression. There is more work to be done. The cycle of this particular performance is not complete yet.

All performances have outcomes, and they are very important, as is the process that brought the performance to an outcome. Some of the outcomes will have been out of the singer's control, for example, the opinions of the critics. But the singer was in control during the performance, and his/her behavior needs an objective analysis and evaluation, to which both the outcome and the process contribute. Both outcome and process need careful thought so as to improve the next performance. Postperformance evaluations form the platform for future improvement. What was done well? How did the preparation go? Where was the focus during the actual performance? How was the singer? What has he/she learned about the self? These answers are the keys to future excellence.

This is not the time for singers to be hard on themselves. It is the time for them to pay themselves compliments for what they did well, to spoil themselves, to learn from experience, and to prepare to go on to bigger and better things next time. If the cycle of performance is completed thoroughly, thoughtfully, and positively, then there is little chance of becoming stale or injured/ill. The completion of this performance cycle should always be viewed as positive and a job well done. The evaluation brings with it a new excitement, more dedication, more challenges, and a knowledge about the personal and performing self. Because singers continue to strive for excellence in all areas of their performance, no one knows how far they will push their boundaries. With the right work, dedication, and talent, they will go far. They aspire; they continue to persevere against many odds. Above all, they have courage to break into and explore their personal boundaries within the full cycle of performance.

What might initially appear to be an end is probably a new beginning, a new means to further goals and achievements. All we have to do is recalibrate our minds to always look for these new beginnings. . . . Performing is the arena in which to show just how far we can take ourselves.

Tom Kubistant,
Performing Your Best

20 Postperformance Management

All performances have an outcome: successful or unsuccessful, a laudable achievement or a stressful experience.

It is important to plan your performances, and most of you will do this, even if just in a general way, such as what to do *before* your performance and what to do *during* your performance. However, the plan for the period *after* the performance, called postperformance, is just as important as the other two plans. At the conclusion of your performance, you will need to devise and utilize some way to relieve the excess emotion caused by performing. The postperformance evaluation phase is critical and should be ongoing. Psychological research (Maslach, 1982; Morgan, 1984) says that performers give themselves a better chance of repeating a good performance or enhancing a poor performance when they are able to evaluate it in an objective manner. After every performance, take time to reflect upon what happened before and during the performance. This is just as important for successful as for unsuccessful performances. A performance is usually unsuccessful in the *head* before the body fails.

Case Study: Postperformance Tension and Emotion

R.P. is a professional singer who, after a break in her career, made a decision to return to musical life.

Following a highly successful tour of Italy in July/August 1993, with recital and orchestral appearances and an especially inspiring last performance, I returned to New York on cloud nine and full of euphoria. Having

253

worked so hard to reach a higher level both technically and in performance, and also having had excellent feedback, I did not want to lose my
momentum and certainly didn't want to "give up" the feeling of euphoria. I thought that in order to keep all the lessons I had learned, I should
try to prolong the performance high in order to use that same energy to
motivate myself.

I gave myself two days to celebrate—I bought five pairs of beautiful
shoes, saw all my friends I had made on the tour, went to a party. Back in
New York, I thought I was just jet-lagged, so I rested a few days. But I
found it extremely difficult to get back my enthusiasm. I spoke about my
wonderful tour in hopes of recapturing the energy so I could use it to
move forward, but that didn't help. By the time I got to my first class I
could barely sing a Poulenc song. I kept digging myself deeper into a
hole, and I was living in the slough of despair. Where was my enthusiasm? Where had all my energy gone?

It took me at least six months before I felt like my old self, able to set
short-term goals and carry out behaviors which were in line with my
middle and long-term objectives.

The preceding case study presents an outline of what is called
postperformance syndrome. Although it took this particular singer
quite a long period to convalesce, the recovery time for singers can
vary greatly. The key is to become aware of your own habits and
behavior following your performances (including auditions). Try to
learn how to deal with postperformance tension and emotion, especially if you want to remain motivated and confident in your forthcoming performances. There is evidence to suggest a strong relationship between postperformance tension and the quality of future
performances; that is, the performer who copes well with the
postperformance tension gives him/herself a better chance of doing
equally well or better in future performances (Henschen, 1986).

Postperformance blues, anger, hilarity, depression, and elation
are all experienced by singers whether the performance was successful or not. Following are the three main emotions experienced
during postperformance: elation, depression, and aggression (which
often manifests itself either as anger with yourself or anger and
aggression toward other people). You can experience any of these
emotions in any order or in any depth. For example, a wonderful
performance can leave you with great elation, yet within hours or
days you can be depressed. You may be encountering a lack of
drive and motivation that makes you lethargic, not really wanting
to do anything at all. Indeed, there are occasions following performances when you might deliberately avoid doing anything linked
to singing. Some of you will suffer all three emotions in your postperformance period.

If you leave any one of these emotions unresolved for any length of time, a state of genuine staleness could be the result. Any of these emotions tends to drain you of all accessible energy. How do you deal with this syndrome and prevent yourself from becoming stale in forthcoming performances?

How to Deal with the Postperformance Syndrome

The first thing that you should do is evaluate your performance. Even if you feel that you deal well with all your emotions following performance, you should still evaluate it in detail. Only if you have planned your preperformance and the performance in detail will you be able to evaluate what you have done. Completing the basic performance plan without making an objective evaluation afterward cannot lead to the desired improvements.

Initially you should give yourself time to recover from your performance. There is no advantage whatsoever to be gained from an evaluation carried out while you are still in a performance-induced emotional state. It is important that the evaluation be done *after* the emotional feelings attached to the performance have decreased. Only then should you reflect upon what happened before, within, and after the performance. This is the process:

1. Get out your preperformance and performance plans. Beginning with the preperformance plan, go over the details and check what was successful and what may need changing as a result of the performance.

   Was my preperformance warm-up efficient?
   Did it do what it was supposed to do?
   Was I as focused as I should have been?
   Was I focused on the right things?
   Was my preperformance routine done in enough detail?
   Do I need to spend more attention on my physical self during this time?
   Is the routine too long?
   Do I have the right balance of technical, mental, and physical in my warm-up?
   What specific things helped me?
   What things need further improvement? And so on.

2. Go through the same process with your performance plans. Ask yourself the same kind of questions, addressing them in detail because the smallest detail could make all the difference to your next performance.

If for some reason your performance was not as good as you think it should have been, then ask yourself some of the following questions:

What happened to make my performance fall apart?
When did it begin?
Why did this happen at that particular point?
Where was my focus when this happened?

Once you have completed this process, then you should be able to change, adapt, and improve your performance plans.

The Voice Teacher and Coach in Postperformance Evaluation

Part of the evaluation process is clear, objective discussions with your voice teacher and/or coach. Your voice teacher may also help you to gauge the timing of this evaluation. You can both learn lessons from any performance. Critique successes as well as failures together, if you can. *It is important to be objective about the imperfections in a good performance and the perfections in a poor one.*

Ideally, if you can also include some objective evaluations from your voice teacher and coach, this will enable you to have a much more "rounded" view of your performance. Voice teachers and coaches are very busy people, but any evaluation that includes their feedback, if at all possible, can only be to your advantage when planning for future performances. After all, you will only be as good as the joint strengths and qualities of all three of you—just the same as being on a team.

TEACHING
POINT
See #17,
appendix 2

Let's use the Super Bowl 1997 winners, the Green Bay Packers, as an example (more people, but the same principle). The Packers' successful team included Head Coach Mike Holmgren, plus the offensive and defensive coaches and a line and backfield coach, as well as the players. Together they had a game strategy, and individually they each had individual strengths and qualities that they brought to the game. There are approximately thirty-three men in a squad, only eleven men from each team on the field at any one time. Together they act as a unit and each individual brings his own personal strengths to the team. The evaluation of this performance (the Super Bowl game) will have included individual coaches' recommendations based on the team's strengths and the overall game strategy, plus the individual input from each player and the players' synergy. "Did it work?" "What could we have done better?" "What should we pay more attention to in the future?" These questions and their answers are all part of the true evaluation of the game—not just how the team played.

This is similar to how your vocal performance functions and how it should be evaluated, when possible. All evaluations should be set against your performance. This way you will get a true picture of what went on and how to improve.

Managing Postperformance Disappointment

If at any time you are suffering from a postperformance disappointment, try to use the following questions for a debate with yourself.

What Do I Do If Things Do Not Turn Out As I Want Them To?

However clear your objectives and specific your action plans, however much time and energy you invest, there are always some factors out of your control that could result in you not getting what
you want. As comedian Sam Levinson put it, "When I finally got
the means to an end, they put the ends further apart."

Have I Tried All the Available Strategies for Getting What I Want?

Whenever you are in a situation that you wish to change, there are
always four basic strategies for managing that situation, as illus-
trated in figure 20-1.

Strategies for Managing Postperformance Disappointment

Strategy 1. Work for Change. The first strategy is often that of
trying to change the situation to make it more as you want it to
be. If you have tried to make changes but to no avail, you are left
with the other three options.

Strategy 2. Leave. You exit from the situation, job, relationship,
or problem.

Strategy 3. Change Yourself. Perhaps if you changed your ambi-
tions, attitude, behavior, lifestyle, et cetera, your situation would
improve.

Strategy 4. Live with It. This means much more than simply
"putting up with it." It requires a conscious strategy (yet another plan!) so that you can minimize the undesirable aspects
of the situation and maximize the desirable ones. Examples

	LEAVE	
WORK FOR CHANGE		CHANGE YOURSELF
	LIVE WITH IT	

Figure 20-1. Strategies for managing postperformance disappointment.

might include: investing more energy in activities outside of your profession (if you are dissatisfied with the work), isolating yourself within a project in such a way that it reduces your contact with troublesome elements, or spending more time doing the things you enjoy and cutting down on time spent on other activities.

Do You Have a Plan B?

Always have a backup plan. If you don't get what you want, it sometimes means that your first action plan was not good enough. Either improve it or change it completely. The two areas to manage are: the emotional and the rational.

The Emotional

The emotional responses, for most people, will have to be dealt with first. This will usually involve:

1. Some way of getting rid of the bad feelings:

   crying
   shouting
   digging in the garden

2. Some appropriate support:

   someone to let off steam with   someone to listen to you
   someone to give you advice   someone to confront you
   someone to share troubles   someone to give you
     with   information
   someone to teach you   someone to do things for
     something   you
   someone to give you   someone to comfort you
     constructive feedback

The Rational

1. Reappraise your action plan.
2. If that does not work, reappraise your original objectives.
3. Ask why it didn't work.

   What was due to your influence?
   What was due to external influences?

4. Ask yourself what you can learn from the experience.

To maximize your chances of managing both sets of responses effectively:

1. Look after yourself physically

   stay fit
   know how to relax

2. Look after yourself mentally

   constructive self-talk
   an occasional treat

Time Out

When dealing with postperformance syndrome try to allow your-self a certain amount of time for recovery. This will vary from per-son to person. Look back over your performances and check how much time you usually take for relaxation. It can be one day, two days, or half a day. This time is very important for your recovery before starting the performance process once again. If your sched-ule allows you to do something completely different from singing, give yourself permission to take time out. Play golf; read a novel; go shopping; visit friends and relatives; go out and have lunch; invite someone for coffee. Above all, have fun. Recharging the bat-teries is very important. No matter how short a time you give your-self, allow it to happen. The body and mind need the change.

This may not be possible, of course, if you are doing a series of performances, either one or two evenings in a row or a run of per-formances two days apart for two weeks. In these circumstances, it is still important to take some time for rest and relaxation, doing something you enjoy that's very different from your singing. Once again, it requires planning. Look at the schedule of performances and note where your free time is and how long it is. Then you can plan how you will use the time. One soprano who was gone from the United States for eight weeks, having traveled to Europe to sing in performances at two different opera houses, had the most suc-cessful tour ever because she used her free time well. She did not let a vacation from constant practicing make her feel guilty. She visited art galleries, went for long walks, slept, watched television, visited friends, and invited other friends to her apartment for cof-fee. When it was time for her to begin preparing for the next perfor-mance, she simply used her preperformance routine once again to start the performance cycle.

Everyone requires time out. Don't fool yourself by assuming that you need to get on to the next practice, voice lesson, or research as soon as possible after the last performance. Even if the time is only one hour, use it wisely. Switch off without guilt. You will feel much better when you begin again.

Postperformance Planning

Another important thing to do following your performance is make sure you always have something *new* to do in your singing. You may not always have another audition planned immediately, nor another imminent stage performance, but there will be plenty of work that you can plan to do. Researching the history of a new role, learning a new part, adjusting your performance programs, setting up appointments with managers, conductors, or your fitness guru, and starting to attend a certain workshop series are all examples of things that can be done.

The process of planning what to do next with regard to your singing changes your focus so that you will not be tempted to cling to the emotions that actually belong to the last performance, wonderful as it may have been. Those emotions belong to that performance, and that is where they should stay. *Gloating indefinitely over a successful performance or succumbing to a prolonged depression over a poor performance can only damage your mental approach to what happens next.* Long-standing emotions may drain you of vital mental and physical energy and lead only to frustration in the end. The performance is gone. You have evaluated it, learned from it, and adjusted your plans. It may have been wonderful while it lasted, but it is now part of the past. This is a new performance cycle, a time to set new goals and decide how those goals should be met.

Your singing should not be pure drudgery and hard toil, but if you *believe* it should be, then there is every chance that you will become bored and stale. Remember to have fun.

Summary

Performers experience one of three emotions following performance: elation, depression, or aggression. Become aware of *your* pattern.

Allow your emotions to subside before commencing the review stage.

Evaluate your performance in an objective manner some time following the performance.

If at all possible, talk objectively to your voice teacher and coach about the performance for a more total view of what happened.

Following the performance, allow yourself some time, no matter how short, for rest, relaxation, and fun.

Postperformance time should be planned.

Leave the emotion elicited by the performance *with* the
performance. Do not be tempted to carry that emotion
forward into the next stage.

Have fun. Your performance and the preparation for it are
meant to be enjoyable, not drudgery.

Always have the next project ready to go to for the time
when you have finished evaluating and recovering.

Further information:

1. On evaluating performances, see chapter 4, "The Performance
Cycle: Plans and Routines."
2. On considering some appropriate support, see "Support Networks Sheet" (chart #17), found in appendix 1.

21 Staleness and Burnout in Performers

Staleness occurs frequently in performance. There are very intense pressures placed on performers in all fields today, and singing is no exception. Often the people around you, your voice teacher, your coaches, your fitness guru, and even you yourself may have difficulty in recognizing and diagnosing what is happening, quite apart from preventing or treating it. Once the process of staleness begins and is left unchecked, it can result in what is known as burnout. Staleness and burnout are interrelated.

Staleness itself refers to an overall physical and emotional state that hinders your ability to put all your energy into your performances. Such things as practice, planning, and researching may all go by the board when you feel stale. This feeling of lethargy and lack of motivation to do what you need to do may be an early warning sign of burnout. However, the harmful route to burnout can be averted if you, or your voice teacher or coach, can recognize the staleness in your performance.

Burnout, on the other hand, is overwhelming. As described by psychologist H. J. Freudenberger and G. Richelson (quoted in Williams, 1986, p. 328): "Burnout's devastating states of physical, mental, and emotional exhaustion result in the development of negative self-concepts; negative attitudes toward work, life, and other people; and a loss of idealism, energy and purpose." This state is frequently brought on by tenacious dedication to your goals although their achievement is perhaps outside the realms of reality. It is easy to see why this condition affects performers of all kinds, particularly people who are motivated to very high standards. Such performers tend to be idealistic, unremittingly seeking perfection. Burnout is the result of striving endlessly toward

263

your goal without reward and without achieving what you really want to achieve.

Periods of staleness, which can result in a slump in your performance, tend to occur when you fail to perform as consistently as usual at the same time that there appears to be no physical or technical reason for such a drop. The real culprit could be your mental perception of what is occurring. You may be performing your vocal and musical skills correctly and well, and yet the outcome never ever feels quite right. Your persistent worry about the quality of your performance may only prolong the slump and the staleness in your performance. If this condition continues, burnout could be the eventual result.

Characteristics and Behaviors That Lead to Burnout

P. A. Shank (1983), in his work on burnout, identified three characteristics and behaviors that lead to burnout in certain people:

1. *Perfectionism.* Perfectionists seem to be at risk simply because they tend to be overachievers. They set very high standards for themselves and also for the significant people around them. They spend more time and effort than is necessary on any one task, simply trying to be perfect.
2. *Being "other"-oriented.* These persons have a strong need to be admired and liked by others and can be very sensitive to any criticism that comes their way. They are unselfish with everybody but themselves. They never give themselves a break, but they drive and drive until the task is done to their satisfaction, which is a rare occurrence!
3. *Lack of assertive interpersonal skills.* Saying no is very difficult for these persons. Even though it puts them under even more pressure, they will do what is requested rather than beg off for lack of time. They also feel guilty about expressing emotions such as anger or saying anything negative to other people.

Factors That Contribute to Staleness and Burnout

If at any time you or your voice teacher suspects that staleness may be occurring, there are physical, psychological, and environmental indications that you can look for. There may be one or two signs or any combination of them. Initially, the key is to recognize that something may be wrong, and the following lists will help you with that. However, it is also important to know whether or not you need to seek further professional help for any one or combination of your symptoms. Indicators that may account for staleness and burnout in performance are as follows.

Physical Indicators

headaches	minor aches and pains	chronic fatigue
stomach upsets	eating disorders	weight loss
impaired breathing	high resting heart rate	bowel disorders
high systolic blood pressure		

Psychological Indicators

continuous worry	sleep disturbances	anxiety
lack of motivation	emotional imbalance	boredom
lack of energy	irritability	depression
apathy	anger and hostility	confusion
low self-confidence		

Your voice teacher or coach can help to recognize this syndrome. If you show any combination of the characteristics listed previously, you should consider the possibility that staleness is the cause. While the psychological signs may appear first, they could also be difficult to detect and more difficult to deal with than the physical signs. One of the key indicators to look for is mood swings. If you find your moods swinging dramatically for no apparent reason, these mood swings being accompanied by some of the physical signs (which are easier to detect), then staleness may be a reason. Try to recognize the early signs associated with staleness before it establishes itself firmly. Dealing with staleness can be a time-consuming job. Prevention is the answer.

Environmental Conditions

The environments in which you live and/or work can be very stressful and can add to the syndrome of staleness and burnout. If you live in poor conditions because you cannot afford better or if you have a difficult and demanding day job, this also adds to your stress. Traveling; packing and unpacking; noise: too many people in a hustling, bustling city; dark, oppressive, small, and claustrophobic studios; cigarette smoke—all these are environmental factors that can also lead to stress and add to the staleness.

Singers are really bound by a catch-22 situation. They need money to survive and to support their basic needs: a place to live, food to eat, money to pay for their lessons, et cetera. Yet the vital energy expended on their daily work, set against the requirements for singing and performance, can contribute to a staleness in performance.

♪
TEACHING
POINT
See #18,
appendix 2
In the performance venue the environmental issues will include size of the room, presence of others, handling of props, assuring ease of movement, and breathing in the stage clothing. If you are interested in pursuing this aspect of your performance, an exercise sheet, chart #16, "Causes of Staleness in Performance," has been provided in appendix 1.

Prevention Is the Key

Voice teachers and coaches can help avert staleness in their singers. There should be a planned program that attends to the following factors:

1. *The length of the season.* Singing almost the year round can hurt you as a performer. Don't ignore or avoid the issue of time constraints placed upon you by such a year. Your day-to-day life often includes working every day of the year to improve your skills while fitting in performances as well. This is not conducive to good, high-level, consistent performance. Plan your year carefully. Take breaks!

   One very renowned tenor of the international circuit *began* to plan his professional year with this thought in mind even before he was in such demand. His manager had instructions never to book him during the month of July, which he planned to spend with his family. After ten years in the spotlight, his personal rule has never been abrogated to this day, no matter the magnificence of the engagement offer. The tenor continues to be the toast of the music world and in fine fettle, vocally as well as physically. He rarely cancels, and he enjoys a well-balanced life.

2. *The monotony of practice and training.* There are times when your practice becomes monotonous and lacks stimulation. You have simply lost the joy of singing. There is something wrong with practice that has become a drudgery. More is not necessarily better. Motor learning research (and singing is a fine motor skill) disproves the axiom that the more you do, the better you become. It would be much more valuable to have fewer, shorter, sharper sessions. If you persist in working hour after hour, then you accept the risk that staleness will be the outcome.

3. *Lack of positive reinforcement, abuse from those in authority (conductors, directors, and others), nowhere to practice, unreasonable rules.* All these elements interact

with each other to cause you to feel out of control. Suddenly your performance doesn't belong to you but to all these other people around you. Often you may feel that it is a hopeless situation. This means that you will tend to go through the motions and not enjoy what you are doing, both of which could be characteristics of staleness. The amount of stress involved in performance makes it important for you to feel some level of success. If you are constantly put down, closed in by yourself and others, then staleness may be your fate. You, your voice teacher, and your coach can help to prevent this condition by:

- *Planning your year carefully.* Don't be tempted to work all the time. This is especially tempting in a profession like singing, where jobs are hard to come by. You may not work again for nine months, but you should still take care.
- *Making sure that you plan some time away from singing, practice, and anything to do with it.* Have fun and enjoy yourself. Make these time-outs an integral part of your planning for the year, no matter how you do it.
- *Making sure that you get a choice in what you do as a performer.* You have the right to make decisions for yourself or at least share in the decision making with the voice teacher and coach. This will heighten your commitment.
- *Being in control.* Staleness and burnout result from conditions that make you feel out of control in your performance or that you have no control over what is happening to you. It is essential to believe that you have, at the very least, some control over your destiny. Try to seek out environments that permit you to do this.
- *Adding variety to your practice sessions.* Try to vary your sessions so that you incorporate vocal, physical, and mental practice periods into the session. This will break up the monotony and allow you to recover from each of the types of practice (without wasting your valuable practice time) before going on to another. In addition, take some time during your vocal practice to work at some form of body relaxation or use imagery to practice your piece or parts of your music. You will return to your work refreshed, and the quality of your work will be enhanced.

If you begin to recognize symptoms of staleness or burnout, but you believe that you can cope without professional help, there are a few ways to help yourself. However, be aware that all cases are different and should be dealt with on an individual basis.

Begin by psychologically reprogramming: Check the year's plans and try to determine which things may be contributing to the staleness.

There are only two courses of action open to you:

1. Remove yourself from activity altogether for a certain length of time. This may not be possible for you, in which case only the second course of action (number 2) remains.
2. Devise a program to help yourself stem the staleness and get yourself back on course.

Try some of the suggestions that follow. Don't give up at the first hurdle. If one combination doesn't work, then try another.

- *Go back and reestablish your goals for performances and for lessons and coachings.* Make these goals exciting, very short-term, day-by-day. If you can't manage that, do it half a day at a time. Give yourself rewards!
- *Really learn how to relax.* Use many different kinds of methods to help you. A text recommended to further your knowledge is *The Relaxation and Stress Reduction Workbook*, by M. Davis, M. McKay, and H. Eshelman (1983).
- *Use positive self-talk to help you return to normal.* Try not to focus on your mistakes or on what *not* to do, both of which are so easy to do at a time like this.
- *Use some imagery to lessen your apathy and increase your motivation.* Imagery can be a great asset when staleness has set in. Try to use all your senses. Here are some examples of imagery exercises for you to use when dealing with staleness.

Exercise 1

Close your eyes. Become aware of the tension in your body; focus on it. Give it a color—red, perhaps. Now become aware of the feeling of relaxation. Focus on that; give it a color—perhaps pale gold. Now try to make the whole body turn from red to pale gold. Work first on parts of the body and then on the whole.

Exercise 2

Go back to your Quiet Place. Enjoy the feelings of freedom, joy, and happiness that the Quiet Place gives you.

Exercise 3

Put on a headset; close your eyes. Listen to your favorite music. Indulge yourself in the music. Let it flow through you. Concentrate on how good you feel. Ignore any negative thoughts that try to invade. Relax.

Summary

The issue of staleness and burnout is a complicated one. This chapter gives you an insight into the issue itself and into the important consequences of ignoring the warning signs. Become aware of the symptoms so that you can recognize them in yourself and in others. The earlier you detect warning signs of staleness or burnout, the better chance you have of dealing with it successfully, either alone or by seeking professional help. Remember that it can be prevented before it happens.

It's a little like wrestling a gorilla. You don't quit when you're tired—you quit when the gorilla is tired.
Robert Strauss in Pat Riley's
The Winner Within

Further information:

1. On avoiding monotony in practice and training by setting short-term goals, see chapter 7, "Setting Goals."
2. On adding variety to your practice sessions by using mental as well as physical skills during practice, see chapter 4, "The Performance Cycle: Plans and Routines," and by using imagery, see chapter 12, "Imagery in Performance."
3. On devising a program to help stem staleness by reestablishing short-term goals, see chapter 7, "Setting Goals," really learning how to relax, see chapter 6, "Physical Well-Being and Relaxation," using positive self-talk, see chapter 8, "Developing Self-Confidence through Positive Thinking," and using imagery, see chapter 12, "Imagery in Performance."
4. On the Quiet Place exercise, see chapter 10, "Distractions."

22 Mental Rehabilitation Following Vocal Injury or Illness

As a singer, you will have always been concerned about your health and will have taken great care of yourself, wanting to achieve the highest you can while remaining injury- and illness-free. Because injury and illness can occur at any time—after performance, from overwork, from intense practice or inappropriate thinking—your ability to rehabilitate as quickly and efficiently as possible becomes an important part of your performance strategy.

Any rehabilitation requires that you be involved in both a physical and a mental program. You will, of course, have sought specialized treatment if the nature of the vocal injury demanded it, but the period of rehabilitation can be shortened considerably if you combine the physical program with a mental program. Your quick return to singing and your future performances will naturally depend upon the nature of the injury/illness, the quality of care by your otolaryngologist and your voice therapist, *the quality of your own mental rehabilitation program,* and your commitment to *adhere* to the program. Vocal injury/illness is not simply a physical loss; it can also cause emotional devastation.

Athletes are stronger, quicker, and presumably sturdier than the rest of us. They seem blessed. We forget that what they do is hard. We so rarely see them at their most vulnerable—in pain and out of commission. And we almost never hear, from their perspective, about those injuries that disrupt their existences and play havoc with their futures.

Harry Stein,
"Brought to His Knees"

Advantages of a Combined Physical and
Mental Rehabilitation Program

Most of you who are injured or ill can find for yourselves a very good physical rehabilitation program to follow. However, if you follow some simple guidelines, you can also plan your own mental rehabilitation program that *builds* on your physical program.

In sport, there is much evidence indicating that if an injured athlete has a mental rehabilitation program that builds onto his/her physical rehabilitation program and the athlete adheres to it, recovery is quicker and much more complete. Bear in mind that what a singer experiences mentally is not very different from what an athlete experiences mentally. Even "[in] the worlds of visual art and sport . . . the mental preparation and attitudes regarding the pursuit of excellence are quite similar" (quoted in Heil, 1993, p. 3). Because you want to return to singing at your preinjury/illness level of performance as soon as possible, your clinicians and therapists will encourage and motivate you to become rehabilitated as thoroughly as possible: "For all performers, medical care is governed by an overriding concern: expedient return to performance and practice. The vigorous use of restorative surgical approaches and rehabilitation for the performer, whether athlete, dancer, singer, or musician, is advocated"(quoted in Heil, 1993, p. 4).

In order to combine a physical and mental program you are encouraged to follow the ideas in this section so that you can learn to design your own mental rehabilitation program with the purpose of speeding up the recovery time. It is important to remember that rehabilitation can be divided into three areas:

1. Psychological rehabilitation
2. General physiological rehabilitation
3. Specific rehabilitation of the injured area

"Without appreciating the psychological aspects in injury and recovery, the injured athlete is unlikely to attain optimum healing, conditioning, and early return to function."

J. R. Steadman, "A Physician's Approach to the Psychology of Injury"

How Do Singers Respond Psychologically to Injury/Illness?

If you become injured or ill, you will commonly experience a sequence of predictable mental reactions. These reactions are similar to those outlined by Elisabeth Kübler-Ross (quoted in Heil, 1993, p. 36).

First, you actually *disbelieve, deny, and isolate yourself.* Aren't you struck by how often, even when you believe yourself to be injured or ill, you continue to sing? You do this because you simply don't *believe* it has happened: "I was doing so well, getting ready for the big day—my recital that I've been preparing for nine months—so it simply cannot be true! I'm not injured, not sick, just tired." Not only do you continue to deny the injury/illness, but you don't even tell anyone about it. This is a normal reaction but can be detrimental in the long run.

Second, you become *angry*: "Why me? How can this happen to me at this time? It's all your fault. If you hadn't made me go to that movie, I wouldn't have got this infection." And so on. Often there is a great anger directed at yourself and at others. Moreover, this is when you may feel your most isolated. You realize that there actually is an injury or illness that will keep you from doing what you do best, and you also become isolated from the people involved in your singing life: your voice teacher, your coach, and your fellow performers.

Third comes the *bargaining*: "Please don't let this happen to me. I will do anything you want me to do, but please don't let me miss this wonderful opportunity that I have worked so hard for." At such a time you will do almost anything, bargain with anyone, to restore yourself to your former fit self, in order to sing.

Fourth can be *depression*. Because of the sense of loss, you become even more desolate. Your normal way of life has been disrupted, and you no longer have the freedom to do as you really want. The length and depth of the feeling of depression tend to vary with the individual and the severity of the injury/illness.

Fifth come *acceptance* and *resignation*: "I am really injured/ill. I have to do something about it." Now you actually enter into the process of planning a successful return to practice and performance.

These steps do vary in time and in intensity and from individual to individual. The diagnostic assessment of your injury should go beyond the crucial objective evaluation and begin to identify what your injury means to you physically and socially as well as mentally. These factors should be viewed in conjunction with your personal needs and the role that singing plays in your life. For example, illness or injury may appear as a complete disaster to you; others may hail it as a break from the incessant practice regime. You may see it as a time to be courageous; others might welcome it because it frees them from the embarrassment and frustration of poor performance and lack of engagements. In sum, the more vital your singing is to you, the more important it is in your life, the more trauma an injury or illness may bring. Moreover, the greater the trauma you have suffered, the greater the likelihood that your treatment will be complicated.

Your Mental Recovery Programs

TEACHING
POINT
See #19,
appendix 2

It is recommended that while you are taking advantage of your specific medical therapy and your physical therapy you also engage in some form of mental recovery program, whether the injury is major or minor. The following suggestions form the outline of your program. However, you need not take advantage of all the ideas; select the ones that are important for you.

1. *Possibly putting a crisis intervention into operation.* Crisis intervention is a short-term intervention method used mainly when your coping capacities are overwhelmed, especially immediately after injury or the onset of your illness, when normal behavior is way off-beam. Crisis management will get you through the initial stages until you can better deal with your crisis and more long-term aid can be implemented. Crisis intervention models are similar to volunteer hot lines. Who are the main people to help you over the first stages of this crisis? Whom would you go to for reassurance? Who would help you attend to the most pressing and practical issues that need to be taken care of *now*, without worrying about the future? Immediately after the injury or the onset of your illness, you need people around you who are able to see all the problems in manageable parts rather than as one overwhelming tragedy. The sports axiom says: "The person who carries you off on the stretcher can be the most important person in the world to you, because the stretcher is very unnerving."

At this time your injury is a real crisis to you. Without the appropriate responses from other people your fears and high emotions can easily be set on the wrong track. Your pessimism or optimism, both of which can be extreme, should be accepted and worked with until you can reckon with either one in a more productive manner.

2. *An emotional well-being program.* Injury or illness produces great emotional stress and may result in trauma. The trauma and the threat to your professional future, together with the demands of your treatment and rehabilitation, result in the need for a program of emotional well-being.

It will be helpful if you have someone nonjudgmental with whom you can talk openly and honestly. You may want (and need) to say much about yourself and your future. This is, after all, your life we are talking about. Your therapist, if you have one, would be a good person, especially if he/she has some understanding of performance function. It is not only the injured part that needs attention. Emotional control will give you the ability to cope more efficiently with the injury or illness.

3. *Social support.* A vital part of any rehabilitation program is your social support. If, like most singers, you have identified totally with your voice and your singing, you will have put together most of your social circle through your singing activity. It may even be that the only friends you have are from the same field. When injury/illness occurs, many of these ties can be broken, and you may no longer see yourself as a singer. More important, others may not see you as a singer either, once you are absent from the "scene" for any length of time.

Your voice teacher and coaches will be helpful in this regard. They will be as reassuring as possible about the recovery of your vocal strengths, beauty, and skills. Try to keep in contact with your teacher and coach as much as possible. You should go to performances, visit the studio, listen to lessons, and discuss them if permissible. Such efforts will help restore you to some equilibrium and reestablish your emotional well-being.

You may find the Support Networks Sheet (chart #17 in appendix 1) helpful when dealing with the areas of your mental rehabilitation covered previously in points 1, 2, and 3.

4. *Viewing your injury from a positive stance.* It is reasonable to believe that your injury is unfortunate and extremely untimely. It is also permissible to feel anger, frustration, and, of course, disappointment. However, it is absurd to tell yourself that this injury is the end of everything you have worked for and that you are in a hopeless situation. An injury or an illness is not a sign of weakness in you.

Try to get as much information about your injury and the ensuing rehabilitation program as possible. Feeling anxious and wondering what is going on during your treatment make it more difficult for you to remain relaxed and positive. Being uncertain about the what and why of your treatment may keep you in denial longer than necessary: "Honest and accurate information coupled with hope helps athletes move into the acceptance phase" (quoted in Williams, 1986; p. 355). It is no different for a singer.

To sum up, here are some important things that can be done following injury/illness:

- Put a crisis intervention into action if needed
- Plan an emotional well-being program
- Become aware of your social support network
- View the illness or injury positively and objectively.

Specific Psychological Rehabilitation Skills

If you wish to plan a mental rehabilitation program for yourself, you will find the following mental skills helpful. Use one from each area of work to fulfill your own needs.

Physical Well-Being and Relaxation

Depending on the nature of your injury/illness, you should do everything possible to keep the other areas of your body fit and healthy. The whole body need not revert to poor physical condition. Enter into a very light physical program to begin with. Walking will do fine. If you are unable to go outdoors, try to do some form of exercise indoors. Relaxation is an important technique in promoting your rehabilitation. It will help to lower anxiety, worry, and depression. Use any of the relaxation methods outlined in this book, or use your own well-trusted methods.

Imagery

Imagery can influence your response to injury and illness. Use your imagery skills for the following:

1. *Mental rehearsal.* This form of imagery can be used early in the rehabilitation process. Focus on coping by using some of the procedures that follow or some that you are already doing. You may image yourself successfully doing the physical rehabilitation exercises that have been given to you. See yourself as free and relaxed and successful. Or include in your mental rehearsal any problems anticipated in your treatment. Both ways build your confidence as you do them and teach you to cope with various obstacles that may arise. For example:

   Sit and relax. Watch yourself leaving the doctor's office, if this is the situation for which you are preparing. Image yourself starting or continuing to do your rehabilitation with a *successful* outcome.
   After your visit to your physical therapist, image yourself doing your exercises *successfully*.
   Image yourself returning to very limited vocal practice. Do some of your favorite exercises in your imagination.
   Image yourself returning to full practicing, even performance.

2. *Healing imagery.* This form of imagery helps you to have a positive attitude relative to the healing process. It is be-

lieved to lead to a swifter and more complete healing process. For example:

> Imagine your blood surging through your veins like a flood, healing as it goes.
>
> Do some deep breathing as outlined in chapter 6, "Physical Well-Being and Relaxation." As you breathe in, imagine that you are breathing in your own healing power. As you inhale your own power, allow it to seep into every part of your injury/illness, then through the rest of your body.
>
> Image the injured/ill part of your body. If you don't know what this part looks like, try to get a picture of it in its *perfect* state, preferably in color. Focus on the injured part. See the injury in vivid detail, in color if possible. (This is why you need as much information as possible from the doctor and physical therapist.) Now image it as becoming healthy, *perfect* as the body part in the picture.
>
> Image the vocal cords, the throat, or whatever body part the illness or injury concerns. See the muscles working *perfectly*. See the cords as wonderful, powerful, healthy sinews, working beautifully.

(Although there is need for further research about the effectiveness of this kind of rehearsal, it appears to be a favorable approach for helping the healing process.)

3. *Emotive rehearsal.* This kind of imagery makes you feel safe and confident in yourself that your own rehabilitation is going well. It also helps to remind you of your positive emotions during performance. For example, image scenes that make you feel positive, self-confident, and proud of what you can do. It could be a very good performance from the past. It could be feeling very excited about your first voice lesson or performance following recovery.

Self-Confidence through Positive Self-Talk

What you say to yourself following an injury/illness will help you to be positive, to remain confident, and to control your thinking. You should be saying things like:

> These exercises are really working; they're doing the job they should be doing.
>
> I'm feeling better and stronger every day. I'm recovering well.
>
> I will be stronger than ever when I return to singing.

Goal Setting

Just as you do in your performance routines, you also need to set goals for your mental rehabilitation routine. Set a variety of goals in each area outlined previously, and keep them very simple, very precise. They will direct your focus and the intensity of your work. Take one step at a time, slowly at first. You will succeed.

Injuries and illness vary from very minor to major, but this distinction does not determine how short or easy your rehabilitation to full recovery will be. As the study by R. J. Rotella and S. T. Heyman declares, "Psychological rehabilitation is necessary to ensure a healthy future for athletes [singers], a future that must include more than just your playing [singing] career" (quoted in Williams, 1986, p. 358). Ideally, your rehabilitation should include both a mental and a physical process. You and the people within your support network should work to make this process as positive as possible and one in which *you* are actively involved. In appendix 1 you will find a Mental Rehabilitation Goal-Setting Sheet (chart #18) to help you.

Returning to Practice and Performance

You should return to performing and practicing only when you are pronounced both physically and mentally well, and in order for the return to singing to be without anxiety you should have utmost confidence in your recovery. Any worrying thoughts or feelings you have about returning to performing should be talked through to alleviate concerns on your part. If you have anxiety about re-injury, you should not recommence singing until you have grappled with the fears and concerns. Remember: the psychologist, the doctor, the teacher, the physical therapist, and you should *all* concur on this readiness to return to action.

> Mentally, there was an incredible amount of anguish and fear. The sheer action of getting up on that foot and turning around twice—sometimes I would just have to go in a corner because I would be choked up and close to tears. It's frustration. But you have to be intelligent about it, because if you pull back in fear from anything in dance, you're going to hurt yourself.
> G. Chryst, "Starting Over,"
> *Ballet News*

Case Study

S. M. is a brilliant musician with a dazzling vocal technique and a great deal of personal fortitude. After having been a professional singer for many years, she had a child. The circumstances of the birth changed her professional life forever. This is her story.

At first I couldn't believe that I had "ruptured my vocal cords." That wasn't one of the things mentioned when I went into labor with my son!

My voice was important to me because it was how I earned my living. In spite of my new son, I knew that if I was going to meet my singing commitments in the months ahead I had to get back to total vocal fitness. Because of the past work I had done in performance preparation, I already was aware that, in addition to my medical and physical therapy, I would need some mental rehabilitation to speed up the whole process to a full recovery.

My reaction to being "injured" (on top of giving birth) was one of real anger and frustration, and of course I was depressed. But I knew that it could all be worse. At least I wasn't required to sing now, so I had time to work.

My mental rehabilitation program was built onto my physical therapy so that they supported each other. I used imagery to see my cords as healthy and to watch myself performing well. I had to keep reminding myself that I was a successful singer and how that felt. I set myself goals daily. They were small, but I knew if I was going to achieve and remain motivated then this was the only way I could do it. (I also had my ongoing physical therapy which had to be completed.) I set goals about technical imagery, self-confidence, healing imagery, and—most important of all—my self-talk. This had to remain as positive as possible. Under the circumstances, it was not easy at all. I was tired; I was injured; I wondered if I would survive the whole process.

My support network was wonderful. I had spent some time putting the whole thing together, but I firmly believe that, without them, I may have floundered many times. Yes, they did relieve me of some of my emotional pressure. With a new baby to care for, I was desperate for some relief. Their help also allowed me to stick to my full rehabilitation program.

I recovered well and speedily, but was left with just a few further chronic problems of the vocal cords, caused by the physical trauma. I now enjoy my singing career as much as I can. I was grateful for the rehabilitation care I received and know that the physical and mental programs working together were very successful.

By the way, my son is just wonderful. He has no vocal problems!

Summary

Your rehabilitation process after injury or illness should include the following mental aspects, as well as the medical and physical treatment:

1. Understanding the process through which you go when you are first injured—denial, anger, bargaining, depression, and acceptance and resignation—and becoming aware of it.
2. Knowing the following important and helpful processes:
   - crisis intervention, if needed;
   - an emotional well-being program;
   - development of a social support network, not just for after injury;
   - viewing your injury from a positive stance.
3. The required key mental skills:
   - physical well-being and relaxation,
   - imagery,
   - self-confidence, through positive self-talk,
   - goal setting.

Further information:

See chapter 6, "Physical Well-Being and Relaxation," chapter 7, "Setting Goals," chapter 8, "Developing Self-Confidence through Positive Thinking," and chapter 12, "Imagery in Performance."

Afterword

Getting Your Act Together, the Ultimate Solution

> If you have worked hard enough to render yourself worthy of going to Olympia, if you have not been idle or ill-disciplined, then go with confidence; but those who have not trained in this fashion go where they will.
>
> Philostratus, Greek philosopher

This book has introduced you to many theories, skills, and techniques that, once learned, will improve and enhance your performance. You have gained an insight into how some singers have used a variety of these techniques and skills. It's not necessary for you to use *all* of the skills outlined. As an individual, you should be selective about those you need in order to develop and enhance your own performance. It is always a good idea to begin with the mental skill for which you seem to have the most urgent need. Armed with this self-awareness, you should develop a performance plan of your own, one designed to meet your own individual needs.

Remember that planning is like going on a journey and that your performance plan is your route map. Just as you would plan your journey from start to destination, which way to go and which roads and turnings to take, so you must create your own performance plan. It must map out the mental journey you have chosen to take to the destination of enhanced performance. Before you begin, there are some important points to remember.

- Design your plan to meet your individual needs, not those of anyone else.
- Make your plan appropriate to your level of performance and skill, and establish how important it is to you.
- Try to keep a record in a mental log of what progress you're making. You are much more likely to remember it if you write it down. In addition, you will need the information to readjust your plan, if necessary.
- Try to integrate your mental practice with your vocal practice and with everyday life as much as you can. This helps to keep you motivated and prevents boredom.

281

At this point your task—to go ahead and plan your journey—will involve you in four activities: designing, implementing, maintaining, and updating and evaluating. Your self-designed plan will require you to carry out several sessions of mental training a week. This will not take much of your time, but it must be done. If the training stops, your mental skills will lose their effectiveness. (Imagine what would happen to your vocal skills if you didn't practice them regularly!) Regular practice will keep your mind well prepared for competition, audition, recital, and stage performances. Achieving well-honed skills will not happen overnight. Even experienced athletes, among whom there is a great acceptance of mental training plans, often fall by the wayside after a few weeks. This is not because they feel that the plans aren't worthwhile—quite the opposite—but either because their time management is poor or because mental training occupies a low place on their list of priorities.

Stage 1. Designing Your Plan

Any well-planned design will take into account those mental areas that your performance requires. First, you should prioritize the areas in which you need to do some work. Your performance profiles will help you with this, as will a talk with your voice teacher and coach about their recommendations.

Use table A-1 to help you take this initial step of prioritizing.

After completing the table, you will have established what you need to do. Choose wisely the things that you think will make an *immediate* difference in your singing, and do only one or two at once. You may have different mental needs in different areas of your work. For example, you might need to work on the development of self-confidence in auditions, but your concentration might need your attention in a staged performance, and during your voice lessons you might need to be more attentive to your goal setting.

Setting Goals

Once you have identified your mental areas needing improvement, you should then set specific goals in relation to each area and the skills that are needed for it. Be thoughtful about your goal setting. Some goals may set themselves in the long term and short term, but you must not set a crazy schedule that would be impossible to keep. This will only lead to frustration. The most important objective is to *persevere* with any program you have set for yourself.

Table A-1 Prioritizing

	Prioritize	
Mental Skills Area	Y(es)	N(o)
Plans and routines		
Preperformance	Y	N
Performance	Y	N
Postperformance	Y	N
The self	Y	N
Preparation skills		
Physical well-being and relaxation	Y	N
Setting goals	Y	N
Self-confidence	Y	N
Concentration	Y	N
Anxiety	Y	N
Imagery	Y	N
Memory	Y	N
Performance techniques		
Exploring meaning	Y	N
Audition skills	Y	N
Competition skills	Y	N
The song recital	Y	N
Staged performances	Y	N
Dealing with fear	Y	N
Postperformance		
Staleness and burnout	Y	N
Mental rehabilitation	Y	N

Priority list:
1.
2.
3.
4.

Organizing the Information into a Mental Plan

Before actually organizing the mental plan, the key question is, "How much time do I have?" Remember to use the time that is at your disposal in the studio, in the practice room, and in your everyday life. Don't overlook traveling to and from work, breaks during the day, or times when you walk or work out. Once you have established what time is available, then you can really begin to organize your plan. Your needs, your mental skills and techniques, and your goals can now be organized. Take one day at a time, and make out a small chart like this one:

Date:

Time of day session to be carried out:

Length of session:

Goals, content of session:

General comments:

Self-rating on quality with a 1–10 scale:

You can apply this kind of outline to one week at a time. Plan ahead for the times when you are going to do your mental training. This will guide your focus and your requirements. It would also be a good idea to select times when you know your focus will surely be on your mental skills. One of the best ways to learn and practice mental skills is to start slowly, working a little bit at a time, but often.

In appendix 1 you will find two examples of mental planners (chart #19 and chart #20). They are only samples; there are many other commercial outlines on the market that you can use.

Stage 2. Implementing Your Plan

The first time you try to establish your mental plan, it can be very time-consuming, mainly because you must also learn the skills first and then practice them. Like all skills, they do take time to learn and have their effect. This cannot be done with a quick fix, but your commitment and your work will be rewarded in the end by an enhanced performance. Take your time. Allow the process of learning and practicing to go on.

Looking carefully at your yearly plan and knowing when your auditions, performances, and competitions are going to take place will help you to decide when you need to begin work on your various mental skills for application during performance. Ideally, your mental skills program should be ongoing, but there will be times when it will be more focused, such as during the approach to the audition season or before a major staged performance. Mental practice should take only about ten to fifteen minutes each session, five to six days a week, but if you incorporate it into your voice lessons, coachings, and practice sessions, you will extract more work from yourself.

Stage 3. Maintaining Your Plan

Your mental skills can be retained at a peak level only if you keep working them, just as you keep your physical and vocal skills honed. The commitment and adherence to your program is also a key factor in its success. If you really want to change, then you must *be aware, plan, prepare, do, and repeat*. Only then will you see the benefits of all your mental training. Your mental program is a very flexible thing. It can have an intensified focus when you need it, but it can also have a more general awareness level to keep it ticking over in between your major commitments to performance. When specific problems arise, you can focus in again to support the present need. It is important that you keep your mental skills "fit." Just because you're not performing doesn't mean that you don't need to practice them. They may take less time per week, but they still need maintenance.

Stage 4. Updating and Evaluating Your Plan

It is a good idea to evaluate your plan occasionally, just as you would your technical vocal program or your acting program. You may be spending time doing something that is not needed now. Keep your program up-to-date, and try to confer with your voice teacher and coaches about whether they think some of your needs may have changed. Performance is a dynamic thing. It will not remain static, and neither will you as a performer. Consequently, you should keep an eye on your development.

To Sum Up Once and for All

You can learn how to develop and use a mental plan to achieve performance excellence. If you commit yourself to it and practice regularly, you will be more able to reach higher levels in the consistency of your eventual performance. It will help you to take control of yourself as a performer; it will help you to tap into your reservoir of potential. It's as easy as *ABC*.

> *A*. Apply the various skills to your own needs and to your own vocal requirements.
> *B*. Believe in yourself and your mental plans at all times.
> *C*. Commit yourself fully to your mental training, which is an important part of your performance preparation.

This is literally your *ABC*, adapted from the ABC in *The Mental Game Plan* (Bull, Albinson, and Shambrook, 1996). Remember it and use it wisely.

Although you can train your voice and your body by sheer perseverance and endurance, it is much harder to train your mind. First, you have to learn *how* to do it, then how to *apply* it, and, finally, how to *use* it.

Good luck!

Appendix 1: Exercise Forms

Chart #1. Preperformance Countdown Plan Sheet

This sheet will help you plan your goals from ten days before the event up to the day before the performance.

Performance, Audition, or Competition:
Venue:
Date:
Date minus 10 days
Date minus 9 days
Date minus 8 days
Date minus 7 days
Date minus 6 days
Date minus 5 days
Date minus 4 days
Date minus 3 days
Date minus 2 days
Date minus 1 day

Chart #2. Day of the Performance and at the Performance Venue Planning Sheet

This planning sheet is geared to record what you want to do (1) on the day of the performance and (2) at the performance venue.

Day of the Performance Plan	At the Performance Venue Plan
A.M.:	Upon arrival:
P.M.:	Two minutes before:
Let's do it!	Let's do it!

Chart #3. Song/Aria/Piece Strengths and Qualities Exercise Sheet

Song/aria/piece:
Date:
Physical strengths and qualities:
Vocal/technical strengths and qualities:
Mental strengths and qualities:

Chart #4. "What If?" Plans Sheet

Identify possible "what if?" situations that may occur before or during your performance. What action will you take?

Performance:	
Date/time:	

Preperformance	
What if?	Action:
1.	
2.	
3.	
4.	

Performance	
What if?	Action:
1.	
2.	
3.	
4.	

Chart #5. Postperformance Evaluation Form 2

A very quick way of evaluating your performance, this can also be used to evaluate single pieces from your performances.

Performance:	
Date:	Venue:

Positive points:	Negative points:

Cross out all the negative points when you have finished deciding what to do about them.

Chart #6. Performance Profile Graph

For your convenience we have provided a blank copy of the performance profile graph so that you can write in the performance qualities (technical, mental, or physical) that you consider most important for yourself. It is quite probable that you will have disagreed with the elements listed in the sample graphs that were included in chapter 7. Fill in the qualities that you find the most important in your own work.

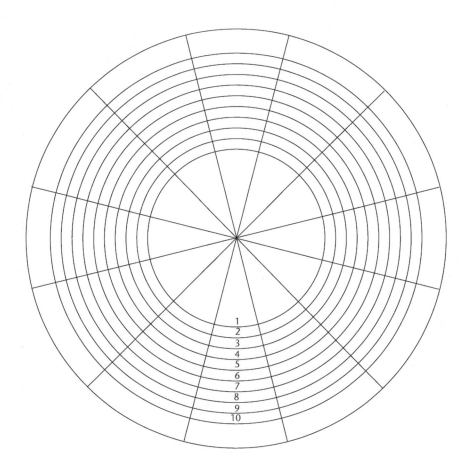

Directions: Label each section of the profile with the technical, mental, or physical skills or factors that you feel are important for this one of your singing performances. Indicate how you perceive yourself AT THE MOMENT on the scale of 1–10 for each skill or factor. Draw a line at that level. A score of 7 or below indicates an area in need of improvement.

Chart #7. Linear Performance Profile for Vocal Skills

Fill in the performance qualities that are meaningful for you.

Name:	Aria:			Date:		
Quality	Assessment					
	0	2	4	6	8	10

Qualities to Work on:

1. _____ 2._____

3. _____ 4._____

Performer's assessment   =====================

Teacher's assessment   /////////////////////////////////////

Chart #8. Linear Performance Profile for Mental Skills

Fill in the mental skills that *you* are concerned with.

Skill	0	1	2	3	4	5	6	7	8	9	10

Key:

Singer's perception of performance   -------------

Teacher's perception of performance   *////////////*

Chart #9a. Questionnaire: Mental Skills for Singing

Feel free to fill in statements in each category that would better apply to *your* singing.

	Strongly Disagree				Strongly Agree

Motivation

1. In performance I usually manage my mental energy well enough to sing my best.	1	2	3	4	5
2. I really enjoy performing when the other singers are of high caliber.	1	2	3	4	5
3. I am good at motivating myself.	1	2	3	4	5
4. I find that I usually try my hardest.	1	2	3	4	5
5. I normally have a clear idea of WHY I sing.	1	2	3	4	5

Goal Setting

6. I always set myself goals in my lessons and coachings.	1	2	3	4	5
7. My goals are always very specific.	1	2	3	4	5
8. I always analyze and evaluate the outcome after a performance.	1	2	3	4	5
9. I usually set goals that I can achieve	1	2	3	4	5

Self-Confidence

10 I suffer from lack of confidence about my performance abilities.	5	4	3	2	1
11. I approach all auditions, competitions, and performances with confident thoughts.	1	2	3	4	5
12 My confidence wavers as auditions, competitions, and performances draw nearer.	5	4	3	2	1
13. Throughout all performances I keep a positive attitude.	1	2	3	4	5

Anxiety and Fear

14 I often experience fears about failing in performance.	5	4	3	2	1
15. I worry that I will disgrace myself when singing in public.	5	4	3	2	1
16. I let my mistakes and omissions distract me while I perform.	5	4	3	2	1
17. My anxiety is harder to control in the presence of other singers.	5	4	3	2	1

Relaxation

18. I am able to relax myself before a performance.	1	2	3	4	5
19. I become too tense before performance.	5	4	3	2	1
20. Being able to calm myself down is one of my strong points.	1	2	3	4	5
21. I know how to relax in difficult circumstances.	1	2	3	4	5

Concentration and Focusing

22. My thoughts are often elsewhere during performance.	5	4	3	2	1
23. My concentration lets me down during performance.	5	4	3	2	1
24. Unexpected noises and sights distract me during performance.	5	4	3	2	1
25. I am good at pretending to be focused even though I'm distracted.	5	4	3	2	1
26. Despite distractions, I can control my focus during performance.	1	2	3	4	5

Imagery

27. I can rehearse my repertoire in my imagination.	1	2	3	4	5
28. I rehearse my musical, vocal and dramatic skills in my head before I use them.	1	2	3	4	5
29. It is difficult for me to form mental pictures.	5	4	3	2	1
30. I can easily imagine how technical vocal and dramatic maneuvers feel.	1	2	3	4	5

Expression and Meaning

31. I am good at personalizing the text of my music.	1	2	3	4	5
32. I have difficulty expressing my intended emotional state with my body.	5	4	3	2	1
33. My face reflects my emotions accurately and expressively.	1	2	3	4	5
34. Without props, costumes, and sets I find it difficult to summon up dramatic truth.	5	4	3	2	1
35. I can usually understand the musical and textual clues that give dramatic meaning.	1	2	3	4	5

Chart #9b. Mental Skills Questionnaire Results

Scoring Instructions: Work out your score by adding up the numbers you have circled in each of the sections. Now calculate your percentage score for each category. Do this by dividing your score by 35, then moving the decimal point two digits to the right. For example, if you have scored 14 out of the possible 35, you will calculate your percentage score as 14 / 35 = .40. Move the decimal point two digits to the right: 40 percent. These percentage scores do not represent a right or wrong score as in an exam. They simply show you where you are now. You should use them in the future to assess whether you have progressed from this starting point.

What to do now? With your eight percentage scores calculated, decide what skills you need to work on.

Date:	Score	Percentage
Motivation		
Goal Setting		
Self-Confidence		
Anxiety and Fear		
Relaxation		
Concentration and Focusing		
Imagery		
Expression and Meaning		
Mental Skills to Focus On:		
1.		
2.		
3.		

Chart #10. General Affirmations: You the Person and Performer

Person	Performer

Chart #11. Performance Achievement Affirmations

Performance:	Date:

Chart #12. Working to Your Strengths Sheet

Physical:

Technical:

Mental:

Chart #13. Triggers or Process Affirmations Sheet

Name of piece: _____ Date: _____

Chart #14. Performance Review List

Performance:
Venue:
Date/Time:
Good Points List
Bad Points List
NOTE: Cut off your Bad Points List and throw it away after using it.

Chart #15. Accompanist Criteria Sheet

Question	Yes	No
Does your coach or accompanist understand all the issues discussed in chapters 14, 16, 17, and 18 and act accordingly?		
Is your pianist a supportive colleague rather than an all-too-observant taskmaster during auditions and other performances?		
Does your accompanist share your ideals about performance?		
Is your pianist unfailingly supportive and understanding during public performance and coaching sessions?		
Does your accompanist do his/her best to accommodate the exigencies of the moment as they occur in performance or does he/she stubbornly cling to the original plan?		
Does your pianist adjust to changes forced on you by the vagaries of live performance, for example, tempos, fermata lengths, breathing spots, ritards?		
Is your pianist then charitable about inadvertent mistakes?		
Does your pianist help you to be your best self in performance?		
Does your pianist abjure the traditional view that singers know nothing about music but are simply bodies into which a fortunate accident of birth placed a singing voice?		
Can your accompanist remember tempos agreed upon in rehearsal?		
Does your pianist understand its importance and make an effort to "breathe with you"?		
Does your accompanist contribute to the performance by his/her stage manner?		
Does your pianist refrain from criticizing repertoire choices for performance unless asked for suggestions?		
Does your accompanist actually *like* singing and singers, especially you?		

If your answers are mostly *yes*, then you probably already know that you have an invaluable colleague. If you must answer *no* many times, then take steps to remedy the situation.

Chart #16. Causes of Staleness in Performance

Write down what you think are the specific causes of your staleness in performance.
Physical (e.g., injury, minor illness, fatigue)
Technical (e.g., perfectionism, nature of practice, performance schedule)
Psychological (e.g., worry, depression, emotion)
Environmental (e.g., living conditions, day job])
Stage Clothing (e.g., room for moving, breathing)

Chart #17. Support Networks Sheet

Whom do I have to talk to? Many of us have this problem: We often expect most of our support and emotional sustenance to come from one or two people. Is it wholly reasonable to expect to get all of our needs satisfied by a single person, a spouse, one's immediate family, or one or two close friends? The following exercise will help you to identify who is in your support network, while making the point that support is a many-faceted thing. You do have a choice. You can extend your support network, plug gaps, and make changes.

Type of Support	In My Singing Life	In My Everyday Life
Someone I can always rely on:		
Someone I just enjoy chatting with:		
Someone with whom I can discuss the exercises in this book:		
Someone who makes me feel both competent and valued:		
Someone who gives me constructive feedback:		
Someone who is always a valuable source of information:		
Someone who will challenge me to sit up and take a good look at myself:		
Someone I can depend upon in a crisis:		
Someone I can feel close to, a friend or an intimate:		
Someone I can share good news and good feelings with:		
Someone who introduces me to new ideas, new interests, new people:		
Someone whose musical judgment I respect:		
Someone whose vocal judgment and musical standards reflect mine:		
Someone who understands the business side of singing:		
Someone I can share bad news with:		

Put an asterisk next to the names of people who can be counted on to be at your side during a time of crisis, injury, or illness.

Chart #18. Mental Rehabilitation Goal-Setting Sheet

Area	Goal	Method Used
Physical well-being and relaxation		
Imagery		
Self-confidence through positive self-talk		

Chart #19. Personal Calendar for One Week

	Monday	Tuesday	Wednesday	Thursday	Friday	Saturday	Sunday
Morning							
Afternoon							
Evening							

Chart #20. Daily Time Log, Divided into Sections That Suit You and Your Schedule

	Time	Activity
Morning		
Afternoon		
Evening		

Appendix 2: Teaching Points

> To teach is to learn twice.
> Joseph Joubert, French moralist and teacher

TEACHING POINT #1. Chapter 2

Knowing that a peak performance is perfectly possible when singing beginning repertoire, you are able to enhance your students' performing ability from the very onset of their studies by encouraging them to "perform" even easy pieces to the best of their ability. Your expectation and encouragement that a *real performance* is part of the study procedure will be very helpful to their development. All the care you expend on finding appropriate repertoire for each student need not be inspired by a fear that inappropriate choices will damage him or her vocally, nor by a concern that while singing repertoire with too many technical difficulties the student will not be able to give a *performance*.

TEACHING POINT #2. Chapter 4

Encourage your students to *plan* their lessons, rehearsals, and performances. It can make a big difference in the quality of their work, if for no other reason than that it will oblige them to think for themselves. If you despair of a certain talented student ever "getting it together," think him/her not persevering, or suspect that he/she does not practice enough, it may just be due to a lack of planning and organization.

TEACHING POINT #3. Chapter 4

Your students may require special attention after they have completed a particular performance that took so much time and effort. It may be difficult for them to deal with this important period without your advice and help. Encourage them to evaluate the performance just completed and then get on with the next performance or preparation.

TEACHING POINT #4. Chapter 5

Continue to give positive reinforcement to your students' efforts, because studies have proven that singers who receive negative appraisals much of the time *lower* their self-estimates, whereas singers who have been given positive feedback *raise* their self-estimates. Some students may be negative not only about vocal technique but also about their self, which attitude can be far more damaging.

TEACHING POINT #5. Chapter 5

This poem (originally written about children) is from an unknown source. This adaptation is particularly germane to this chapter, although it has import for all of them.

> If a singer lives with criticism,
>   That singer learns to condemn.
> If a singer lives with hostility,
>   That singer learns to fight.
> If a singer lives with ridicule,
>   That singer learns to be shy.
> If a singer lives with shame,
>   That singer learns to feel guilty.
> If a singer lives with tolerance,
>   That singer learns to be patient.
> If a singer lives with encouragement,
>   That singer learns confidence.
> If a singer lives with praise,
>   That singer learns to appreciate.
> If a singer lives with fairness,
>   That singer learns justice.
> If a singer lives with security,
>   That singer learns to have faith.
> If a singer lives with approval,
>   That singer learns to like him/herself.
> If a singer lives with acceptance and friendship,
>   That singer learns to find love in the world.

TEACHING POINT #6. Chapter 7

Try to discourage your students from setting outcome goals. Encourage them to set objective performance goals for lessons and practice sessions, and help them to follow through on their goals. You may find that your vocal technical work with them will proceed much faster and much more efficiently.

TEACHING POINT #7. Chapter 7

One of the real strengths of performance profiling is that it can be used as an exercise to be shared among you, your student, and the coach. This in turn makes your work easier and more productive. It also encourages your students to think in objective terms about where they are at the present moment and where they would like to be, say, at the end of the year. It will clarify their understanding of their teachers' opinions about their current status and what needs to be done to improve it.

TEACHING POINT #8. Chapter 12

As a teacher, you constantly seek to devise ways in which your students can experience that vocal skill, placement, or kind of tone that you are attempting to teach them. It is your students' job to remember it, to repeat it, to excel at executing it. In this endeavor, imaging is a great help. Imaging the exact physical movements of the skill, imaging the total kinesthetic feedback of the properly executed maneuver, and imaging the sound of the tone accompanying the well-done skill will make it much more efficient and faster to reproduce.

TEACHING POINT #9. Chapter 12

There are many different approaches to teaching voice, but the one thing that unites all voice teachers is their use of concepts to help instill proper vocal habits in their students. Many teachers use concepts such as "singing those high notes right out of the top of your head," which are actually imagery. You may not call them that. The more students are encouraged to use imagery, the more their skills improve.

TEACHING POINT #10. Chapter 12

In order to make the imagery much more vivid for your singers, it is helpful to speak or recall in the present tense during the lesson. For example: "Now you *are* walking across the little bridge. What color *is* the water?"

TEACHING POINT #11. Chapter 12

When using imagery, there is real potential for more efficient technical learning (e.g., if your singer cannot get the hang of keeping the ribs out when the air supply begins to diminish, seeing the ribs extended like an expanding balloon at the end of the phrase may help), undoing bad habits (e.g., if you have told the singer numerous times to open the mouth on certain notes, but he/she cannot remember, imaging the open mouth like a baby bird awaiting food may help correct this), and improving performance (e.g., if your singer persists in keeping an inexpressive face, even while singing expressively, imaging his/her own face smiling, being happy, beaming, may help to change this).

TEACHING POINT #12. Chapter 14

An important consideration for any teacher is: *When* should you allow your student to work with a coach? Is there any point to the student working with a coach before the student has developed both a reasonably workable range and sufficient breath support and endurance so that vocal difficulties are no longer insurmountable? What kinds of demands can a coach make upon a singer who has not yet learned fundamental singing skills? Perhaps the best answer is: No coach at all until the time is right.

TEACHING POINT #13. Chapter 14

It may be very helpful to your students, especially the less-experienced among them, if you are able to find time to help them locate a proper coach. It would also be useful to them if you can confirm the practice of performance mode, as well as teaching your students *how* to practice for performance. These activities are wise investments in the development of your singers.

TEACHING POINT #14. Chapter 15

As a voice teacher, you always attend first to your primary responsibility, providing technical help. But under the pressure of time, not to mention the responsibility (for you are always the one with whom "the buck stops" when the technical skills show up poorly in performance), there is a tendency just to remind the singer to "be sincere" or to "make sure you understand the words" when he/she is facing performance. The students' attention should be

directed to *how* to find the meaning behind the texts of their repertoire. The quality of the performance hinges upon meaning, and
this is their responsibility.

TEACHING POINT #15. Chapter 16

It is well-known that a competition can be either a powerful mo-
tivator or a destructive and humiliating experience. You naturally
want your singers to walk away from a competition feeling empowered, thinking, *This experience was truly valuable, and I'm
glad I sang.* In order to help your singers to feel empowered, you
may find the following techniques useful:

- Share with your students your thoughts on which competition they should enter and the reasons why (e.g., just for
  the experience in competing or because you are convinced
  that they will do well).
- Remind them that it is not useful to try to outguess the
  reaction of judges to the repertoire ("if I sing this, they will
  then choose that").
- Encourage your students to spend their time and energy in
  working at their performance rather than worrying about
  the judges.
- Persuade your singers to sing what they *can* sing.
- Teach your singers to understand that only the judge can
  decide who wins and it is unimportant whether or not it
  seems "fair" to the singers.
- Evaluate the student's work before the competition and after
  the results are announced—for example, what the student
  did well, and what areas (physical, mental, or technical)
  need further work.

TEACHING POINT #16. Chapter 19

Every performer experiences fear at one time or another. Therefore, it becomes crucial that students are encouraged to focus on
what they can do and the goals that allow them to succeed. The
secret of success in dealing with fear is to view mistakes not as a
threat but rather as a challenge to push the performance further.
Because lack of fear is an important ingredient in mental toughness and will almost guarantee excellent mental performance, any
help or guidance given to students so that they can evaluate their
performances in an objective manner will assist them in overcom-
ing their fears.

TEACHING POINT #17. Chapter 20

Sharing your students' performance evaluations will guide their understanding of how best to prepare for future performances. The more efficient they are in planning and evaluating their preparation and performance, the more effective and independent they will become as performers.

TEACHING POINT #18. Chapter 21

There is a suspicion abroad that singers have been lost to the profession because of staleness and burnout, not because of anything the teacher did or did not do, but because many singers are trained in such a way and operate in such a way that they fit very nicely into the personality type that is highly susceptible to this syndrome. Your vantage point probably makes you uniquely qualified to observe the whole student and detect the problem early.

It is helpful to have the clinical signs of staleness and burnout identified, so that you can help your singers when they are afflicted with the (heretofore) mysterious malady. (Perhaps this would be helpful to coaches as well.) Just as one of your duties as a voice teacher is to send your students to a speech therapist or to the otolaryngologist when the circumstances indicate the need, so you may have to be ready to refer your students to a professional counselor or psychologist if they consistently experience some of the psychological symptoms of staleness, whether or not accompanied by physiological symptoms.

TEACHING POINT #19. Chapter 22

Naturally, your most fervent wish as a teacher has always been to have the ability to guide your students through the rough spots, whatever they may be. Of course you can conjecture, surmise, and intuit because of your continuous experience working with singers, but being informed about mental rehabilitation equips you with more knowledge to use when helping your students in their neediest hours.

Bibliography

Bernstein, Seymour. 1981. *With Your Own Two Hands*. New York: Schirmer.

Blair, Gary. 1993. *What Are Your Goals?* Delmar, California: Wharton.

Bull, S. J. 1991. "Personal and Situational Influences on Adherence to Mental Skills Training," *Journal of Sport and Exercise Psychology*, Vol. 13, pp. 121–32.

Bull, S. J., J. G. Albinson, and C. J. Shambrook. 1996. *The Mental Game Plan*. Eastbourne: Sports Dynamics.

Burns, R. B. 1988. *The Self Concept*. London and New York: Longman.

Butler, Richard J., and Lew Hardy. 1992. "The Performance Profile: Theory and Application," *Sports Psychologist*, Vol. 6, pp. 253–64.

Cohen, Robert. 1978. *Acting Power*. Mountain View, California: Mayfield.

Craig, David. 1993. *A Performer Prepares*. New York: Applause.

Cross, M. J., L. A. Pinczewski, and D. J. Bokor. 1989. "Acute Knee Injury in a Rock Musician. A Case Conference," *The Physician and Sports Medicine*, Vol. 17, No. 7, pp. 79–82.

Davis, M., M. McKay, and H. Eshelman. 1983. *The Relaxation and Stress Reduction Workbook*. Oakland, California: New Harbinger.

de Mille, Agnes. 1956. *Martha: The Life and Works of Martha Graham*. New York: Random House.

Emmons, Shirlee. 1990. *Tristanissimo*. New York: Schirmer.

Emmons, Shirlee, and Stanley Sonntag. 1979. *The Art of the Song Recital*. New York: Schirmer.

Fanning, Patrick. 1988. *Visualization for Change*. Oakland, California: New Harbinger.

Floyd, Ray. 1989. *From 60 Yards In*. New York: Harper Perennial.

Graham, Martha. 1974. "A Modern Dancer's Primer for Action." In *Dance as a Theatre Art: Source Readings in Dance History from 1581 to the Present*, S. J. Cohen, ed. New York: Dodd, Mead, pp. 135–42.

Green, Elmer, and Alyce Green. 1977. *Beyond Biofeedback*. New York: Dell.

Hardy, Lew. 1990. "A Catastrophe Model of Performance in Sport." In *Stress and Performance in Sport*, J. G. Jones and L. L. Hardy, eds. Chichester, England: Wiley.

Hardy, Lew, and Dave Nelson. 1990. "Sports Related Psychological Skills Questionnaire" (SPSQ). Developed 1990, as yet unstandardized.

Harris, Dorothy V. 1986. "Relaxation and Energizing Techniques for Regulation of Arousal." In *Applied Sport Psychology, Personal Growth to Peak Performance*, Jean M. Williams, ed. Mountain View, California: Mayfield.

H'Doubler, M. N. 1968. *Dance: A Creative Art Experience*. Madison: University of Wisconsin Press.

Heil, John. 1993. *Psychology of Sport Injury*. Champaign, Illinois: Human Kinetics.

Henschen, K. P. 1986. "Athletic Staleness and Burnout." In *Applied Sport Psychology, Personal Growth to Peak Performance*, Jean M. Williams, ed. Mountain View, California: Mayfield.

Hook, Ed. 1989. *The Audition Book*. New York: Back Stage Books.

Humphrey, Doris. 1951. *The Art of Making Dances*. New York: Grove.

Jacklin, Tony. 1970. *Jacklin, T.* New York: Simon and Schuster.

Jacobson, Edmund. 1974. *Progressive Muscular Relaxation*. Chicago: University of Chicago Press, 1929, Midway Reprint.

Kretch, D., R. S. Crutchfield, and E. L. Ballachey. 1962. *Individual in Society*. New York: McGraw-Hill.

Kubistant, Tom. 1986. *Performing Your Best*. Champaign, Illinois: Life Enhancement Publications.

Leonard, G. 1975. *The Ultimate Athlete*. New York: Viking.

Loehr, James E. 1984. "How to Overcome Stress and Play at Your Peak All the Time," *Tennis,* March, pp. 66–76.

———. 1987. *Mental Toughness Training for Sports*. Harrisonburg, Virginia: R. R. Donnelley and Sons.

Mahoney, M. J., and M. Avanel. 1977. "The Psychology of the Elite Athlete: An Exploratory Study," *Cognitive Therapy and Research*, Vol. 1, pp. 135–42.

Martens, Rainer. 1987. *Coaches Guide to Sport Psychology*. Champaign, Illinois: Human Kinetics.

Maslach, C. 1982. "Understanding Burnout: Definitional Issues in Analyzing a Complex Phenomenon." In *Job Stress and Burnout: Research, Theory, and Intervention Perspectives*, W. S. Paine, ed. Beverly Hills: Sage, pp. 29–40.

McKay, Matthew, and Patrick Fanning. 1992. *Self-Esteem*. Oakland, California: New Harbinger.

Miller, Saul. 1992. *Performance under Pressure*. Toronto/Montreal: McGraw-Hill Ryerson.

Moir, A., and D. Jessel. 1991. *Brain Sex: The Real Difference between Men and Women*. New York: Dell.

Mordden, Ethan. 1984. *Demented*. New York: Simon and Schuster.

Morehouse, L. E. , and L. Gross. 1977. *Maximum Performance*. New York: Simon and Schuster.

Morgan, W. P. 1984. "Selected Psychological Factors Limiting Performance: A Mental Health Model." Paper presented at the Limits on Human Performance Symposium, Olympic Scientific Congress, Eugene, Oregon.

Murphy, M., and R. White. 1978. *The Psychic Side of Sports*. Reading, Massachusetts: Addison-Wesley.

Nicklaus, Jack. 1994. *Golf My Way*. New York: Simon and Schuster.

Orlick, Terry. 1986. *Psyching for Sport: Mental Training for Athletes*. Champaign, Illinois: Leisure Press.

————. 1990. *In Pursuit of Excellence*. Champaign, Illinois: Leisure Press, 2d edition.

Otto, H. 1970. *Guide to Developing Your Potential*. North Hollywood, California: Wilshire.

Ravizza, Kenneth. 1977. "Peak Experiences in Sport," *Journal of Humanistic Psychology*, Vol. 17, No. 4, pp. 35–40.

————. 1986. "Increasing Awareness for Sport Performance." In *Applied Sport Psychology*, Jean M. Williams, ed. Mountain View, California: Mayfield.

Riley, Pat. 1993. *The Winner Within*. New York: Putnam.

Rotella, Robert J., and Steven R. Heyman. 1986. "Stress, Injury, and the Psychological Rehabilitation of Athletes." In *Applied Sport Psychology, Personal Growth to Peak Performance*, Jean M. Williams, ed. Mountain View, California: Mayfield.

Shank, P. A. 1983. "Anatomy of Burnout," *Parks Recreation*, March, Vol. 17, pp. 52–58.

Stanislavski, Constantin, and Pavel Rumyantsev. 1975. *Stanislavski on Opera*. New York: Theatre Arts.

Steadman, J. R. 1993. "A Physician's Approach to the Psychology of Injury." In *Psychology of Injury*, J. Heil, ed. Champaign, Illinois: Human Kinetics Publishers.

Stein, Harry. 1984. "Brought to His Knees," *Sport*, September, p. 64.

Syer, John, and Christopher Connolly. 1984. *Sporting Body, Sporting Mind*. London: Cambridge University Press.

Teyte, Maggie. 1958. *Star on the Door*. New York: Arno.

Titze, Ingo R. 1994. *Principles of Voice Production*. Englewood Cliffs: Prentice-Hall.

Unestahl, L., ed. 1983. *The Mental Aspects of Gymnastics*. Orebro, Sweden: Veje.

Waitley, Denis. 1984. *The Psychology of Winning*. New York: Berkley.

Williams, Jean M., ed. 1986. *Applied Sport Psychology, Personal Growth to Peak Performance*. Mountain View, California: Mayfield.

Williams, Mike, and Alma Thomas. 1994. *The Exam Game.* Sevenoaks, England: Baccalaureate Press.

Worrell, Teddy W. 1992. "The Use of Behavioral and Cognitive Techniques to Facilitate Achievement of Rehabilitation Goals," *Journal of Sport Rehabilitation*, Vol. 1, No. 1, February, pp. 69–75.

Yenne, Vernon. 1996. "Competing." Address before the National Association of Teachers of Singing/Ohio State University Master Teacher/Intern Teacher Program, July.

Index

accompanist. *See* coach
anxiety
   distractions, resulting from, 127
   the effect of planning on, 53
   and its ideal arousal zone, 150–1
   identifying its causes, 153–5
   as an internal factor, 148–9
   low level of, 158–9
   managing, controlling, and
     recognizing symptoms of, 151–9
   means of reducing, 155–8
   and negative self-concept, 61–2
   types of, 147–50
auditioning
   control when, 217–8
   and fatigue, 218
   food, drink, and vocalizing before,
     215–6
   and presentation of self, 217
   psychological overview of, 207–8
   repertoire for, 212
   strategies for, 211–2, 215–20
   vocal overview of, 208–9
awareness
   of body, 66–8
   developing, 127–9
   and distractions, 144–6
   exercises for achieving, 16–8, 68
   identifying where you need to focus,
     126–7
   and mental toughness, 27–9
   and peak performances, 11, 15–6
   of performance level, 81–91
   and self-identity, 57–61

body-mind link. *See* mind-body link
burnout. *See* staleness and burnout

case study
   of auditioning, 220
   distractions, of dealing with, 144–6
   of imagery, 163
   of mental rehabilitation after vocal
     injury, 279
   of mental toughness, 29–30
   of peak performance, 18–9
   of performance cycle planning, 53–5
   of postperformance tension, 253–5
   of self and performer, 62–3
change, 249–50
clothing, 216, 231–2
coach
   accompanists, two kinds of, 241–2
   burnout, staleness. or mental
     rehabilitation and his/her help
     with, 266–8
   criteria for judging stability and
     supportiveness of, 241–4
   and evaluation of your performance,
     256
   function of, on a singer's team, 191–
     2
   parameters of the profession, 181–4
   performance work with the help of,
     241–4
collaborative pianist. *See* coach
communication
   and brain activity during
     performance, 203–5

317